Through My Enemy's Eyes

Envisioning Reconciliation in Israel–Palestine

Salim J. Munayer and Lisa Loden

Paternoster:
thinking faith

Contents

Foreword

Visitors to my home city of Belfast are quick to remark on the not infrequent flying of Israeli and Palestinian flags by each side of our divided community. The red, black, white and green in Catholic, Nationalist, Republic areas. The blue star of David in Protestant, Unionist, Loyalist streets. Such is the resonance of the Israeli-Palestinian conflict around the world.

Wherever peoples are in conflict, while there is much that is particular to their place and story, questions of contested identity, precarious belonging and disputes over land are a shared experience. When combined with a deep rooted religious narrative and the dynamics of a post-colonial legacy, those of us who have been nurtured among such people, know instinctively how it feels and have an intuitive sense of what it costs for those involved. We are also, less helpfully, quick to identify our cause with those we perceive to be on our side of history.

A common weakness of Christian reconciliation ministries is not to take seriously our incarnational belonging, embedded as we all are within a community and culture, with its political realities, ancestral voices and wounded history. Even when we do address such matters it is often to spiritualise profoundly human needs and desires to belong to a place and a people. To embark on the path of reconciliation with the assumption that if we affirm our new humanity in Christ often enough then we are indeed reconciled.

Church history shows us that without the really hard work of confronting the prejudices and fears, misunderstanding and wilful misrepresentation, then spiritual revivals can sweep through leaving intact the infrastructure of our divided societies, even within the body of Christ. If we are to envision a reconciled future for our divided communities, then we in the body of Christ cannot risk leaving unexamined those things which do not make for our peace.

This journey of faith can only be undertaken in the company of others, specifically those that are the other to us. It is only together that we can engage in the honest remembering, hard telling and humble listening that create the space for hope to flourish.

The ministry of Musalaha is something I have admired for a number of years. Those involved not only take seriously their rootedness in a complex landscape but also Jesus' invitation to love our enemies and in so doing know the things that make for peace. One of the joys on arriving at Coventry Cathedral in 2008 was to discover they are part of the Community of the Cross of Nails network and to have the opportunity to get to know Salim and the passion and vision that he holds. I first met Lisa in Pattaya, Thailand, on the Reconciliation working group of a Lausanne consultation in 2005. The experience profoundly affected all of us who were part of that group as we shared a deep understanding of the cost of reconciliation in our divided world.

In this book we are given an insight into and benefit from the fruits of the conversation between Lisa and Salim as they bring the hurt of their world into their relationship as sister and brother in Christ. Such conversations are always holy ground as the peaceable kingdom is built and the children of God come into their own, as peacemakers.

They have learnt much about God's mission of reconciliation and this is a refreshing oasis in a barren landscape. We have much to learn from them, not least in our willingness to follow their example in our journey towards our other.

Canon David W. Porter
Archbishop of Canterbury's Director for Reconciliation
Community of the Cross of Nails, Coventry Cathedral
Advent 2013

Introduction

Few conflicts in the world command attention like the Israeli–Palestinian conflict. For Palestinian Christians and Israeli Messianic Jews, this entangled dispute engages a variety of important subjects: theology, identity, eschatology, ethics and the interpretation of Scripture. These issues shape the convictions of individual believers and congregations who try to make sense of the conflict and its relationship to Scripture. In spite of our own challenges, Israeli Messianic Jews and Palestinian Christians can be agents of hope within our historic, national and regional conflict. This makes the process of reconciliation between our communities all the more precious to God.

Issues of theology, land, politics and justice are not mere academic subjects for our communities, but rather, existential realities in the midst of this conflict. We are believers who have committed our lives to God and believe in the authority and relevance of Scripture. Further, we believe God calls us to be ministers of reconciliation for his sake. As we, a Palestinian Christian and an Israeli Messianic Jew, live together in the land of our ancestors – the land of the patriarchs, prophets, and our Lord's birth, death and resurrection – we see each other as brother and sister in our Messiah. We have been entrusted with the ministry of reconciliation. For us, this is a sacred trust and a personal calling. In the writing of this book we are expressing what it means to actively live out the reality of reconciliation. From our vastly different personal histories, perspectives and community affiliations, we have struggled to be gracious to one another and unbiased in our presentation.

As authors and friends, writing this book together has been a fascinating adventure. It has not always been easy or even pleasant, but it was an adventure we chose to experience together. Our relationship was forged through our personal friendship dating back to the mid 1970s. During the following years, we connected through our joint passion for building up the body of Messiah in this land and through our mutual concern for healing the many wounds and divisions in his body. We later connected through Musalaha, a non-governmental organization based in Jerusalem that promotes practical, grassroots-level reconciliation in the context of the Israeli–Palestinian conflict. Musalaha seeks to create non-threatening settings in which Israeli and Palestinian believers can meet, develop relationships, and intentionally and honestly discuss theological and political ideas, including issues of land, justice, eschatology, and identity. Creating and maintaining such a space provides a framework for both of our communities to over-come hindrances to our reconciliation.

The main focus of the book is to explore the obstacles to reconcil-iation and present a vision of what reconciliation looks like between our faith communities. Our goal in this book is to facilitate discussion between our respective communities that would serve as a catalyst for our appropriation of what God has done for us in Christ. We see this book as vital for any movement forward through the impasse we daily experience in our Middle East, Israel-Palestine context of conflict. Despite our common commitment to Jesus/Yeshua as Lord of our lives, our communities are estranged. To help defuse the estrangement, we have chosen to directly face and explore the difficult and divisive issues of history, narrative and theology.

To clarify our terms of self-designation, when we speak of 'Israeli Messianic Jews', we are referring to Jewish believers in Yeshua (Jesus) the Messiah. We also broadly include non-Jewish followers of Yeshua who identify with the Messianic movement and who live in Israel. By 'Palestinian Christians' we refer to Palestinian Arabs who believe in Jesus Christ as their Saviour and who live within Israel and the Palestinian territories. Some Pales-tinian Christians in Israel prefer the terms 'Palestinian-Israeli', or 'Israeli-Arab', to designate their identity. We respect whichever signifier they prefer.[1] For our purposes, however, we include them when we refer to 'Palestinian Christians'.

The origins of this book began with a lecture Salim gave in England on the theology of reconciliation and the need to develop it more comprehensively. Among those in the audience was Robin Parry, then an editor at Paternoster and now with Wipf & Stock. Robin asked Salim to consider co-authoring a book on this subject with an Israeli Messianic Jew. After some misfires, Lisa Loden emerged as the candidate for the task. On account of the tested friendship between the two, Lisa's long-term involvement and commitment to the work of reconciliation, and her previous writing on the subject, Salim approached her with the proposal to join him in the project.

The process of writing has involved moving our relationship to new levels as we met together to discuss the progress of the book. Both of us have been stretched and have learned a great deal through the process. The views in this book are our own, and do not represent an 'official' position of Musalaha or of our individual congregations. We do not in any way claim to be official representatives of our respective communities, but rather, are writing as individuals within those communities. As far as we know, this book is *sui generis*: a Palestinian Christian and an Israeli Messianic Jew, as co-authors of a book on a theology of reconciliation.[2] Looking back, we can both say that we experienced a sense of discovery as we ventured into the thick of this project. We can also say our personal relationship has deepened and been enriched by the process of writing together.

The book is organized to first introduce the reader to the historical background of the Israeli–Palestinian conflict. Chapter one is a brief chapter on the history of the conflict. We have consulted many sources for the statements made in this chapter. As much as possible we have tried to use sources that are local Israeli or Palestinian with the majority of our references being taken from books used in Israeli universities. We have most often referred to the works of Israeli Jewish historians, most of whom are from the 'revisionist' camp of contemporary historians who write on these issues. The reason for this is twofold. One is that we wished to maintain a high level of contextual integrity; to be faithful to the context. The second reason is these historians had greater access to recently unclassified original sources than did earlier historians whose work necessarily expressed a more partial view of the subject. We are aware we will be criticized for our seemingly limited choice of sources. Nonetheless, we felt an obligation to mainly use more recently published works.

History is exceedingly complex and is never reported comprehensively or objectively. Historical reporting needs to be nuanced by an understanding of the narratives of the people whose history is being related as well as by an understanding of how historians write history – historiography. For this reason we devote three chapters – a brief history, narrative and historiography – to give our readers an understanding of the historical background of our current conflict.

In the following four chapters we introduce the reader to our two faith communities. Two chapters discuss the identity of the respective communities and two chapters discuss the way in which each community reads Scripture. We then turn to the theological differences that divide us. We discuss how both communities approach Scripture and their understanding of how Scripture relates to our situation in Israel-Palestine.[3] Since both communities look to Scripture to ground their theological positions, the issue of hermeneutics is critical to understanding how theology relates to the conflict. We then summarize some examples of divisive issues between Israeli Messianic Jews and Palestinian Christians, together with two prevailing theologies that impact our communities.

As the conclusion to the book, we present a theology of reconciliation as a model for our communities to consider. Finally, we conclude with a teaching of Jesus and a challenge to our communities. Each co-author is responsible for those sections that represent their individual and community views, and those views are not necessarily shared by both authors.

This has been an ambitious project, and the more deeply we engaged with the subject, the more complex the picture became. The issue of identity became a major theme that is integrated and interwoven throughout the book. We quickly recognized we would be unable to exhaustively cover the many relevant issues that emerged. We therefore limited our presentation. Two of the outstanding areas we were unable to address in depth are the issues of justice and a scriptural meta-narrative in which to frame our discussion of history.

The authors would like to especially thank Joshua Korn for his dedication to this project and for his research assistance. We gratefully acknowledge the contribution of A. Ben-Shmuel and Mark Calder. We want to thank our friends who read, commented and offered suggestions for various portions of this book. You know who you are. Heartfelt thanks also go to both Robin Parry for his vision for the book, and Mike Parsons at Paternoster for his encouragement and patience. Special thanks goes to Richard Harvey who, during a noisy open taxi ride in Bangalore, India, brainstormed with us to come up with this book's great title. Finally, we would like to thank our spouses and families, who lovingly and sacrificially supported us as we laboured together to see the work completed.

Our prayer for our readers is that they will read the following chapters with open hearts. Our prayer for this book is that it will be used to help bring 'glory to God in the highest heaven, and on earth peace among those whom he favours' (Luke 2.14).

Salim J. Munayer and Lisa Loden
Jerusalem
2013/5773

1.

A Brief History of the Israeli–Palestinian Conflict

The history of the Israeli–Palestinian conflict is long and contentious. The modern historical narratives of the two peoples have emerged over the course of more than a century of conflict, and debates rage among academic historians as well as the general public. The details of these arguments are well beyond the scope of this book; there are many resources from many perspectives on this history. Our more limited goal here is to provide the reader with a factual overview of the conflict between Israelis and Palestinians. Without some kind of understanding of the past, we will not be able to work towards the future. No historical account can hope to include every significant event for each community, and the history offered here is admittedly selective. We focus on the earlier, foundational period, especially the war in 1948 and its aftermath.

While this limited focus may be puzzling at first, there are a number of reasons for this asymmetry. First, to make sense of the conflict, we must carefully look at its beginnings. The national myths developed in this foundational period have fed the conflict ever since, and these continue to define the discourse today. Second, in terms of reconciliation, the significance of the conflict's beginnings outweighs the events that followed it. Acts of aggression committed by both sides during the early period continue to figure prominently in the conflict. Finally, from a practical perspective, we simply know more about this period than we do about what came after it. Historians have contributed much, and we are able to gain insight from their efforts. All historical work requires humility, but when we attempt to address the more recent past, we tread on especially uncertain ground. We need the perspective the passage of time provides. This is particularly true in a setting of conflict, where truth is often sacrificed for the sake of political expediency and legitimacy. To be sure, our understanding of the early period of the conflict is far from being either perfect or complete, but it remains, nonetheless, fuller and perhaps more accurate than our understanding of more recent events.

The Origins of Zionism

Throughout their Diaspora the Jewish people have retained spiritual and historical attachment to *Eretz Yisrael* (the Land of Israel) and have longed to return to their ancestral homeland. This desire for a physical, national restoration was coupled with Messianic aspirations of spiritual redemption; both are evident in Jewish liturgical literature. The daily repetition of prayers for the restoration of Zion was a constant reminder of the Messianic hope of a future in the Promised Land. Until the middle of the nineteenth century, this hope was primarily an eschatological longing for the 'days of the Messiah' to come when all would be restored, including the return of the Jews to their ancient Promised Land. An example of the centrality of this hope can be seen in the fact that at every wedding of Jews there is a moment when the loss of Jerusalem is remembered. No Jew was ever allowed to forget that his or her people were in exile from the ancestral land and would one day return.

Although exiled from Jerusalem in 135 CE, the Jews were not exiled from the rest of Roman Palestine.[1] They lost their political independence but maintained a spiritual and physical connection to the land that was revived prior to the Crusades. During the Byzantine era, from the fourth to seventh centuries, there was a vibrant Jewish presence in Palestine. This is evidenced by the large number of synagogues built during this period. To date, over 100 synagogues have been excavated, many of them located in areas where there was no previous Jewish presence.[2] It is estimated that up to 300,000 Jews were in Palestine in 1000 ce. With the recapture of Palestine by Saladin after the Crusades, only a thousand Jewish families remained. The rest were killed or exiled:[3]

The Jewish community in Palestine waxed and waned with the vicissitudes of conquest and economic hardship, and invitations by different Turkish rulers to displaced European Jews to settle in Tiberias and Hebron. At different times, there were sizeable Jewish communities in Tiberias, Safed, Hebron and Jerusalem, and numbers of Jews living in Nablus and Gaza. A few original Jews remained in the town of Peki'in, families that had lived there continuously since ancient times.[4]

However, other than pilgrims visiting the small remnant of pious Jews who had remained – mostly in the four Jewish holy cities of Jerusalem, Hebron, Safad and Tiberias[5] – there was no systematic communal effort to return. It was not until the nineteenth century, when religious sentiment found a partner in a growing sense of secular Jewish identity, spurred on by the rise in European anti-Semitism and the development of other European nationalisms, that modern Zionism was born.[6]

In both the Muslim East and the Christian West the Jewish people were viewed suspiciously, as inferior outsiders who were merely tolerated. They were subject to discriminatory treatment in the best of times and often lived under the threat of pogroms,[7] massacres and expulsion. A wave of violent pogroms[8] in Russia prompted Jews to establish settlements in Ottoman-ruled Palestine.[9] European Jews despaired that they would ever be able to live in peace until they had a homeland of their own. When Theodor Herzl emerged as a significant leader, modern Zionism began to be a viable Jewish political and nationalist movement.

A journalist for the Viennese daily *Neue Freie Presse*, Herzl was a thoroughly assimilated and secular Jew. He rarely thought about the 'Jewish problem' and knew little of Jewish customs or traditions. But he was shaken by the outburst of anti-Semitism he witnessed while covering the Dreyfus affair in Paris. Alfred Dreyfus was a Jewish-French army officer who was falsely accused of treason, and his trial triggered serious animosity towards Jews in France.[10] That this took place in France was significant; ever since the French Revolution, Jews had considered France to be the symbol of liberal tolerance. Herzl became convinced that assimilation would never be enough to save the Jews. In 1896 he published *Der Judenstaat* (The Jewish State), advocating the establishment of a Jewish homeland in response to the problem of anti-Semitism.[11]

It is significant and well documented[12] that Herzl was influenced and encouraged in his incipient Zionism by Puritan Christians who held to an understanding of Scripture that Jews would return to Israel before the second coming of the Messiah.

The First Zionist Congress was held in Basel, Switzerland, in 1897. It defined Zionism as a movement that 'seeks to secure for the Jewish people a publicly recognized, legally secured home in Palestine for the Jewish people.'[13] Nearly 200 delegates from all over Europe attended the congress. While there was much debate about how the new movement should proceed, even at this early stage Herzl confidently wrote in his diary, 'At Basel I founded the Jewish State.'[14] He would not live to see it actually established. Not long after Herzl's death on 2 November 1917, the British government issued the Balfour Declaration, articulating its support for the establishment of a Jewish homeland in Palestine. Although Palestine was still in Ottoman hands, it would not be long before the British took control of it. The Zionists understood the declaration as international recognition of the legitimacy of their movement.[15] When the British succeeded in conquering Palestine in 1918, the Zionists viewed it as a promise that would soon be fulfilled.

The Origins of Palestinian Nationalism

The area called Palestine changed hands numerous times from the end of the Roman Empire until the twentieth century. It was invaded and occupied by Persians, Arabs, Crusaders, Mamluks and, from the early sixteenth century, the Ottomans.[16] From 1831 to 1840 the Ottomans lost control of Palestine to the Egyptian Muhammad Ali and his son Ibrahim Pasha.[17] This rebellion, a minor footnote in the long history of the Ottoman Empire, would prove to be catalyzing in the development of Palestinian identity.

The local Arab population of Palestine quickly turned against the Egyptian occupation, protesting the various reforms implemented as well as the demand for conscripts into the Egyptian army. Their resistance stemmed from their awareness that 'conscription was little more than a death sentence: The term of service was frequently for life and, given the sanitary conditions and military technology of the day, there was little chance parents would ever see their sons again.'[18] In 1834 important families from Nablus, Jerusalem and Hebron refused to cooperate with the Egyptians. This sparked riots, repression and, eventually, a full-blown rebellion. The revolt brought together a cross section of society; it 'united dispersed Bedouins, rural sheikhs, urban notables, mountain fellaheen, and Jerusalem religious figures against a common enemy. It was these groups who would later constitute the Palestinian people.'[19]

Although the revolt was finally suppressed, the Ottomans resumed control of Palestine in 1840. However, this hardly brought about a return to the status quo. A number of factors converged, bringing about far-reaching changes, including the establishment of a more centralized government, general migration to the cities, and the land law of 1858. The centralized government was able to increase the efficiency of taxation, which mostly affected the rural population. This triggered a steady flow of migration into towns and cities, and 'by 1881 a third of Palestine's Arab population was urban – up from only 22 percent in 1800.'[20] Many of the notable urban families grew wealthy in their roles as Ottoman tax collectors, and they were able to take advantage of the 1858 land law by buying up large tracts of land. Traditionally, ownership of land was demonstrated simply by cultivating it; however, the new law required ownership to be registered. The law also permitted the registration of uncultivated land. As a result, even the villagers who did not move to the cities lived and worked, for the most part, on land they did not own. The large *effendis* (landowners) were content to allow the peasants to stay and work the land, provided they turned over the profits. Many of the effendis were absentee owners, living outside Palestine.[21]

Towards the end of the nineteenth century, there was a growing sense of pan-Arab solidarity and Arab nationalism from within the Ottoman Empire, which was reinforced by the emergence of the Young Turks, whose 1908 revolt led to a process of 'Turkification'.[22] Anti-Arab sentiment spread throughout the Ottoman Empire, providing the context of the 1915 wartime correspondence between the British High Commissioner Sir Henry McMahon and Hussein ibn Ali, the Sharif of Mecca. The British offered to support self-determination for the Arabs if they would rebel against the

Ottomans. When the British defeated the Ottomans, the Arabs viewed the McMahon–Hussein correspondence as a mandate for independence.[23]

Early Conflict

The conflict between the Zionists and the Arab Palestinians began as soon as Jewish immigrants started arriving and establishing settlements. Early on, the two communities tolerated each other and sometimes worked together, but the tensions between them intensified with each new wave of Jewish immigration. The Arab Palestinians' chief fear was that the Zionists wanted to take their land. This fear was, to a large degree, justified, as the Zionists purchased around 400,000 dunams – approximately 100,000 acres (US) – of land between 1878 and 1908 and viewed land acquisition as their primary objective.[24] The Zionists, for their part, viewed the Palestinians as a part of the local landscape and mostly ignored them. Their focus was on internal Zionist matters. When they did think about the Palestinian Arabs, they either considered them an obstacle to overcome or reflected on how they stood to benefit from the Zionist project.[25] Increasingly, the two communities began to clash, usually over the issue of land. Eventually these clashes became violent and laid the groundwork for future conflict.

As a result of the Ottoman land reforms, land was available for sale and usually not by the people who lived and worked on it. For the first time 'a peasant could be deprived not of formal title to his land, which he had rarely held before, but rather of the right to live on it, cultivate it, and pass it on to his heirs – rights that had formally been inalienable.'[26] Some of the Zionists purchased land and allowed the Arab Palestinians to continue to work and live on it, especially during the first *aliyah*, or first modern wave of Zionist immigration, generally dated 1881–1903. But often the local Arabs were evicted so that the Jews could work the land themselves. Many Palestinians viewed these purchases as illegitimate and resisted eviction.[27]

The Jews arriving during the second aliyah, beginning in 1904, were influenced by the organized massacres that swept through

Russia in 1904–6 and, consequently, were far more militant in their outlook and dedicated to the ideals of self-defence and Jewish labour.[28] Jewish labour was the idea that the work done in the Jewish settlements should be done only by Jews and not by hired workers, an idea that was controversial among the Zionists. There was no consensus on the exclusive nature of this principle, and it was often not strictly enforced as the Jewish workforce was too small to sustain the amount of labour needed.[29] It did, however, have an effect on Jewish–Arab Palestinian relations, which were beginning to deteriorate. While initial resistance to Zionism came from the *fellahin* (the rural peasants), soon the urban notables joined in, especially through the establishment of Arabic-language newspapers that provided a public platform in which to denounce Zionism.[30] Their shared opposition to Zionism served as a link between the rural and urban Palestinians and strengthened their will to resist the Zionists.[31]

One of the earliest examples of this confrontation occurred in the Zionist settlement of Petah Tikva, which was formed on purchased land that the Arab Palestinian village of Yahudiya considered its own. Tension mounted between the village and the colony, and finally, in March 1886, a group of peasants attacked Petah Tikva, vandalizing houses and crops, killing one inhabitant and injuring several others.[32] Because of this and other similar attacks, a Jewish paramilitary group, *HaShomer* (the Guard), was formed to defend the *Yishuv* (the Jewish settlements). They rode on horseback, often adopted the language and dress of Bedouin Arabs, and consciously set out to reverse some of the stigmas related to diasporic Jewish identity (the Jew as weak and defenceless). Most importantly, they were defending their land.[33] HaShomer was seen as an important forerunner to the Israeli army. Eventually the iconic images of both HaShomer (the armed Jew on horseback, defending his land against the Arab hordes) and the fellahin (the *kaffiyya*-clad peasant, resisting dispossession by the colonial occupier) would become archetypal figures for Israelis and Palestinians respectively, representing the struggle and inspiring future generations of fighters.[34]

The British Mandate

While the British had ostensibly promised both the Jews and the Arabs a measure of self-determination during the First World War, through both the Balfour Declaration and the McMahon–Hussein correspondence, they had also made a secret agreement with the French. The Sykes–Picot Agreement of 1916 essentially divided the Middle East between the British and their French allies, with Palestine falling under British control.[35] From the beginning of the British Mandate, the British were commissioned to fulfil the Balfour Declaration, as embodied in the League of Nations. Some in the Zionist camp were disappointed that their homeland would not include territory east of the Jordan River. Arab Palestinians, however, opposed the mandate, which they saw as granting the Zionists a homeland at the expense of the Palestinians, undermining their national aspirations. Both Jews and Arab Palestinians harboured resentment against what they saw as British duplicity and colonial realpolitik.

There were a number of violent riots between the Jews and the Arabs that the British chose to selectively intervene in or ignore in the early 1920s. Lack of British intervention on behalf of the Jewish population led to the founding of the *Haganah*, a Jewish defence organization that would eventually become the Israeli Defence Force (IDF). In attempts to appease the Palestinian population, the British restricted Jewish immigration, leading to a breakdown in Zionist–British relations. However, Jewish immigration continued, often illegally, and a relative calm dominated the political realm throughout the mid to late 1920s.[36]

The tensions still existed, but the industrialization and modernization that the British brought in their wake helped to turn both Jewish and Palestinian attentions away from the conflict and towards the building up of their respective societies. This peaceful interim, however, came to an abrupt end in 1929, when riots and fighting broke out all across the country. Leading up to this, Muslims and Jews were engaged in a fierce argument regarding ownership of the Western Wall. On the Jewish side, the Western Wall was one of the four walls that housed the Second Temple compound; the closest many could come to the site of the destroyed temple, the holiest site in Judaism. For Muslims, the Western Wall (or *al-Buraq*) is named for Muhammad's horse, which he tethered there prior to his heavenly ascent. The Western Wall is one of the four sides of *al-Haram al-Sharif* (the Noble Sanctuary) where the Dome of the Rock and al-Aksa Mosque were built, marking the third-holiest site in Islam. While the Jews were allowed to pray and worship at the Wall, the Muslims owned the Wall and regularly tried to assert their sovereignty of this site.

Skirmishes at the Wall led to deteriorating relations between the two parties who both came to view the Wall as a symbol of religious–national struggle against the other side. Some right-wing Zionists even advocated rebuilding the Temple. On 14 August, six thousand Jews gathered in Tel Aviv, chanting 'The Wall is ours', followed by Jewish demonstrations at the Western Wall on 15 August. These actions sparked rumours spread by Muslim leaders that the Jews were planning to take over al-Haram al-Sharif. Violence ensued, and the British lacked the manpower to address the escalating situation.[37] The worst of the violence occurred on 23 August 1929 in Hebron, where sixty-four Jews were massacred. In all, 133 Jews and 116 Palestinians were killed in the violence, and many more were wounded.[38]

The British eventually restored calm, but it did not last long. In the early 1930s, Sheikh Iz-al Din al-Qassam launched an armed uprising in the Haifa–Lower Galilee region against both the Zionists and the British, and consequently became something of a folk hero for Palestinians. In November 1935 he was killed by British troops, and his funeral sparked massive nationalist demonstrations.[39] The following year more violence broke out, which culminated in the Arab Revolt. Directed more towards the British than the Jews, the revolt saw the establishment of the Arab Higher Committee, headed by Amin al-Husseini. The committee advocated a general strike, demanding an end to Jewish immigration, an end to land sales to Jews, and independence from the British.[40]

Rural bands of guerrilla fighters roamed the hills, including volunteers drawn from Iraq, Syria and Transjordan. Some areas were wrested from British control, and Palestinian flags were seen flying in these 'liberated' zones.[41] The British repression of the revolt was brutal. They increased their troop presence and ultimately had more troops stationed in Palestine than in the entire Indian subcontinent.[42] They also recruited and armed Jewish police. Soon the revolt deteriorated into communal warfare between different Arab Palestinian factions and families. Assassinations became frequent, and political reasons were often given for what was actually the settling of old scores. Many of the urban elite began to flee, resulting in a leadership vacuum.[43] Historians have emphasized the inner-Palestinian struggle, but this fails to take into account the deliberate strategy of 'divide and conquer' employed by the British, who actively encouraged the divisions within Palestinian society.[44]

In response to the revolt, the British initiated the Peel Commission, which concluded that Palestine should be partitioned between the Jews and the Arab Palestinians. The Zionist leadership was not pleased with the suggestion, but ultimately accepted it, whereas the Arab Palestinians rejected it and continued with the revolt, which was eventually suppressed in 1939.[45] The revolt proved disastrous for the Arab Palestinian people, who had incurred serious casualties: between 3,000 and 6,000 killed, another 6,000 in detention, and many more exiled. They were left weakened, leaderless and exhausted.[46] The Jewish Yishuv, on the other hand, benefited from the Palestinian revolt. The Palestinian strikes had helped them develop economic self-sufficiency, and politically the Zionists only gained by the Palestinian revolt against the British. The Zionists were given a free hand to strengthen the Haganah and other paramilitary groups.[47] These factors would prove decisive for both communities in the 1948 War.

In an attempt to be even-handed and appease the Palestinians, the British issued the White Paper in May 1939, which limited Jewish land purchases, proposed an independent Palestinian state, and, most importantly, severely limited Jewish immigration. The Palestinians rejected the White Paper as insufficient, and the Zionist leaders saw it as a betrayal, shockingly ill-timed as many Jews were seeking to escape Nazi Germany.[48] The Yishuv continued to bring immigrants in illegally, and some of the more extreme factions began attacking the British through acts of terrorism. However, with the outbreak of the Second World War, the Zionist leadership called off these attacks. Ben-Gurion famously said, 'We shall fight the White Paper as if there is no war, and we shall fight the war as if there is no White Paper', and many Jews volunteered to fight in the British army.[49] Once the war ended, however, the

Jewish revolt against the British was renewed, and the different Jewish military organizations, including the Haganah, joined forces. In addition to normal military actions, they committed various acts of sabotage and terrorism, the most destructive being the bombing of the King David Hotel in Jerusalem, which killed ninety-one people.[50]

The British, still reeling from the war, decided to end the Mandate and bring the issue of Palestine before the United Nations. The United Nations Special Committee on Palestine (UNSCOP) began an investigation and recommended that Palestine be partitioned between the Jews and the Arab Palestinians, while Jerusalem would become an international zone. Land ownership during this period is a difficult and complex subject. Jews owned 7% of the land while the remaining 93% was owned by private individuals, villages and Bedouin shepherds, or came under the category of tenant rights.[51] Jews, who comprised 37% of the population at the time, were to be allotted 55% of Palestine.[52] This recommendation eventually became UN Resolution 181, also known as the UN Partition Plan, which called for the creation of two independent states in Palestine. It was passed through the General Assembly on 29 November 1947.[53] The Zionist leadership accepted it, seeing it as a great accomplishment; the Palestinians rejected it as unfair, demanding to know why, for example, the Jews, who were a minority, should be given a majority of the land.[54]

The War of 1948

The day after the UN resolution was passed, violence escalated between the Arab Palestinians and the Zionists. This violence began a civil war between these two communities, which would last until 15 May 1948, when Israel declared independence and was invaded by the armies of Syria, Jordan, Egypt, Lebanon and Iraq.[55] The first part of the war was characterized by inter-communal violence, terror and massacres, and left both communities traumatized.

During this early stage of the war, both the Israelis and Palestinians used terrorist tactics against one another. For example, in December 1948, two bombs killed thirty-seven Palestinians in Jerusalem. In March the headquarters of the Jewish Agency was bombed, killing twelve Jews. Often one violent act would trigger retaliation, which would in turn trigger more retaliation, each event bloodier than the first, raising the stakes and contributing to the escalating cycle of violence.[56] As the official date for the British withdrawal from Palestine grew closer, the British were content to retreat from the violence and leave the opposing sides to attack one another. They did very little to prevent the killing, even though their mandate was officially still in place. The roads of Palestine became the scenes of some of the most intense fighting, especially on roads that led to isolated Jewish outposts that were susceptible to Palestinian ambush. The road to Jerusalem, in particular, saw a number of major battles.[57]

In the early months of the war, the Haganah adopted a defensive strategy, coupled with retaliatory attacks. Nevertheless, beginning in April 1948, they began an offensive that aimed at taking over areas that the British would leave behind, and conquering additional territory that had not been allotted to them in the UN Partition Plan. This plan – Plan D – had been drawn up in March and was supposed to be implemented in May. When the British left, it was put into action in April.[58] Plan D (for *Dalet* in Hebrew) has caused controversy among historians. Palestinian historians and most of the Israeli 'new historians' agree with Walid Khalidi, Ilan Pappé, and others, who argue that it specifically called for the expulsion of Palestinians and, therefore, constitutes a clear case of ethnic cleansing.[59] Other historians disagree with this claim.[60] What is certain is that the implementation of Plan D did include massacres and caused the mass flight of thousands of Palestinians. The most infamous of these attacks occurred on 9 April 1948, when the Irgun, one of the smaller extreme militias, attacked the village of Deir Yassin near Jerusalem. After the village was taken, following a fierce battle, a massacre occurred, and between 100 and 110 men, women and children were murdered.[61]

During this period, both prior to Israel's declaration of independence and in the war following, massacres occurred on both sides. On 13 May 1948, the day before the Israeli Declaration of Independence, a massacre of 129 Jews by the Arab Legion occurred in kibbutz Kfar Etzion. There were only four survivors of this massacre and the kibbutz was destroyed.[62]

The events at Deir Yassin and elsewhere caused panic to spread among Palestinians, and induced many of them to flee. This flight, Pappé argues, was the intention of the Zionist leadership all along. Other historians disagree, but it certainly was the intention of the Irgun.[63] The expulsion of Palestinians during the years 1947–9 came to be known as the *Nakba* (catastrophe). There were four stages of expulsions,[64] and by the end of the war, around 700,000 Palestinians had either fled or been expelled and became refugees, most of them living in refugee camps in what became known as the West Bank (under Jordanian rule), the Gaza Strip (under Egyptian rule), and in neighbouring countries such as Transjordan, Syria, Lebanon and Egypt.[65] In June 1948 Israelis officially barred the return of Palestinian refugees, a policy that was enforced by the army.[66]

The second stage of the war began on 15 May 1948, when Israel declared independence and was attacked by the surrounding Arab states. It lasted until 1949 when armistice agreements were signed. Although it had not won a decisive victory, the new state of Israel had emerged victorious.

For the Israelis, the War of Independence was the fulfillment of their greatest hope; after two thousand years of tumultuous history in the Diaspora, the Jewish people finally had their own country in their homeland. Droves of Jewish refugees from Arab countries began arriving in Israel, often after expulsion from their homes.[67] Israel began the task of resettlement, and these newly arrived Jewish immigrants were often sent to live in abandoned Palestinian homes. After the trauma of the Holocaust and a gruelling war, Israelis were cautiously optimistic. The agreements they signed were not peace treaties, but rather ceasefires. It was clear that, although the formal fighting had stopped, the conflict was far from over.

The Nakba of 1948 changed the Palestinian way of life for ever and left an indelible mark on the identity of Palestinians.[68] To them, it represented an end of their meaningful political agency. Israel signed armistice agreements with other Arab countries but not with the Palestinians themselves. They were unrepresented and ignored. Their interests would now be represented by the various Arab regimes (with varying degrees of sympathy for the Palestinians' plight), a situation that would last until the 1960s when the Palestinian Liberation Organization (PLO) emerged as the voice of the Palestinian people.[69]

After the War

The Palestinians who remained in the state of Israel were viewed with suspicion and lived under martial law that restricted their rights of expression, movement, organization and equality. This law remained in place until 1966.[70] One tragic example from this period occurred in 1956, when the Israeli border police murdered forty-nine Palestinian-Israelis in the village of Kafr Kasim. The village had been put under curfew, but many of the villagers had not been informed. They were shot by Israeli police for violating the curfew.[71]

The Palestinians outside Israel, most of whom were living in refugee camps, came to be completely dependent on the newly created United Nations Relief and Work Agency (UNRWA), which provided them with employment and subsidies, and helped in the construction of more permanent refugee camps, schools and medical centers. The despair over their situation, along with the absence of leadership from the traditional leading families, led to the emergence of a younger generation of nationalist leaders who emphasized the necessity of a Palestinian right of return.[72]

In the years immediately following the war, there were clashes between Palestinians who infiltrated the Israeli border and the Israeli military.[73] Many of these infiltrators only wanted to return to their home village or visit relatives, but others attacked Israelis. Between 1948 and 1956, in addition to scores of Israeli soldiers, infiltrators killed approximately two hundred Israeli citizens. In response, Israel instituted a policy of shooting infiltrators on sight and began laying landmines along known infiltration routes. In the same years, at least 2,700 infiltrators, many of them unarmed, were killed by the Israelis.[74] The infiltrations continued in spite of Israeli actions, with many infiltrators coming from the Egyptian-controlled Gaza Strip.

From the time of the seizure of power by Gamal Abdel Nasser's Free Officers Movement in 1952, Egypt became Israel's most outspoken opponent. When Nasser secured a major arms deal with Czechoslovakia, Israeli fears of Egyptian aggression intensified.[75] In 1956, Nasser nationalized the Suez Canal. Israel saw an opportunity to deal him a blow and launched an invasion, together with the British and the French, to counter Egyptian control of the canal.[76] Israel conquered the Gaza Strip and the Sinai Peninsula, but eventually agreed to withdraw after pressure by the United States. Nasser became the hero of the Arab world as well as an icon of the global anti-colonial struggle, as Egypt retained control of the canal. The Arab world, and especially Egypt, stepped up their anti-Israeli rhetoric, although the cross-border infiltrations from Egypt slowed to a trickle.[77]

The Six Day War and After

In May 1967, Egyptian forces began deploying in the Sinai, a move that put the Israelis on alert.[78] The peninsula had been mostly demilitarized since the 1956 war and was patrolled by UN troops. Nasser ordered the UN troops out and moved in Egyptian troops. A few days later he announced the closure of the Straits of Tiran to Israeli shipping, completely cutting off Israeli access to Asia. In response to these measures, Israel began preparing for war.[79] Tensions heightened when Egypt signed a mutual defence pact with King Hussein of Jordan and Iraq, and inflammatory statements calling for Israel's destruction were repeatedly sounded in the Arab press. On 5 June 1967, Israel launched a surprise attack on Egypt, and the Six Day War began.[80]

Israel swiftly took control of the entire Sinai Peninsula and the Gaza Strip. When Jordan joined in the war, Israel took the Jordanian-occupied section of East Jerusalem as well as the West Bank. On the northern front, Israel drove the Syrians back and secured possession of the Golan Heights.[81] Taking control of this territory more than tripled the size of Israel. In the aftermath of the war, the decision was made to keep the newly acquired territories.[82] Thousands of Palestinians from the West Bank and Gaza fled to Jordan and Egypt. Many of them were refugees from 1948 and were fleeing for the second time. Those that stayed behind – around one million – came under Israeli occupation. By 1 June the war was over, and within a week, the political and military landscape of the entire Middle East was dramatically changed.

The reunification and subsequent expansion of Jerusalem, which had been divided in the 1948 War, was especially significant for the Israelis. For the first time in nearly twenty years, they were now able to return to the Old City and to the *Kotel* (Western Wall). East Jerusalem was officially annexed by Israel soon afterwards. For many Jews, the dramatic capture of Jerusalem as well as the West Bank was perceived as a sign of God's deliverance. The religious nationalist movement, inspired by Israel's military victory, began planning the annexation and settlement of Palestinian territories. Within a few years these plans began yielding results. By 1973, aided by the government and military, the religious nationalists successfully established seventeen settlements in the West Bank, including re-establishing Jewish communities lost during 1929 and the 1948 War. In 1977 when the right-wing, pro-settlement Likud Party came to power, the settlers' movement gained mainstream political support.[83]

In 1967, in response to Israel's conquests in the war, the Arab League Summit met in Khartoum, Sudan, and passed the Khartoum Resolution. This resolution advanced the position of the so-called 'Three No's': no peace with Israel, no recognition of Israel, and no agreement to negotiation with Israel.[84] The UN passed Resolution 242, which called for Israel to withdraw from territories taken in war, and for the Arab states to acknowledge the state of Israel. It also called for a solution to the Palestinian refugee problem. Although ignored by both Israel and the Arab states, the resolution nonetheless continues to be one of the possible bases for a peace negotiation.[85]

The Palestinian territories have been under continuous Israeli military occupation since 1967. Military occupation 'may be provisionally defined as a form of government imposed by force or threat thereof that establishes a type of mutual obligation between the occupier and the occupied, but without bringing about any change in allegiance'.[86] All military occupations are founded on force and implemented through fear. Israel's occupation of the West Bank and Gaza often violates the rules of military occupation according to the Geneva Convention. Under occupation, the Palestinian populace is regularly subjected to intimidation, brute force, repression, humiliation, beatings and manipulation.[87] The dismal reality of occupation, coupled with the failure of the Arab states in the war, raised the status of the Palestinian Liberation Organization (PLO), which had been established in 1964 by the Arab League.[88] Originally, the Arab states sought to control the PLO, hoping to prevent the Palestinians from initiating their own struggle against Israel, which could prove to destabilize their interests. The failure of the Arab states to control the PLO allowed the Palestinians to wrest control of their own political agency for the first time since 1948. This resurgence of Palestinian leadership was most evident when Yasser Arafat's *Fatah* (the Palestinian Liberation Movement), founded in 1959, took control of the PLO.[89]

Palestinian organizations such as Fatah began launching attacks on Israel from Jordan, threatening the Jordanian government's authority and inviting Israeli reprisals on Jordanian territory. Increasingly, the Palestinians began challenging the Hashemite monarchy in Jordan, and clashes between Palestinian guerrilla fighters and Jordanian soldiers became a regular occurrence. Following assassination attempts on King Hussein's life, the Palestinian terrorists significantly challenged his authority by hijacking planes and holding hostages on Jordanian soil. In response, King Hussein declared war on the PLO in September 1970. This war became known as 'Black September', and the crackdown was especially brutal. By the end of the struggle, close to 5,000 Palestinians[90] had been killed, most of whom were civilians. Part of the tragedy of the Palestinian refugees who fled to the surrounding Arab countries has been at the hands of some of their Arab hosts. Palestinian refugees were welcomed in Jordan, but the situation in Syria and Lebanon was hostile to the refugees. Life in refugee camps often exposed the people to repression, beating, torture, intimidation and humiliation. Many guerrilla fighters escaped to Lebanon, which had come to be called 'Fatahland' by the Israelis.[91] A number of other Palestinian terrorist organizations continued their assaults against Israelis elsewhere. These attacks included the kidnapping and murder of Israeli Olympic athletes at the 1972 Munich Olympic Games and the capture and detainment of Israeli passengers on an Air France flight in Uganda, which led to the dramatic Israeli rescue raid on Entebbe in 1976.[92]

From the October War to the War in Lebanon

Following the Israeli seizure of the Sinai, Egypt began a war of attrition with Israel that would prove costly to both sides in terms of casualties, but would do much to bolster Egypt's confidence after its humiliating defeat in 1967. From 1968 until Nasser's death in 1970, Egypt continually bombarded Israeli positions in the Sinai from across the Suez Canal, resulting in Israeli incursions into Egypt.[93] Although the Sinai remained in Israeli hands, the War of Attrition prepared the way for the October War (or Yom Kippur War), when Egypt's new leader Anwar Sadat and Syria's leader Hafez Assad attacked Israel in order to regain the territory they had lost in 1967.

The Egyptian and Syrian forces strategically attacked on 6 October 1973, which that year fell on *Yom Kippur* (the Day of Atonement), the holiest day in the Jewish liturgical year. As part of the national observance of the holy day, all businesses in Israel were closed and all private and public transportation was suspended. The attack had the desired element of surprise and caught the Israelis completely off guard. After initial defeat and a number of costly battles, Israel was able to repel Syria and Egypt, and push deeper into Syrian and Egyptian territory. Still, it was clearly not an overwhelming victory in the mould of the 1967 war. Although they eventually retreated, the Arab forces were pleased with the outcome of the war; they had faced the Israelis and restored a measure of dignity to their military and national pride. In addition, their actions forced Israel to come to terms with the fact that military force alone was not enough; they would also need to seek peace with their neighbours.[94] The war also demonstrated Israel's growing dependence on the United States and the Arab states' dependence on the Soviet Union in the larger ideological conflict of the Cold War.[95]

Soon after the war, Sadat expressed his willingness to break with the status quo and begin peace talks with Israel. This led to his historic visit to Israel in 1977, when he addressed the Israeli Knesset.[96] The following year, Sadat and Israeli Prime Minister Menachem Begin met with US president Jimmy Carter for the Camp David Accords, and in March 1979, Israel and Egypt signed a peace treaty. Only a few years later, in 1981, Sadat was assassinated in Egypt by Islamist activists from the 'Muslim Brotherhood'. Nevertheless, and at the time of the writing of this book, the treaty between Egypt and Israel has held[97] and serves as the basis for future peace agreements between Israel and Arab states.[98]

With peace secured on the southern border, the Israelis were now able to turn their attention to defending their northern border, where the PLO continued to attack Israel from Lebanon. The Palestinians had been able to further entrench themselves in Lebanon and had essentially turned the Palestinian refugee camps in southern Lebanon into a Palestinian 'state within a state'. During the Lebanese Civil War, which began in 1975, the Palestinians found themselves allied with Lebanese Muslims. This opened the door for Israel to create a strategic alliance with the Lebanese Maronite Christians – an Eastern Church in full communion with the Holy See in Rome – and their Phalange militia.[99] Begin's government was looking for a pretext to invade Lebanon and deal with the PLO once and for all. When a Palestinian terrorist not directly affiliated with the PLO attacked Shlomo Argov, Israel's ambassador to the United Kingdom in June 1982, the Israeli cabinet met and made the decision to invade.[100]

The Israeli forces fought their way to Beirut, and eventually managed to put enough pressure on the PLO to make Arafat concede defeat. The PLO evacuation began in August 1982 as the PLO leadership set sail from the Beirut harbour bound for Tunisia, where the new PLO headquarters were established.[101] A few days later a Christian, Bashir Gemayel, was elected president of Lebanon. He was assassinated on 14 September, leaving the Maronite community devastated and hungry for revenge. The Israeli army invaded the Palestinian stronghold of West Beirut, and on 16 September, their Phalange allies began massacring Palestinians in the refugee camps of Sabra and Shatila. The massacre lasted for three days.[102] Between 700 and 800 men, women and children were killed. When news of the massacre reached Israel, waves of anger swept through both the Israeli and the Arab population. Sizeable demonstrations were held, calling for the government to resign, and Ariel Sharon, then the Minister of Defence, was forced to step down.[103]

By the end of September, the Israelis withdrew from Beirut, but still occupied southern Lebanon. Now that the PLO was gone, they faced a new enemy in Lebanon: the Iranian-backed Hizbullah (the Party of God), a radical Shi'ite militia. For the next two years Israel continually battled with Hizbullah, and eventually pulled back into their 'security buffer' in the south in June 1985. Hizbullah was still not satisfied; they wanted the Israelis out of Lebanon altogether and continued attacking them. Israel refused to withdraw under fire, as doing so would have been an admission of failure. Nonetheless, periodic fighting was common until Israel's eventual unilateral withdrawal in 2000 under the leadership of then Prime Minister Ehud Barak. The PLO had been ejected from Lebanon, but clearly, the goal of bringing peace to the northern border had not been achieved.[104]

Intifada and the Peace Process

In December 1987, the first Palestinian *intifada* (uprising) began in Gaza, and quickly spread to the West Bank. Immediately prior to the outbreak, both the Gaza Strip and the West Bank had experienced an economic decline. Most of the labour pool in these territories was forced to seek employment in Israel due to the absence of indigenous industrial or agricultural development. The Israeli government stifled Palestinian economic development by not permitting Palestinians to develop resources that might compete with Israel. Usage of resources is an issue between Israel and Palestine, with water and land being the most contested. The rise of the Likud Party in the Israeli government in 1977 and its subsequent settlement expansion only served to confirm Palestinian fears of displacement.[105]

That the intifada began in Gaza was no coincidence. Gaza was and remains one of the most densely populated places in the world. The living conditions faced by Gazans were cramped and squalid, and a third of the population was unemployed. Only a spark was needed to ignite the populace to rise up against the Israeli occupation, and that spark was provided when an Israeli army vehicle accidentally killed four Palestinians.[106] The intifada was marked by boycotts against Israel, and Palestinian youth agitating against Israeli soldiers, throwing rocks and Molotov cocktails. The repression of the uprising was harsh; many Palestinians were killed and many more injured.[107] Early on in the intifada, Hamas (an acronym for *Harakat al-Mukawma al-Islamiya*, the Islamic Resistance Movement) was created as an offshoot of the Egyptian Muslim Brotherhood, and it began to plan and execute attacks against the Israeli military and civilian population.[108]

Because of the intifada, Israeli morale and international standing were damaged. Pressure increased, both domestically and internationally, to make peace with the Palestinians. Secret talks began between the Israelis and the PLO, and finally, a document entitled the 'Declaration of Principles' was signed on 13 September 1993 at the White House in Washington, DC. This document, signed by Yasser Arafat and Israeli Prime Minister Yitzhak Rabin, was to guide the final status negotiations between Israelis and Palestinians, eventually leading to a peace agreement. In addition, the Palestinians gained a degree of autonomy with the establishment of the Palestinian Authority (PA), which assumed control over the Gaza Strip and part of the West Bank.[109]

These years were hopeful, especially as Israel and Jordan signed a peace treaty in 1994. Israelis and Palestinians were optimistic about the peace process. There seemed to be a real chance that the long conflict would end. But these hopes proved to be short-lived. On 4 November 1995, Israeli Prime Minister Rabin was assassinated at a peace rally in Tel Aviv by an Israeli Jew opposed to the peace process. Soon after, Hamas and other radical Palestinian Islamic groups began a campaign of suicide terror attacks against Israel. These were partially in response to a massacre of Muslims that took place at the Cave of the Patriarchs in Hebron in 1994. Consequently, the peace process began to lose momentum and popularity on both sides.[110] Throughout the late 1990s, neither side implemented the terms they had agreed upon, with Israeli and Palestinian extremists doing everything possible to provoke each other and thwart the possibility of peace.

The 1999 election of Ehud Barak, the leader of the Labour Party, brought renewed hope for peace. The following year, he met together with Arafat and US president Bill Clinton for another attempt at negotiation at Camp David in July 2000. In the end, the talks failed, and both sides blamed each other for intransigence. Shortly after, in September 2000, Israeli defense minister Ariel Sharon, accompanied by armed bodyguards, visited the Temple

Mount. The Palestinians perceived this as an act of provocation and a demonstration of Israeli sovereignty at their holy site. Some claim that this triggered the subsequent violence, while others argue that Sharon's visit provided the excuse Arafat needed to launch the second intifada, or the *al-Aksa intifada*. This was a more violent and bloody sequel to the first uprising, and it profoundly terrorized the Israeli civilian population.[111]

In October 2000, Israel's Palestinian citizens began to protest in solidarity with Palestinians in the Occupied Territories and Jerusalem; the Israeli police killed thirteen Palestinian-Israelis during these protests. The new intifada, and the anger and death that it brought to both sides, effectively killed the peace process. For the next few years, the continuous violence left many Israelis and Palestinians dead, and many were permanently traumatized, sceptical and opposed to attempts to make peace.

In the decade since the beginning of the second intifada, many dramatic events have occurred. In March 2002, the Arab League presented Israel with the Arab Peace Initiative. This was an offer to end the Israeli–Arab conflict and to normalize relations, based on an Israeli withdrawal to the 1967 borders. Israel and Hamas agreed that Israel would stop targeted assassinations and Hamas would stop suicide bombings. The damage to Ḥamas's reputation, Israel taking control of all West Bank cities for a limited period of time, and the Palestinian Authority's cooperation with the IDF all contributed to the elimination of the flood of suicide bombings and other terror attacks against Israelis. However, Israel's construction of the controversial separation barrier around the West Bank has further solidified the divide between Israelis and Palestinians. Most Israelis view the wall as a necessary security measure to defend them against Palestinian terrorist attacks, while most Palestinians view it as part of an Israeli land-grab and a symbol of Israel's oppressive occupation.

Israel's disengagement and unilateral withdrawal from the Gaza Strip (September 2005) was followed by the election and rise to power of Hamas in Gaza. Following the Gaza withdrawal, the whole south of Israel, including Netivot, Ashkelon, Beer-Sheva and the Israeli city of Sderot, was subjected to years of missile barrage originating from Gaza, further terrorizing the civilian population. Subsequent wars in Gaza and Lebanon have also played a role in shaping the current situation, and Israel's growing fear of a nuclear Iran, the current deteriorating situation along the Syrian Israeli border, together with the 'Arab Spring' revolutions that spread across the Middle East and North Africa in 2011, are factors which may well bring about far-reaching diplomatic changes. It is still too early to interpret these events, but they are sure to leave a lasting mark.

The history offered here provides background and gives insight into the larger stories that Israelis and Palestinians tell about themselves, to themselves and to their children. These stories are their narratives, and it is to these narratives we now turn.

2.

History and Narrative

Working out a theology of reconciliation presupposes a context of conflict. In the words of David Augsburger, human conflict is 'essential to, ineradicable from, and inevitable in human life'.[1] When people experience conflict, either as a member of a group or individually, they instinctively look for witnesses who can testify to their suffering and whose testimony can secure their vindication. They tell stories to make sense of their suffering. The telling and retelling of the stories of life, including but perhaps especially those of pain and conflict, contribute to the formation of history, an important source of identity and legitimacy. History is not a simple linear recounting of facts, although it accounts for and incorporates facts into a broader web of meaning. History is also a carefully guarded expression of a people. The way a people tell their history reveals how they perceive themselves, their past and their future.

Historians increasingly recognize that the once-clear distinction between the academic study of the human past (history) and the story a group tells about itself (narrative) has blurred. Indeed, the poststructuralist critique has upended methodologies within the social sciences, permitting new space for the accounting of narratives. Many historians now discount the notion of 'objective history' or even whether a kind of detached objectivity is a worthy goal for historical study. Not all, though, see this critical hermeneutic as an incontrovertible good. While acknowledging the limits of 'objective' historical study, some historians continue to argue for preserving a notion of that ideal, even if the clear conceptual distinctions between narrative and history are now less precise.

Balance is needed. While it is true that narrative shapes history, affirming the distinction between the two is still valuable. Not all canonical history represents the fraudulent narratives of the victors over and against the silenced voices of the vanquished. History and narrative, working together, serve a larger purpose in human meaning. They simultaneously inform and are informed by each other. Indeed, there could be no history without narrative, just as there could be no narrative without history. They are separate but intertwined. Imagine history without narrative. It would be comprised of statistics and graphs, without a connecting story that would give those facts coherency and meaning. Similarly, narrative without historical input lacks an accounting in the wider world; the story, while resonant with meaning, might not reflect reality.

Our concern here is not to classify the historical events that comprise the larger story of the Israeli–Palestinian conflict. There are many historians and culture-shapers working towards that end. It is simply a matter of time before all classified, hidden or lost documents are declassified, uncovered or brought to light. When this happens, the historical record will be more fully orbed. What interests us here is that which will continue to be contested long after any 'facts' are revealed – the finger-pointing and selective memories, whether codified in school textbooks or recounted by grandparents; in short, the narratives.

In their studies of narrative, Shlomith Rimmon-Kenan and Matti Hyvärinen explore the many aspects of narrative in life. For this discussion, we will use a simple definition of narrative as 'someone telling someone else that something happened'.[2] The important question we are asking is whether the Israeli–Palestinian narrative is essentially a struggle in which both groups tell their own story of conflict as an objective version of history recounting a sequence of events; or whether the narrative is an effort to establish an ideological position.[3] Rimmon-Kenan challenges this particular use of the word 'narrative', citing the lack of an obvious narrator – the 'someone' from our definition: 'Who, for example, *narrates* the ideological construct in question?'[4] That is, narrative presumes the presence of a narrator, when lived experience does not readily locate narrators in the making of narrative meaning.

It seems fair to appropriate the concept of narrative for our discussion of the Israeli–Palestinian conflict. Furthermore, the conflict *can* be spoken about as a struggle over narrative within the parameters of our definition. There *are* narrators, speaking through the currents of culture, media, family members, schools, political and religious leaders; blaming the 'other side' while vindicating their own side. Within a conflict, the dominant party can afford to narrate explicitly – or choose something else. Regardless, there are voices, and they are telling their version of what has happened.

Narrative – someone telling someone else that something happened – is an important, even essential, part of human life. It helps us understand the world around us, for 'man is . . . essentially a story-telling animal' which means that people can 'only answer the question "What am I to do?" if [they] can answer the prior question, "Of what story or stories do I find myself a part?"'[5] To deprive children of narrative through stories would impoverish their lives and leave them without a context for understanding either their actions or their words.[6] Even if one accepts that narrative contributes to an understanding of the world, there remains significant debate over how exactly narrative exerts its influence. For some, the concept of narrative reflects how people perceive life. People 'emplot' or assign a narrative-like structure – with a discernible beginning, middle and end – to events that are not already structured this way. 'Stories are not lived but told. Life has no beginnings, middles, or ends; there are meetings, but the start of an affair belongs to the story we tell later, and there are partings, but final partings only in the story.'[7] From this perspective, it is the occurrences that precede the telling of the stories so that the later narratives provide a framework for understanding the events.[8] This view of narrative distorts the reality of what actually took place, causing an undesirable effect on both history and memories of personal experience.

Some scholars suggest that the human mind organizes data through narrative because life itself is organized in a narrative fashion.[9] Others maintain that narrative structure is an inherent part of how life is experienced and therefore is integral to what it is to be human, regardless of whether the story is actually told.[10] This understanding of narrative exceeds our selected definition and denies the need for a narrator. If one accepts the idea that there is a narrative quality to all of human experience, then this also influences an understanding of history. Reality is easier to understand if it has a beginning, middle and end. It is also easier to embrace if it is organized through a simple moral division of the forces of good and evil.

If we accept that historical facts are, in fact, moulded into the shape of a narrative, interpreted and constructed, and not primarily discovered through historical research, then it is possible for alternative constructs to exist. Making room for a narrative that challenges the dominant account can be positive. It can be a way of empowering the powerless, 'a way of giving voice to minorities or disadvantaged groups, generally repressed and silenced by the hegemony.'[11] Nevertheless, while alternative narratives can provide a platform for repressed voices, narratives themselves are not without risk. An extended quote illustrates the point:

> Even when accounts remain rooted in a critique of hierarchy, storytelling has real dangers, one of which is accepting a place at the margin. Storytelling as method originated in powerlessness and can bring a fear of power with it. Instead of telling power it is wrong, tell it a story. Avoid finger pointing. No offense; everyone can be right. Storytelling can be ingratiating in ceding reality to power this way, presenting itself as just another version, becoming a grace note to the main account. When one dare not argue, storytelling can be a strategy for survival. But it can ask too little. Dominant narratives are not called stories. They are called reality.[12]

Furthermore, to challenge the dominant account of history – 'reality' – out of a foundational conviction that there is no truly neutral or objective historical position is to expose the alternative narrative to the possibility of severe critical challenges. Storytelling, narratives, and the like can sustain the powerless. However, they can also act like a coping mechanism, offering a kind of panacea rather than fostering wise human agency and political responsibility in the midst of a conflict.

One reason groups guard their narratives closely and defend them so strongly when challenged is because their narratives are intricately linked to their identity. Individual and group identities are formed through given or adopted narratives. This view is shared by many scholars.[13] How a person or a group responds when their narratives are directly challenged reveals much about who they perceive themselves and their group to be. A challenge to a narrative may, paradoxically, strengthen an uncritical belief of a group's narrative, in which 'we' represent 'the good', and 'we' are the hero of the story. Legitimacy is also at stake, and in order to protect a group, its narrative must function at times like a sacred text. A threat to one's story can be perceived as a threat to life itself. It is human nature to situate oneself and one's people as the central, heroic figure of the tale one tells about oneself, regardless of its accuracy.

Elements of Narrative

Narratives provide many of the things that give life meaning, such as a sense of identity, belonging and place, a paradigm through which to understand the world, and even a set of moral values. Each of these elements adds to the richness of life. However, when these are threatened in the midst of a conflict, they can reinforce the inflexibility and exclusivity of narratives that oppose each other. Opposing narratives reflect more than a simple dispute regarding past events. Simple disputes, like agreeing on basic facts of history, still play a big part within the conflict of narratives. Opposing narratives are, rather, perspectives on life that are fundamentally different from, and in strong, even judgmental disagreement with, each other. To accept one narrative often necessitates denying the other. Accepting one narrative leaves no room for the consideration of the opposing narrative: narratives 'morally exclude each other and devalue and dehumanize their enemy's narrative. If the opponent's narrative is described at all, it is presented as morally inferior and irrational. The enemy is depicted as faceless, as well as immoral, espousing manipulative arguments.'[14]

A number of traits are particularly characteristic of narrative accounts, and these elements are present in most intractable conflicts. In the case of the conflict between Israelis and Palestinians, these traits often contribute to the perpetuating of strife and impede opportunities for reconciliation. For while narrative supports identity, it also provides a sense of legitimacy, functional truth, a motivating rationale for participating in a conflict, as well as the rationale for significantly resisting new information that may challenge the totalizing aspects of a narrative.

Therefore, narrative grounds personal and collective identity, and then it steadily reinforces that identity. It focuses on positive in-group images and tends to exclude, or tellingly omits, any in-group blame for violence and conflict. The burden of guilt for provoking and maintaining the conflict is reserved for the other side. This reassuring message is not difficult for an in-group to believe. It reinforces the group's own belief that it consists of good, reasonable people who value peace and harmony. The narrative reinforces the already existing sense that the group members are not the aggressors but the victims. Indeed, the narrative endlessly presents the in-group with the factuality of its own innocent victimization. It should come as no surprise that both Israelis and Palestinians see themselves as the true victims of the conflict and see the other side as the aggressor. This belief is maintained on both sides by their respective narratives of the historical past and 'proven' – i.e. reconfirmed and reinforced – every time the conflict escalates.[15] The narrative explains the conflict and, in doing so, strengthens its capacity for explaining the future.

In a conflict, legitimacy – a sense of the rightness of a cause – is a crucial resource. If either side loses its legitimacy, the members will also forfeit the conflict. Legitimacy, in this case, means the belief among the members of an in-group (Israelis, Palestinians) that they are right and not necessarily that their belief in their own rightness is universally legitimate by virtue of international law or public opinion. In fact, both the Israeli and Palestinian narratives lack this element of universal legitimacy. Interestingly, both sides feel misunderstood and persecuted by the world, which seems indifferent to their suffering at best, and aligned against them at worst. In the narratives of both communities, this sentiment only reinforces their own sense of legitimacy and perceives any challenge to the narrative as betrayal.

Each side has built a case for their claim to the land based on their own sense of legitimacy and the grievances committed against them. These sentiments also necessarily delegitimize the narrative of the other side. 'History is the reservoir of resentment, the fount of blame. History legitimizes; history thus sanctifies . . . Without an acceptable recourse to the past, gaining legitimacy for rebellion and hostility, plus terror, is impossible. No contemporary cause, however implausible, achieves widespread following without such legitimation.'[16] For both Israelis and Palestinians, the proof of their rightness and the other side's 'wrongness' is found in the past just as much as it is found in the present.

As an aspect of any narrative, functional truth is a partial truth that serves a purpose, offering legitimacy, while serving truth itself is a secondary goal. For example, the Israeli and Palestinian narratives both claim to offer the definitive truth of the conflict, but both are often one-sided, biased views. However, these functional truths have a powerful purpose: they strengthen the claims and further entrench the victimization of both sides. A functional truth may not always be a truthful recounting of history; instead, it may be a description of past events that reinforces the group's ability to function and survive. 'It is a story that is biased, selective, and distorted, that omits certain facts, adds others that did not take place, changes the sequence of events, and purposely reinterprets events that did take place. In short, it is a narrative constructed to fit the current needs of the group.'[17]

Because of the way conflicting narratives are constructed, they lend themselves to presupposing a zero-sum universe mentality on both sides. Each narrative tries to make sense of the same events and the same history, but each interprets these events and history in fundamentally different ways. For the adherents of either narrative, any interpretation that differs from their own narrative is seen as a grave, potentially mortal challenge to the narrative in its entirety. Since so much depends on narrative, when any part of it is challenged the challenge feels categorical. In the case of Israelis and Palestinians, each has the sense that if they were to accept the identity of the other, this would nullify their own identity and even endanger the basis of their claims for legitimacy and statehood. The claims and aspirations of each group are seen as fundamentally incompatible. For one to exist, the other must disappear. In a land that is contested, each side sees the aspirations of the other to achieve autonomy on the land as a threat to the existence and autonomy of the other. For one side to establish independence would jeopardize the position of the other side concerning their mutually exclusive claims to the land.[18]

A collective narrative comprises the story a people tell about themselves as a group. As a collective endeavour, it functions in the same way as a personal narrative. In fact, collective and personal narratives often merge as people connect historical events from the distant past to more recent events and to their own personal experiences. In the merging of the past and present, together with the personal memories of the individual, the memories can become part of a larger historical narrative that increasingly strengthens as conflict continues. This narrative memory is a potent force that frequently affects and even alters current behaviour, attitudes and perceptions.[19] As a collective narrative, it serves as a unifying factor; people 'remember' who they are *together*. In this way, for example, Jewish people from all over the world, who have relatively little in common with each other, are still able to identify personally and collectively with the dramatic stories of Passover, Masada and the Holocaust. Similarly, Palestinians worldwide, from South America to the West Bank, are able to relate personally and collectively to the collective memory of the Nakba, whether or not they actually experienced it.

No less important to narrative is what is actually remembered, and therefore incorporated and retained, and what is forgotten. In this sense, narrative faces the same problem of selection as does the discipline of history. Selection is an inevitable process, but it can also be revealing. From a historical perspective, selection is an unfortunate limitation to discovering the whole truth about the past. But from the perspective of narrative, selection is not necessarily a limitation. Indeed, it is a useful, if not fully conscious, process that nurtures the legitimacy of one side as it raises doubts about the legitimacy of the other. Again, this is true for the Israeli–Palestinian conflict.[20]

No matter how objective a people think their narrative is, it still reflects who they are as subjects. Therefore, it can properly be called 'subjective', even if this word has become a byword meaning 'not factual'. Subjectivity, however, is a fundamental part of narration in which someone tells somebody what has happened. This process is evident when one contrasts Israeli and Palestinian views on the war of 1948. Israelis are quick to point out early in their narrative that Arab nations attacked Israel first, and, tellingly, most likely exclude (or forget to include) Israeli offensives throughout the war. On the other hand, Palestinians usually emphasize the fact that Israel aggressively expelled many Palestinians from their homes, and, tellingly, exclude (or forget to include) the attack by surrounding Arab nations on Israel. Both narratives contain factual elements, but neither of them accounts for all relevant historical facts. What these narratives do preserve, though, is the 'truth' of the legitimacy of their in-group, while at the same time excluding other parts of the historical record that challenge or discount their role as 'pure victim' in the narrative.

The use of collective narrative can also be an effective tool in garnering moral and material support for one's side in a conflict. If a group's narrative can successfully portray its own side as the innocent victim and the other side as the aggressor, the in-group members will be more willing to vote for an extreme leader, serve in combat, and commit acts of violence in the name of their people. Again, this plays out in both Israeli and Palestinian societies. People are willing to commit acts of injustice for their narrative in-group when they would likely never commit such injustices for themselves alone. 'It is enough to say "we" instead of "I" – and we already have a ready-made easy conscience'.[21] This is true especially if 'we' are simply defending ourselves against aggressors who threaten us with extermination. A firmly established narrative is a powerful tool. It justifies the eruption and continuation of conflict and gives a powerful *raison d'être* for mutually exclusive goals. The group's narrative highlights the importance of achieving its goals and emphasizing that the result of failure to achieve them may in fact endanger the group's very survival. In so doing, the goals of the other side are denied, ignored, and seen as irrational and indefensible.[22]

Whenever a narrative is created, repeated and handed down over generations, it grows stronger and develops resistance to challenge. The more often it is repeated, the more it comes to be accepted as the whole truth. In intractable conflicts, enduring for generations, it is told repeatedly, gaining strength and formality. Once a narrative is rooted deeply in the collective psyche, it is very difficult to convince an adherent that they may not be seeing the whole truth. Any new information that may call the narrative into question is automatically rejected and labelled as lies and propaganda.[23] In this way, narratives not only prevent an in-group from seeing the situation from the perspective of the other side, which is essential to reconciliation, but they also help the conflict to continue.[24] This is a vicious cycle that can only be broken through willingness to be mindful of the role of narratives and their tendencies to capture our imagination to the exclusion of other narratives, including God's narrative.

Bridging the Gap: Narrative and History in Conflict

Israelis and Palestinians, like all participants in any conflict, foster their own representative narrative about the history of the conflict that discloses which side is innocent and which is to blame. However, if reconciliation is the goal, what is to be done with these narratives? There has been considerable debate among academics on this topic. The debate ranges from whether it is best to try and bridge the gap between the two narratives, forming them into a third, shared narrative that could serve as the foundation for reconciliation and a platform for the future; to whether it is better to accept that the two narratives will never be bridged and to focus on criticizing areas of weakness in both narratives.

Some historians believe it is possible to bridge the gap between the Israeli and Palestinian collective narratives. This bridging can be accomplished by putting a renewed emphasis on social and interdisciplinary history, rather than on political and military history, which tend to dominate the narratives of the conflict. Perhaps a common narrative could emerge if lesser-known voices and testimonies of ordinary people from both sides of the conflict were given respectful attention. Stress should also be placed on the attempts Palestinians and Israelis have made, personally and politically, to work and live together in peace. The goal of this created narrative is to 'install in their pantheon of heroes and heroines men and women of peace and reconciliation rather than generals and politicians of war and destruction.'[25]

Other historians believe that bridging the narrative gap is impossible, if by 'bridge' one means reaching a point where both sides agree on what happened in the past. As an Israeli historian, former IDF chief education officer, and an advocate of the Israeli–Palestinian peace process, Mordechai Bar-On takes the example of the 1948 war between the Israelis and the Palestinians as an indicative symbol of the futility of bridging narratives. Israeli Jews call this war the War of Independence. From their perspective, this name is both a factual description and the means whereby they understand their entire collective existence. Yet Palestinians call these same events the *Nakba* (catastrophe), which is, from their perspective, a factual description of what they actually individually and collectively experienced.[26] Bar-On explains that not only is it unreasonable to expect these perceptions to change through bridging, but it is also undesirable to try and force both narratives to blend into one. He objects to bridging efforts because they lead to, in his opinion, 'an attempt to reassert the "truth" of one's own narrative against the "falsehood" of the other.'[27] This is not to say that historians have no role to play in the work of reconciliation. Indeed, they should seek to challenge the exclusivity of narratives during conflict, and focus on their own narratives. To require or demand a revision of the narrative of the other side exacerbates rather than resolves conflict. As scholars debate the validity of conflicting narratives, this venture can only bear fruit if each side is self-critical and non-condemnatory towards the other side.[28] Additionally, by trying to use relatively value-neutral terms, like 'War of 1948', historians can help to bring calm to an already painful, heated discipline.

Can the gap between the Israeli and Palestinian narratives be bridged? Should it be? If so, how can this bridge be built? It is beyond the scope of this book to weigh in on these questions, but they are important questions that are being asked by those living in Israel-Palestine. It is enough for us, here, to ask them as a way of understanding how narratives affect the process of reconciliation.

A theology of reconciliation must be created and lived by Israelis and Palestinians involved in the conflict. The theology cannot be removed from the context of the conflict. In the meantime, Robert I. Rotberg suggests three steps that can help in working towards reconciliation. The first step is to learn the opposing narratives, the second step is to bring them together and bridge them as much as is possible, and the third step is to 'assist both sides to acknowledge and hopefully to even respect the legitimacy of the opposing narrative.'[29]

The first step involves actual encounter with views that are easily dismissed or considered suspect. Since most people already know their own narrative, it is helpful to the cause of reconciliation to sincerely seek to learn and empathize with the opposing narrative, even if one strongly disagrees with it. This discipline facilitates more coherent discussion between the sides, but it also enlarges the capacity to hear divergent views without a sense of danger or scandal. For many people within the conflict, simply hearing the narrative of the other side is scandalous, in part because they often have little opportunity to do so.

Many difficulties stand in the way of the second step of trying to bridge the gap between the two opposing narratives. One way to attempt this is by being self-critical of one's own narrative, rather than focusing on telling the other side how their narrative is wrong or deficient. This endeavour is facilitated whenever new evidence becomes known, such as the declassification of documents by the Israeli government or the resurfacing of documents from the Palestinian archives. Although a complete bridging of the narratives might be impossible, it is possible to make considerable progress in narrowing the gap.

The third step involves cultivating a sense of empathy with the opposing narrative. While one may never agree with one's enemy about the past, one can come to understand more fully the way the other side thinks, and regard them as human beings with hopes, dreams and aspirations for themselves and their children. Granting acceptance and respect to an enemy's narrative, even if one does not agree with it, can foster reconciliation. It can even gain a respectful hearing of one's own narrative. This respect can, in turn, affirm opposing identities normally secured by exclusive narratives and prepare the way for fuller reconciliation. This process is essential, for 'in meeting the other, we do not deny our own reality, but seek to include the reality of the other . . . within our own reality, to integrate the other's story, point-of-view, fears, joys, and hopes within our own story. In confirming the other's "presence" – or existential reality – we invite him or her to confirm our own.'[30]

To Rotberg's three steps we add a fourth, which is to invoke the narrative that Israeli Messianic Jews and Palestinian Christians share: the narrative of the cross of Jesus and the coming of his kingdom. The narrative that God continues to tell the world through his Holy Spirit, his word, and his church, is the bridge upon which both in-groups can stand and move towards one another. The greater biblical narrative reminds each community that they, together with all human beings, are created in the image of God. There is even a narrative of the Holy Land that both communities share. Each side loves the land, and each side must learn to love each other in that land.

To some, this understanding of history and narrative is problematic, even threatening. By casting doubt on the idea of history as the means of discovering the truth about the past, it might seem as though we are questioning the very idea of truth. There are, however, facts that one can know unequivocally about what happened. We both affirm that truth – absolute truth – exists, but we equally acknowledge the noetic effects of sin – the effect of sin that corrodes knowledge and even the capacity to know. As sinful and finite human beings, we are limited in our ability to fully know or even *truthfully* know the truth. The problem lies not with the truth, nor with God, but with us.

As biblical evidence of this reality, we offer the two different accounts of King David's life found in 1 Samuel and 1 Chronicles. Each narrative offers a very different image of David. That these two narratives exist within the biblical canon does not cast doubt on the truth of either, nor does it call into question the sufficiency or veracity of Scripture. They are both true and yet are told from different perspectives and with distinctive purposes in mind. The same could be said of the four gospel accounts of Jesus' life. Each narrates a story; each is plainly true on its own terms. Yet they are very different from one another and, at times, even seem contradictory. However, each witnesses truly to the Truth, to the one who called *himself* 'the Truth'.

The wise posture for those of us who acknowledge the noetic effects of sin is epistemological humility. This kind of humility must also extend to our own historical narratives, which, we must admit, do not encompass the whole truth and are, at times, severely mistaken. One biblical example of this is in the life of King Saul, who pursued David's life in the belief that David, despite David's careful overtures to the contrary (1 Sam. 24.9), was intent on overthrowing and killing him. While there may be divergent and even conflicting accounts of history, it is best, out of our love for Truth, to stand humbly before 'the Truth' and ask him to enable us to honestly and bravely, truly hear narratives other than our own.

3.

Israeli–Palestinian Historiography

Simply stated, historiography is the writing of history. The simplicity of the statement belies the multifaceted density of the subject. In ancient times, history was considered to be a branch of literature. This understanding of history and historiography gradually changed. From the late eighteenth century, history has been considered a science. As a term, history can either mean the actions and events that comprise humanity's past, or the accounts of the past and the methods of study and investigation used to arrive at its reconstruction. Historiography as a systematic discipline did not appear until the nineteenth century.

The task of the modern historian is to reconstruct as accurate a record as possible of both the activities and events of humanity with the aim of attaining a deep understanding of them. Modern historiography incorporates narrative elements combined with data from many other sources, including public and private documents, oral history and archival materials. A grasp of the importance of historiography is vital for any understanding of the complex history of the Israeli–Palestinian conflict.

No less important than the sources for historiography are the agenda and the motivation of the historian himself. As we have repeatedly emphasized, no one comes to any subject *tabula rasa*. Historians are influenced by many factors, including the socio-economic and political realities of the situations they write about. Many factors contribute to the way history is written, understood and interpreted. Impartiality, while desirable, is not ever completely possible. This is very much the case in contexts of conflict when historians from both sides, with their own agendas and often preconceived views, are writing about the same events.

Individuals have a need to live in a setting that is meaningful, comprehensible, organized and predictable. This need also applies to groups, and collective experiences have a significant influence on individual experiences.[1] The Israeli–Palestinian conflict is considered an intractable conflict, and this context has influenced the historical narratives of both sides. Nationalist agendas are often selective, simplistic and self-serving,[2] and to some degree, the histories written by both sides often mirror these agendas.

Israeli Historiography

Traditionally, Israeli historiography has been articulated in the following terms. This presentation of history is the predominant narrative and it has shaped generations of Israelis. Israeli Jews see their presence in Palestine as a return to their historical homeland, a restoration of their ancient birthright, which was given international approval and legitimacy through the Balfour Declaration and the United Nations Partition Plan. Zionism was a liberal national movement[3] that sought compromise with the Arab Palestinians in hopes that they could live peacefully side by side. The Jews accepted the United Nations partition plan for two states in Palestine; the Arab League and surrounding Arab states, including the local Arab Palestinians, rejected it. Great Britain attempted to thwart the establishment of a Jewish state through offering political and military assistance to the Arabs. After Israel declared its independence, five Arab countries invaded the new state with the aim of total destruction. Israel was like a Jewish David fighting against a stronger, larger Arab Goliath. Israel fought back heroically and miraculously emerged victorious. Throughout the war, approximately 700,000 Palestinians voluntarily fled their homes at the behest of Arab leaders, even though Jews pleaded with them to remain in Israel. After the war, Israel sought peace, but the surrounding Arab nations refused any such gestures.[4] From 1948 to the present, Israeli historiography continues to characterize the Palestinians as marked by rejectionism that categorically rejects any peace initiative.

Israel's new historians

The view articulated above has experienced significant changes since the late 1980s and the emergence of what has come to be known as the 'new historians'. The methodologies employed by the new historians are as diverse as their political leanings. Benny Morris claims that the job of historians is to look at the facts in front of them and present the most objective story possible based on the available evidence. He argues that objective detachment from the source material is possible, and historical truth should be attempted.[5] He believes documentary evidence[6] is the best source material available in this conflict and argues that this presents the truest picture of what actually happened. He argues that historians must 'seek truth, not justice' and that historians should refrain from moralizing. Instead they should analyze events based on multiple sources and then allow the reader to employ their 'moral compass' and draw their own conclusions.[7]

Other new historians argue that it is the role of the historian to moralize, to look at the facts before them and pass judgement on them. This perspective is easily reflected in their works.[8] They believe that history dealing with more contemporary issues such as the Israeli–Palestinian conflict is best constructed based on interviews, memoirs and oral history rather than documentation from military and political establishments. While reliance on an interdisciplinary approach in history may result in a loss of 'objectivity', historians should represent themselves as 'parliamentarians who represent different points of view' rather than as a 'priest who represents the only existing truth'.[9] True engagement with source material cannot be detached, and historians must be consciously aware of their engagement and involvement in historiography, and construct it accordingly.[10]

In December 1988, Benny Morris, a relatively unknown author, published an essay entitled 'The New Historiography: Israel Confronts Its Past' in the Israeli journal *Tikkun*. In this article he recounted a number of reports from the 1948 War detailing Israeli aggression against Arab Palestinians, from killing to expulsion. He contrasted this with Israeli historical accounts of these incidents published between the 1950s and 1970s. These accounts often contained partial truths, misleading descriptions, and at times blatant propaganda portraying the IDF in an excessively flattering light. Morris's argument is that the traditional, or Old History, was a pro-Israeli propaganda attempt to simplify and interpret the past in a way that avoided staining Israel's pristine image in the West. He discounts the methodology used by the traditional historians since they relied on interviews and memoirs, and often engaged in self-censorship. Many of these first historians were in fact themselves chroniclers and active participants in the 1948 War.[11]

Benny Morris reflected a significant shift in Israeli historiography, a shift that did not occur in a vacuum. There are a number of reasons for the emergence of a new narrative in the late 1980s. First, Israel follows the British policy of document declassification after thirty years. In the late 1970s and early 1980s, Israel released much documentation that had previously been classified.[12] These documents provided copious amounts of primary source material that was previously censored and thus unavailable to the Old Historians. Second, prior to, during and after the 1948 War, the Old Historians were often active participants or ideologically committed to the Israeli cause. They were therefore unable to separate themselves from events to engage in more objective historical inquiry. The new historians, on the other hand, were born close to or after 1948. They were willing to engage in self-criticism, thus providing a more impartial approach in their methodology.[13] Third, the 1982 Lebanon War changed the political climate of Israel.

Historically, the Israeli public, including the government, argued that Israel only engaged in wars of 'no choice' as a last resort as opposed to engaging in wars to further national ambitions. Then Prime Minister Menachem Begin gave a lecture discussing wars of choice and wars of no choice. He compared Israel's engagement in Lebanon to the Sinai War of 1956 and said both were wars of choice for the attainment of national objectives.[14] This opened the door for further self-criticism and self-examination of Israel's past and present actions. One of the final reasons for this historical shift in academia is timing. The shift emerged during the first intifada that began in 1987. People were receptive to hearing Morris's accusation that laid blame for the Palestinian refugee problem on the Israelis. At that time there was increasing discomfort with the

Israeli occupation,[15] and this new research was made accessible due to widespread media coverage.[16]

The New History was introduced into academia and political journalism by scholars like Benny Morris, Avi Shlaim, Ilan Pappé and Simcha Flapan. Their findings challenged the way Israeli society viewed itself. A variety of interpretations of Zionism emerged from the new historians. Some maintained that Zionism was a national liberation movement while others argued that it was a settler–colonialist movement.

The narrative as told by the old historians was challenged at almost every point by the new historians' interpretation of events and the motivations of the major players in the drama of the foundation of the state of Israel. The new historians often argue that the Zionist movement was involved in political machinations that attempted to undermine and/or usurp the rights of the indigenous Arab Palestinians. Some argue that Zionist leaders expressly intended to ethnically cleanse the new state of its Arab Palestinian inhabitants. Though the Jews accepted the partition plan, some new historians argue that the Jews always intended to increase Jewish land allotment in the war that everyone expected. The British, contrary to previous assumptions, did not thwart the establishment of a Jewish state, but they thwarted a Palestinian state. The 1948 War was not a story of an outnumbered Jewish force against larger Arab forces; the Jews outnumbered Arab forces in Palestine, and superior arms were also available to them. Palestinians did not flee their homes voluntarily, or at the request of Arab leaders; Arab Palestinians were forced from their homes. At times Israel engaged in expulsions and massacres; on other occasions psychological warfare was used to frighten populations into flight (although those that left had every intention to return to their homes following the fighting). Israel's success in the 1948 War was a logical outcome of their preparation.

The new historians maintain that, following the war, peacemaking was impeded due to Israel's actions and decisions more than by Arab refusal to come to terms of settlement.[17] These are a few of the sweeping claims made by the new historians. They felt these claims were confirmed by Israeli and British documentary evidence. In his groundbreaking 1988 article, Morris goes so far as to say that Israel was born in sin – the sin being the expulsion of

Palestinians – and therefore Israel is no more deserving of Western support and approbation than are the surrounding Arab states. Morris closes his article praising the New History as a sign of a 'maturing Israel', with the hope that this new endeavour would 'serve the purposes of peace and reconciliation'.[18]

Right-leaning critics often label the new historians as post-Zionist or anti-Zionist, but these historians' ideological commitments are diverse. Some actively identify as Zionist, others as left-wing Zionist, and yet others as post-Zionist. Some claim they do not have a political agenda, and their findings are not meant to delegitimize Israel, but rather to reveal what actually happened. One of the new historians, Shlaim, argues that the New History does not have political motives but it does have political consequences, which he hopes will create a context more conducive to the peace process.[19]

Critique of the new historians

The new historians have been critiqued from various positions. Some argue that the new historians are too left wing, and that they are post- or anti-Zionist. Hillel Halkin, a frequent commentator on Israeli and Jewish culture and politics, argues that some of the new historians (Morris, Shlaim, and Segev) seek to delegitimize Israel. He also says that their claims are a classic case of a bark being bigger than a bite. His primary concern is that the new historians undermine the justness of Zionism and alienate Israeli youth from identifying with Israel. He contends that Israel's attempts to use some of the new historians' conclusions in school curricula will have a detrimental effect. While he says the claims of the new historians seem fearsome, in a careful reading of their works it is possible to find that 'more conciliatory leaders with more conciliatory policies would not have made any difference'.[20]

Anita Shapira, professor of Zionism at Tel Aviv University and a critic of the new historians, argues that their ideas are unoriginal and comprise yet another Zionist anti-narrative such as those that have always been present alongside the Zionist movement (usually from Arab critics). While the new history initially critiqued Zionist figures, Zionist ideology eventually became the 'culprit'. She disapproves of the methodology that relies almost exclusively on Israeli diplomatic and military documentation. She asserts that every far-fetched idea is considered 'conclusive evidence'; the new historians make little to no mention of the political, social and cultural dimensions of the conflict; and they barely (or rarely) use Arab sources.[21] She accuses Shlaim of moralizing when he discusses Israel's actions, but of taking a realpolitik approach when he discusses the Arabs.[22]

Efraim Karsh, professor of Middle East and Mediterranean Studies at King's College in London, is a vocal critic of the new historians in numerous publications, most notably his book *Fabricating Israeli History: The 'New Historians'*. He argues that the new historians 'fashion their research to suit contemporary political agendas; worse, they systematically distort the archival evidence to invent an Israeli history in an image of their own making.'[23] A number of scholars have commented on Karsh's work, discounting his efforts due to sloppy and unreliable research, and claiming it is unbalanced in its rhetoric.[24]

On the Palestinian side, the information released by the new historians was not entirely new. While the documents cited provided more specific information, Palestinian historians had long challenged Israel's traditional narrative, so the New History's conclusions did not come as a shock. Palestinian historians acknowledge that the new historians were 'more critically aware and less ideologically oriented than their predecessors'.[25] Edward Said wrote, 'The great virtue of the new historians is that their work at least pushes the contradictions within Zionism to limits otherwise not apparent to most Israelis, and even many Arabs'.[26]

In the main, the Israeli new historians were 'cold-shouldered' by Palestinian historians who were insulted by the view that Israeli archives and historiography were a superior 'gate to the past' – something they found condescending and neo-colonialist in its approach. While Palestinian academic Nur Masalha recognizes the contribution of the Israeli new historians, he finds the self-criticism it contains to be a form of 'Zionist catharsis' in which Zionism is renewed and the 'Israeli domination' is reinforced. He sees this in the critical elements of New Historian scholarship as well as in the work of other Israeli Jewish intellectuals. He argues that their contribution promotes a 'fallacy of balance . . . between the colonized and the colonizer'.[27] He sees no legitimate contribution in the writings and moral narrativization of Zionism unless the ideology is specifically anti-Zionist.[28] Masalha faults the liberal Zionist understanding of Israel's 'original sin' as dating to 1967, in addition to the new historian dating of this to 1948. From his research, he sees this 'original sin' emerge between 1882 and 1948 when ethnic cleansing plans began to take shape.[29]

When the new historians argue that Palestinians share in the responsibility for what happened in 1948 and that the refugee problem is partly their burden to bear, Masalha responds that the idea that 'Palestinians should share blame for their own Nakba' is uncalled for in the same way as the idea that 'Germans and Jews might have a shared responsibility for the Jewish holocaust would rightly be considered deeply offensive'.[30] In conclusion, Nur Masalha sees the new history as liberal Zionist euphoria and catharsis that aided 'the Israeli settler state to move to the next stage of colonization and suppression of the Palestinians' in the late 1980s and 1990s.[31]

Palestinian Historiography

The evolution of Palestinian historiography is not as pronounced as the old and new historiography on the Israeli side. There is no harsh break in Palestinian scholarship, and its critique has grown more subtly.

Palestinian historiography began during the *nahda*, the cultural renaissance of the Arabs during the late nineteenth and early twentieth centuries. As the British, French and Russians began establishing churches, hospitals and schools in Palestine; this, coupled with Ottoman educational reform, provided Arabs in Palestine with new educational opportunities. During this period Arab nationalism was on the rise, and Ottoman ruler Abdul Hamid II sought to stifle any sort of pan-Arab identity through censoring Arab ideological and intellectual publications, sometimes driving Arab intellectuals into exile. In 1908, Arab Palestinian exiles returned from Egypt and Europe and launched newspapers and journals between 1908 and 1914. During this period Palestinian writers began to address the issue of Zionism. With the establishment of the British Mandate and the changes that came with it, Palestinian historiography was influenced by the debate between the Arab Palestinians and Zionists regarding history and the historical right to the land. This debate became increasingly complex as history and national identity became linked.

The writing during this period reflects a marked shift from antiquarian interests (focusing on specific aspects of history or culture) to national interests. While scholarly works continued to be written, the spirit of the work was often nationalist. During this period, historians gradually increased their focus on city and countryside history and ethnography, which 'constitute a kind of land survey where the authors seek to repeople the terrain with the thick presence of ancestors, as if in response to the continuing obliteration of Palestine by Zionist settlements'.[32] Publications ranged from geographical studies, to accounts of culture and city historiography. In cities the source material was comprised of diaries, family documents from family archives and libraries (many of which were confiscated and destroyed in 1948), English accounts, and records from the Jerusalem Sharia court. Historical subjects of inquiry during this period reflect the increased interest of Palestinians in recounting their ancient past that predated the Israelite period. This was an obvious polemic with the Zionists who also encouraged national unity.[33] The publications during this period reflect Arab Palestinian awareness and angst regarding the political changes occurring in their midst.

Prior to 1948, Palestinian historiography concentrated on the ancient roots of the Palestinian people as connected to the land through which many cultures and empires passed. Similar to Israeli foundational myths that ignore or marginalize Palestinian identity, Palestinian foundational myths pay little attention to a Jewish presence and its connection to Palestine. This historiography argues that the local national identity of the Palestinian people began to coalesce prior to the appearance of the Zionist movement in the land. This history emphasizes the significance of Palestine in the Arab and Muslim world as an important centre of worship and religious devotion.[34] Much of the historiography also ignores the importance and influence of Arab Christian presence in the Holy Land.

Palestinian historiography since 1948 has two main strands. One focuses on the surrender and defeat of Palestinians, and the other focuses on Palestinian heroism and resistance.[35] The first strand often hearkens back to the 1834 Palestinian Revolt against Ibrahim Pasha in which the local population protested various infrastructural and agricultural reforms, as well as new taxation methods and conscription. This revolt failed, as did the revolts and uprisings against the Zionists who began to come to Palestine in the 1880s. This narrative also records the failure of the Palestinians to prevent the British implementation of the Balfour Declaration, their failure in the 1936–9 Arab Revolt in Palestine, and their failure in the 1948 War, or Nakba. The defeat narrative continues, recounting Palestinian resistance after the establishment of Israel, Black September and its aftermath in Jordan, the civil war in Lebanon and the First Lebanon War, Sabra and Shatila, the first intifada, and the Oslo accords. In all these events, Palestinians are portrayed as the defeated party.

The second strand is approached from a different perspective, explaining how Palestinian interests were thwarted due to the historical circumstances they faced. This narrative presents the Palestinians as victims of outside forces who are concerned with their own national interests, and who conspired to steal their land and exile their people. Focusing on the uniqueness of the Palestinian tragedy, with outside forces and history against them, Palestinian heroism, resistance and sacrifice only resulted in the further stripping of their national rights.[36]

Palestinian history concerning the 1948 War is much more nuanced and diverse. Palestinian and general Arab historiography agree on the following: 'the superpowers, especially Great Britain, are responsible for the creation of the Palestinian problem by virtue of their installing a Jewish state in the heart of the Arab world; the 1948 war was inevitable because of Zionist intentions to build an exclusively Jewish state; and Israel is fully responsible for the refugee problem'.[37] Additionally, Arab historiographers are much more inclined to label Israel's actions toward Palestinians in the 1948 War as premeditated ethnic cleansing, whereas Israeli historiographers generally see them as a by-product of war. The Arab historiographers' main areas of disagreement surround the national agendas of the Arab states that entered the war against Israel, the leadership and roles of King Abdullah of Jordan and the Mufti of Palestine, and the military capabilities of Israel in 1948.[38]

Appropriation and destruction of memory

This third and final point is the least discussed in academia, but it is very significant when trying to understand Palestinian historiography. The following quotation from Saleh Abdel Jawad describes this issue at length, a portion of which we quote here: 'Essentially the 1948 war was a project of ethnic cleansing. It included not only the destruction of 80–85 percent of the Palestinian villages that fell under Israeli control and the expulsion of approximately 60 percent of the Palestinian people, but it was also directed at silencing even the memory – uprooting even the landscape – of the people being dispossessed.'[39] Eleven Palestinian cities came under Israeli control, five of which were completely depopulated, five others partially depopulated.[40] The Arab part of Jerusalem was also completely depopulated. Only Nazareth, due to public opinion from the Christian world, including the Vatican, remained intact. The destroyed cities comprised the 'intellectual core of the Palestinian society'.[41] Israel

'destroyed or confiscated all public libraries, printing presses and publishing houses, the land registry, the archives of municipal councils, hospitals, schools and cultural centres. Private libraries, family papers, and personal diaries of intellectuals were also taken. *In the areas that fell under Israeli control, which included the main cultural and intellectual centers of Palestinian society, the totality of a written cultural heritage disappeared.*'[42]

The confiscation of Palestinian documents continued in 1967. When Israel occupied the West Bank and the Gaza Strip, it 'seized all political documents of the National Palestinian Movement from 1948 to 1967 that were found in the headquarters of the Jordanian administration and intelligence service in the West Bank and in the Egyptian administration in the Gaza Strip.'[43] Israel has many of these documents in its state archives, but Arab historians are limited in their ability to access them due to language barriers and travel restrictions.

Another prominent example of Israel's confiscation of Palestinian documents occurred during the invasion into Lebanon in 1982.[44] Although documents from this archive were returned during a prisoner exchange, it is unclear how much was returned. In 2001, records were confiscated from the Arab Studies Society archive at the Orient House in East Jerusalem.[45]

Due to the paucity of documents available to them, Palestinian historiography has had to rely on oral testimonies and eyewitness accounts. While oral narrative is considered of questionable value in traditional Western historiography, it is slowly gaining credence in contemporary methodologies. Middle Eastern history values this form of recollection. Oral history is troublesome as our memories are finite, often selective, and our ability to remember and recount events in perfect detail is limited. At the same time, however, oral tradition plays a prominent role in Palestinian collective memory. When we speak of oral history in the Palestinian context, we are not speaking of ancient history. Palestinian oral history is comprised of the memories of Palestinians who lived through 1948, like co-author Salim Munayer's parents and grandparents. Secondarily, documents can be destroyed, falsified and restricted, and when this happens, oral history can aid in filling in the information gap. Holes and fabrications in documentary evidence have been filled and countered with the aid of oral history, only to be vindicated, or not, when other sources become available. Jawad maintains that 'all new works about the 1948 War, including those that make extensive use of Israeli archival material, are validating Palestinian eyewitness accounts.'[46]

Critique of Palestinian historians

Palestinian history combines the oral history of families and communities, along with personal memoirs, with new archival evidence (primarily from Israel). The Palestinians are more aware of what happened to Palestinians than are the Israelis, who often have little knowledge of expulsions, massacres, etc. The Palestinian stories relating these actions are told by families and friends, and with the opening of the archives it has become clear just how systematic and premeditated some of these actions were.

Abdel Jawad argues that Arab historians have failed to produce a comprehensive narrative of the 1948 War. This is largely due to the fragmentation of the history along national (Palestinian, Jordanian, Egyptian, Iraqi and/or Syrian), class (the narrative of the elite Palestinians who held prominent positions in society versus that of the peasant population) and sectorial lines (military versus civilian);[47] 'the inability of Arab historians to disentangle themselves from Israeli formulations' (such as the actual beginning of the war, the acceptance of the myth of 'eternal enmity' between the Arabs and the Jews, etc.);[48] and finally the limited or prohibited access to documentary and archival evidence from which to draw their scholarship.[49]

Some Israeli historians have contrasted Israeli historiography's reliance on documents with Palestinian reliance on oral history, arguing that documents more accurately represent the facts and are less subject to distortion.[50] Most prominently, Benny Morris has made note of this, commenting on the lack of 'state papers' from Palestinian sources between the years 1947 and 1949 and the Arab states' refusal to release their papers from the 1948 War.[51] Morris notes that interviews are often unreliable (from both Jewish and Arab sources), and while documents 'may misinform, distort, omit or lie, they do so, in my experience, far less than interviewees recalling highly controversial events some 40–50 years ago.'[52] While oral testimonies can provide 'color', they often fail to provide 'facts', Morris argues. Faded memories, partial recollection, together with more recent political developments and ideological commitments hinder accurate historical research.[53] The inaccessibility of Arab documents that have not been released for research is lamentable. Interviews can provide legitimate source material so long as they are used alongside documents.[54]

Another area of critique revolves around the emergence of a distinctly Palestinian identity. While Palestinian historians trace it back to a distant past, sometimes preceding the Israelites, most historians have focused on the formation of a 'unique and particular non-politicized Palestinian identity' which they have dated to various periods, from the eleventh, seventeenth, eighteenth, nineteenth and pre-1914 twentieth centuries.[55] Researcher Zachary Foster has argued that only in the 1930s did a distinctly Palestinian political identity begin to coalesce, as is evidenced by the number of histories focused on distinctly Palestinian issues. Prior to this period, the primary identification of residents in Mandatory Palestine was Arab, and Arab Palestinians viewed themselves as part of the Arab nation more than as a distinct ethnic group apart from the Arab nation.[56]

Benny Morris also remarked that even into the 1920s and 1930s 'the Arabs of Palestine did not see themselves and were not considered by anyone else a distinct "people". They were seen as 'Arabs' or, more specifically, as 'southern Syrian Arabs'". He makes these remarks in the context of a discussion of transfer in Zionist thought. The Zionist leaders thought that if they compensated the Arab Palestinians for such a move, it would not be considered exile, but instead '"Arabs" would merely be moving from one Arab area to another.'[57]

More recent Palestinian historiography has levelled harsher critique towards Palestinian leadership, recognizing its failures and shortcomings more readily than did older critiques. After reflecting on the new historians' contribution to Israeli historiography, Said offered the following observations on Arab historiography:

> Speaking self-critically, I feel that as Arabs generally, and Palestinians in particular, we must also begin to explore our own histories, myths, and patriarchal ideas of the nation, something which, for obvious reasons we have not so far done . . . Nevertheless, as intellectuals and historians we have a duty to look at our history, the history of our leaderships, and of our institutions with a new critical eye. Is there something about those that can perhaps explain the difficulties as a people that we now find ourselves in? What about the conflict between the great families or hamulas, the fact that our leaders have traditionally not been elected democratically, and the fact, equally disastrous, that we seem to reproduce corruption and mediocrity in each new generation? These are serious, and even crucial matters, and they cannot either be left unanswered or postponed indefinitely under the guise of national defense and national unity.[58]

An issue that is often overlooked is the focus of Palestinian identity on the Nakba. Yet Palestinian identity was forged before the Nakba, regardless of the date of the emergence of Palestinian national identity. Arab people living in present-day Israel and Palestine share a rich and complicated past. The prominence of the Nakba in Palestinian historiography casts a looming shadow over all other aspects of Palestinian identity, and hides aspects of culture and history that predated 1948.

Historiography and the Present Challenge

Historians are not objective figures examining an ancient past. They are always subject to a particular perspective, and selective in their choice of resources as they construct their arguments. This is especially true in Israel-Palestine. Historians here detail the history that their parents and grandparents lived through. Their knowledge comes not only from research and study, but through family stories and cultural legacies. Our recent past has a marked effect on the present, and how we choose to present and view the past has implications for our present and our future relations with one another.

Historical discourse has very tangible political implications for our peoples, which is why it is often controversial. It is not uncommon for Israeli and Palestinian historians to give interviews and make political statements to the media. We believe that Israeli and Palestinian historians must take responsibility for their role in public discourse, whether they are optimistic or pessimistic about the future.

As two individuals invested in reconciliation efforts, we the co-authors believe that historiography should be written with hope for the future. We do not believe that our peoples are doomed to repeat their mistakes; nor do we believe that we are forever locked in cycles of violence and political impasse. What Israelis and Palestinians believe about themselves is a reflection of our changing historiography. We must look at our past and our present in light of our hope for the future. This is part of our eschatological hope as believers in the Messiah. We know that God can bring his magnificent future into our present. He has already done this by sending his Son into the world to reconcile humanity to himself. The history and historiography presented in the past few chapters often deconstruct one another's identities, make light of each other's pain, and ridicule the other's struggle. Additionally, historians on both sides engage in condemning the other and they often see little to no room for redemption. There is no space in these kinds of discourses for the mutual identity affirmation that we believe is essential to a reconciliation process.

Practically, there are three steps we can take that will aid in the process of reconciliation. First, we can learn one another's narrative and history. Simply being open to hearing the other side's account of what happened will bring the sides towards one another. Second, we should bridge the narratives as much as possible. While there are many impasses in our accounts of what happened and what caused these events, we can focus on shared social and cultural history and be open to challenging our own narrative. Finally, we need to accept and respect the other narrative. This does not mean we will completely agree on the past, but it does mean we will develop empathy for one another, and respect the importance each narrative has for each side.[59]

Regardless of the history we read, or the history we know from our own people and families, we must learn to listen to each other. We must hear each other's pain. Our perception of what happened is often just as influential as the truth of what happened. Through listening to one another and hearing each other's stories, we can minimize the gap between what we think and what we know. In the following chapters we will begin to articulate a message of hope for our two communities. A message that seeks to recognize the other's pain, affirm the other's identity, and help bring us closer to the goal of reconciliation gained at the foot of the cross.

4.

An Introduction to Palestinian Christianity

Many in the West think of all Palestinians as Muslims and are surprised to learn of the existence of an ancient, longstanding, still extant Palestinian Christian community that predates Islam, residing both in Israel-Palestine and around the world. Bernard Sabella, a leading academic researcher of Palestinian Christians, estimates that there are roughly 400,000 Palestinian Christians worldwide that make up around 6.5 per cent of the entire Palestinian population, many of whom trace their ancestry to the early church.[1] For example, the Greek Orthodox patriarchate of Jerusalem, the oldest and perhaps most important Christian institution in the Holy Land, has existed in unbroken succession since the Roman period.[2]

The Holy Land has been witness to a great many conquests and invasions, and the Palestinian Christian community has been significantly influenced by its interactions with these different cultures throughout the centuries, including Jewish, Greek, Roman, Islamic and European. In spite of the many influences from the outside, the Palestinian Christian community sees itself not as Christians living in Palestine, but as Palestinian Christians. While most Western Christians view Christianity in 'individualistic, personal and doctrinal terms', Palestinian Christians, and Eastern Christians in general, 'tend to see themselves as a community with an ethnic or cultural background and defined traditions.'[3]

Significant challenges face this community. First, Palestinian Christians need to find a way of dealing with the Jewish people and the state of Israel in a way that does not invalidate the historical and religious attachment the Jewish people have to the Holy Land but that also confidently asserts Palestinians' legitimate attachment. Second, Palestinian Christians need to learn to relate to Islam in a way that addresses the differences between Christianity and Islam frankly, but that also avoids 'Islamophobia' and hatred of Muslims. Third, Palestinian Christians need to address the hermeneutical threat posed by the Christian Zionist and some Messianic Jewish approaches to the Bible that claim exclusive, ethnically Jewish owner-ship of the land. Finally, Palestinian Christians need to re-evaluate their communal identity, especially in light of the growing numbers of Muslim-background believers and the increasing ethnic diver-sity of the Christian population in the Holy Land, due to the influx of immigrants from Russia and Ethiopia, along with other foreign national workers.

Throughout their history, Palestinian Christians have identified with the Holy Land and its sacred sites, along with an inherited sense of stewardship for the task of the sites' maintenance and preservation. There can be no separation between Palestinian Christians and the Holy Land. As Gabriel Baramki writes, 'the land is central to the life of our people . . . you cannot separate the geography from either the whole panorama of history nor the spiritual experience of belonging.'[4] Palestinian Christians have a special sense of pride in belonging to the land in which Jesus was born, raised, lived, taught, died and was resurrected – a land often referred to as the 'fifth gospel'.[5]

For many Palestinian Christians, their privileged position in the Holy Land also influences their view of the Western church. When Christians from the West encounter Palestinian Christians, they are, at times, surprised to learn of this old and continuing Christian community with its own rich history and theology as evidenced in the Eastern church. There is a clear bias in Western seminaries and Christian institutions favouring the development of Western Chris-tianity. Often when Western Christians come to Israel-Palestine, they come to teach their positions as opposed to being informed by local theology, a position Palestinian Christians find offensive.[6] Palestinian Christians consider themselves to have a:

> first-birth right because of the formative role they had in the devel-opment of Christian theology. They have a strong sense that they

have suffered for centuries under Islam to defend their faith and all it entails: liturgy, theology, icons, saints, and monasteries. This makes it the more painful for them when their members defect to Churches that are seen as newcomers from the Western World.[7]

Because of the importance of this history for Palestinian Christian identity, we will first present a historical overview of the Palestinian Christian community and then consider the community's current situation.

Historical Overview

The Palestinian Christian community dates to the time of the early church. Like the early church, this community has always been remarkably cosmopolitan, comprised of many different people groups, languages and cultures. Culturally Hellenized, Palestinian Christian ancestry draws from different ethnicities, including Jewish, Greek, Armenian, Aramaic, Phoenician, Samaritan and, of course, Arab. In the seventh century, following the conquest of Islam, Palestinian Christians and other locally based peoples underwent the process of Arabization, in which the Arabic language and culture's influence grew significantly, eventually overtaking locally used languages and cultures. Yet Arabs were already living in the region of Palestine before the arrival of Islam and were playing a significant role in the development of the church. For example, in 374 CE Musa, the first Palestinian Arab bishop, was appointed in Jerusalem.[8]

Of course, the Arab people predate Christianity and are found throughout the Old Testament narrative.[9] Although the modern Arab world includes most of the Middle East and North Africa, encompassing around 250 million people, in biblical times the Arab people were only found in the Arabian Peninsula. The Arab people appear in three early genealogical lists in the Bible: among the descendants of Joktan (Gen. 10.25–30), the descendants of Abraham through his son Ishmael (Gen. 25.12–18), and the descendants of Abraham through his wife Keturah (Gen. 25.1–6), each occupying a different region of the peninsula.

Eventually, by the 'end of the first millennium BCE, Ishmael and his line had become the dominant representatives of north and central Arabia.'[10] A commonly held view in the Arab world, put forward by the Arab genealogist Hisham ibn Muhammad al-Kalbî (737–819? CE), associates Ishmael and his descendants with the Arab people generally, and with Arab Muslims in particular, by linking Ishmael and the prophet Muhammad. Although many researchers find this connection dubious, the claim that the Arab peoples are the descendants of Ishmael is not without its proponents. It was widely assumed that this was the case in the ancient world. For example, writing in the first century, Josephus refers to the Arab Nabataeans as part of the Ishmaelite tribes. And as Tony Maalouf argues, 'Whether or not there is a strong ethnic basis for his classification, no one can deny that Ishmael had become a great symbol for north Arabian tribes by the first century AD.'[11]

Arabs in the biblical account are often presented in a positive light. These include the queen of Sheba, who came to visit King Solomon and most likely represented a whole 'confederation of other petty Ishmaelite tribal kingdoms' in the Arabian Peninsula (cf. 1 Kgs 10:1–13). Another is Job, who according to the biblical narrative, was 'the greatest of all the people of the east' (Job 1.3), a phrase which was typically used to describe 'nomadic dwellers of the Syro-Arabian Desert.'[12]

Matthew's narrative of Jesus' birth includes magi who arrive from the east (Matt. 2.1–2). Although some consider the magi to be Persian Zoroastrians, many of the church fathers specifically identified them as Arabs. Justin Martyr wrote about the magi who 'came from Arabia'. Around 155 CE Tertullian, Clement of Rome, and others made comments that support this view.[13] Additionally, the gifts brought by the magi – gold, frankincense and myrrh – would have been easy to find in the Arabian Peninsula at the time because of its importance on the spice trail. The Roman historian Herodotus in the fifth century BCE wrote that Arabia 'is the only country that yields frankincense and myrrh', and biblical as well as classical sources note the abundance of gold in Arabia.[14]

According to the historical narrative of the Palestinian Christians, their origins lie in the earliest days of the church. Writing from an Orthodox perspective, Baramki explains it very simply: 'The Orthodox Church is the indigenous church of the land where

Christianity itself originated', and he describes Palestinian Christians as 'the people who have lived there from time immemorial . . . At times, we were the majority, at others, we were simply part of the larger society', but at all times they were 'Palestinians, and felt as one would expect an indigenous people of a land to feel anywhere else in the world.'[15] Arabs were among the first converts to experience the Spirit of God at Pentecost (Acts 2.11), and belief in the Messiah spread eastward just as quickly as it did westward, so that by 50 CE, the apostle Thomas had already found his way to the Indian subcontinent through the Arabian Peninsula.[16] Paul himself mentions going to Arabia (Gal. 1.17).

There are different theories about the origins of Arab Christians. Some scholars, especially those with Arab nationalist sentiments, are eager to claim that the Arab Christians of today are the descendants of the Christian Arabs who lived before the advent of Islam. They draw a direct line of continuity from then until now, and the emphasis is on the Arab ethnicity of these communities. For example, Irfan Shahîd writes that in the fourth century a number of Arab Christian kingdoms existed in Mesopotamia and Syria under the sponsorship of the Byzantine Empire, and that other Arab Christian communities could be found in the southern Arabian Peninsula, now modern-day Yemen. These Christian communities developed a lyrical Arabic for their liturgy and poetry, and through it the Christian Arabs influenced the development of Islam.[17] Others, including Milka Rubin, have argued that, with the rise of Islam, most Arab Christians either converted to Islam – many were forced to convert and others converted for socio-economic reasons – or left and scattered around the region and mixed with other ethnicities. Therefore, Arab Christians of today are a mixture of Arab as well as other Semitic ethnicities, and are also of Greek and Armenian descent.[18]

Throughout the Middle East, different church authorities began to develop, most of them tracing their roots to the time and place of the life of Jesus.[19] The Church of the East (later known to Western detractors as 'Nestorian') was already developed by the third century.[20] The Coptic Orthodox Church in Egypt developed even earlier when, according to tradition, St Mark the Evangelist was martyred in Alexandria sometime between 62 and 68 CE. The Syriac Orthodox Church traces its origins to the early Christian community at Antioch, mentioned in the book of Acts, and the Orthodox Church established Jerusalem as one of the four ancient Eastern patriarchates; the other three were Constantinople, Alexandria and Antioch.[21]

When the Romans destroyed Jerusalem in 70 CE, they renamed the city *Aelia Capitolina*, and all Christian activity went underground. Archaeological evidence indicates that, in spite of these challenges, Christian pilgrims were already secretly coming to Jerusalem in the first century. However, when the emperor Constantine converted to Christianity, pilgrimage became an established trend.[22] The Church of the Holy Sepulchre was built during this period which witnessed a great flourishing of Christian thought and development throughout the Holy Land, including the arrival of the Desert Fathers and the establishment of various monasteries and churches in Jerusalem and the surrounding wilderness. This golden era, which was to last until the Muslim conquest of the Holy Land, also saw the establishment of the Jerusalem patriarchy at the Council of Chalcedon in 451 CE.[23]

The Muslim conquest of Palestine in 638 CE led to many changes for the Palestinian Christian community. As a result of this conquest, 'a determined cultural shift took place during the early Islamic period; Christians learned how to pray in the language of their conquerors, they produced devotional and theological literature and translated the Gospels into Arabic.'[24] For some Palestinian Christians, however, the arrival of the Muslims represented a kind of liberation. The Byzantine rulers had often come into conflict with the Eastern churches, which had rejected the christological formula agreed upon at Chalcedon. Special taxes were levied on the local population, and they were persecuted for their supposedly heretical beliefs. The oppression was so intense that when the Muslims conquered Jerusalem, some of the Palestinian Christians fought alongside them.[25]

The arrival of Arabic-speaking Muslims provided a linguistic opportunity as well. At the time, the Christian community was ethnically mixed and used a variety of languages for different purposes. They spoke Aramaic or Arabic but used Greek and to a lesser extent Syriac, a written form of Aramaic, for their liturgy. Although Greek was their dominant liturgical language, Hellenistic culture had not truly penetrated all segments of society. Some of the churches still clung to their Aramaic or Arabic linguistic identity. Various segments of the Christian population were already calling for the use of Arabic before the Muslims arrived. For example, the preacher Quss ibn Sa'idah, the bishop of Najran in the sixth century, was the first to start using Arabic in his sermons.[26]

With the arrival of Islam, many of the monasteries in the Judean desert began translating the Greek liturgy into Arabic through Aramaic. In this way they developed a dialect of Arabic that was distinct from classical or Qur'anic Arabic and was unique to the Christian community. It was, in effect, a new form of Arabic that was heavily influenced by Aramaic. Even though many of the community members were not originally or ethnically Arab, being Arab became an important part of their identity, although not without some tension. Especially in the early period of Islam, there was a strong sense that to be Arab was to be Muslim. Muslims actively promoted this idea. However, through their dialect, the Christians were able to carve out a niche for themselves as both Arab and Christian. Writing about this linguistic development, Joshua Blau has shown that the Arabic dialect developed by the Christians in Palestine consisted of Arabic words and grammar with Aramaic words and roots. It was not only a matter of different vocabulary, but also represented a fundamental shift in the structure of the language so that it could be legitimately called Aramaic written in Arabic.[27] This Christian Arabic began to replace the Greek and Aramaic liturgy – except within the Syriac Church, which continued, and continues, to use Aramaic. The Melkites were among the first to make a complete linguistic switch to Arabic in their worship.

This unique kind of Arabization was especially evident in the intellectual and apologetic aspects of Palestinian Christian life. The 'monks in the monasteries of Palestine began to write theology and the saints' lives in Arabic, the language of the Qur'an, and to translate the Bible, liturgical texts, hagiographies, patristic texts and other ecclesiastical works from Greek and Syriac into the lingua franca of the Islamic caliphate.'[28] Writers such as Theodore Abu Qurrah, Anthony David of Baghdad, and Stephen of Ramlah contributed to this cultural renaissance that only occurred once the Eastern Christian community came under the control of Islam.

Kenneth Bailey has pointed out that next to Latin and Greek, there is more Christian literature in Arabic than in any other language.[29]

The violence and destruction brought on by the Crusades, as well as the injustice suffered by the Muslims and Jews, has been well documented. Less well documented was the calamitous impact the arrival of European Christians had on the local Christian population. For example, the Orthodox were expelled from Jerusalem by the Crusaders, and because of the merciless actions of the Crusaders, the Palestinian Christians incurred a damaging yet largely undeserved association with the Crusades.[30] This false association stirred resentment against them among the Muslim and Jewish communities, which would have significant repercussions in later centuries. Christian–Jewish and especially Christian–Muslim relations were so damaged by the Crusades that they have yet to recover. The Crusades also exacerbated the split between the Eastern and Western churches, a division that grew more entrenched with the arrival of Protestant missionaries.

Additionally, the Mongol invasion of the thirteenth century devastated much of the Middle East and ended the Abbasid dynasty. The sack of Baghdad in 1258, the cultural and political centre of the Muslim world, continues to be viewed as one of the most traumatic defeats the Muslims have ever suffered. Muslims perceived the Christians as allied to the Mongol invaders, and indeed, the Christians harboured some hope about the Mongols. They thought their new rulers might change the status quo, especially since some of the Mongol invaders viewed Christianity favourably. Philip Jenkins writes that 'Christian leaders dreamed that Baghdad itself might be the capital of a new Christian empire'.[31] The Mongols brought with them a measure of religious tolerance that benefited the local Christian communities. But any dream of a Christian empire was dashed when the Mongols adopted a particularly militant version of Islam and began to persecute Christians as well as many Muslim groups they considered suspicious. This manifestation of Islam within the Mongol Empire was to have a long-lasting effect on Christian–Muslim relations, and the effects of the Mongol conquest are arguably 'even more critical for the long-term relationship between Islam and Christianity than the original Arab conquests of the seventh century.'[32]

However, unlike their dominance of the north-western Caucasus, Iran, and Iraq, Mongol control of Palestine was more tenuous. The Mamluk sultan Beybars defeated the Mongols in 1260. At the end of the fourteenth century, Timurlane temporarily regained much of the territory and subjected it to brutal rule, but his territory disintegrated with his death in 1405. Within fifty years of his death, however, the marginal Ottoman kingdom of Anatolia had captured Constantinople from the decaying Byzantine Empire. Fifty years later, they were the rulers of most of southwest Asia, a rule that continued for four hundred years.

The Ottoman period was characterized by the millet system,[33] which organized aspects of life for the non-Muslim communities that were recognized as 'people of the book'. In this way the Christians of the Holy Land were somewhat protected and granted a certain amount of religious freedom as long as they accepted the domination of Muslim rule, paid special taxes, and agreed to certain restrictions in order to mark their inferiority, such as wearing distinctive clothing or abiding by prohibitions against carrying arms and riding horses.[34] This system was in place throughout the Ottoman period until it began to give way under pressure to reform in the nineteenth century.

These reforms coincided with a renewed colonial interest in the Holy Land from the West, brought about by increased religious interests as well as a sense that the 'sick man of Europe' (i.e. the Ottoman Empire) was crumbling and would be easy to pick apart. A 'scramble for Palestine' ensued, in which each of the great European powers – Britain, Russia, Germany and France – sought to gain a presence in the Holy Land, usually through the establishment of religious institutions. By the end of the nineteenth century, the Roman Catholics alone had established in Palestine 'some 30 religious orders, brotherhoods and associations, with 29 convents, 18 hospices, 6 higher schools, 16 orphanages, 4 industrial schools and 5 hospitals.'[35] And the Catholics were not alone. They were joined by the Anglicans, Lutherans, German evangelicals and other Protestant sects, all of which built churches, schools, hospitals, and other institutions throughout the Holy Land.

Ottoman rule ended with the start of the British Mandate for Palestine. The Palestinian Christian community embraced an emergent Palestinian nationalism and pan-Arabism. Palestinian

Christians were influential in this movement and, to some extent, led the way towards a national, secular independence movement characterized by opposition to British and Zionist political goals. For the Palestinian Christian minority, Arab nationalism seemed to provide the best 'opportunity to break the yoke of their marginality and to create an ideology and community sufficiently broad to encompass them as full and equal participants.'[36]

One of the earliest and most significant expressions of Palestinian nationalism was the printing and distribution of Arabic newspapers. The two most important papers – al-Filastin and al-Karmil – were both run by Palestinian Christians. There were even isolated calls by Palestinian Christians to embrace Islam as their true cultural heritage. An example of this is the pamphlet written by Khalil Iskandar al-Qubrusi, which 'denounced European Christianity as a corrupt religion which oppressed eastern Christianity, and European monks and missionaries as sowing dissention between the Muslims and Christians of Palestine.'[37] This Western Christianity contrasted with Islam, which was portrayed as a 'benevolent egalitarian and democratic religion which formed the basis of Arab nationalism and unity.'[38]

Few Palestinian Christians responded to this call, but it is indicative of the internal pressure Palestinian Christians felt. 'They tried to prove good Arab nationalists bearing the conviction of their deficiency for being non-Muslims, which prevented them from becoming fully accepted as equals.'[39] Eventually, many Palestinian Christians became disillusioned with Palestinian nationalism when they realized that 'although the Arab national movement was explicitly secular, the Arabs could not separate nationalism from Islam according to the ideas of European nationalism'.[40] This truth became increasingly evident over the years through the rise and increased influence of radical Islam.[41]

The traumatic events of the Nakba in 1948 greatly affected the Palestinian Christian community. Many became refugees, either internally displaced in what was later called the West Bank and Gaza or living under military occupation.[42] Although in some cases Palestinian Christians were treated differently from Palestinian Muslims by the Israeli army, they also went through the 'same process of uprootedness and change. Tens of thousands of Christians either ran away from their villages in order to escape, or avoid the consequences of military occupation.' Palestinian Christians faced the same violence and threats of violence that their Muslim neighbours faced and suffered the same results. It is estimated that around 700,000–800,000 Palestinians were displaced during the war, 50,000 of whom were Christians.[43] In Jerusalem for example, more than 13 per cent of the land in the western part of the city was owned by different Christian churches, some of which was confiscated and much of which was difficult to access.[44]

After 1948 the Israeli government viewed Palestinian Christians with suspicion, both because they were Arab and because they were Christian. Because of Arab Christian connections to the global church, and especially to the Vatican, the Israeli government felt limited in how it could deal with the Palestinian Christians. Israel did not want to upset the Vatican, which they also viewed as an anti-Semitic, hostile entity, but it was clear that from the beginning, the Zionist leadership viewed the Palestinian Christians as a potentially subversive group.[45]

The Israeli governing authority has employed a number of tactics in its dealings with the Palestinian Christian community since Israeli independence in 1948. For the most part, the relationship has been tense, but functional. The divisions between the different denominations presented an advantage to the Israelis; the government had no interest in making enemies of the local Christians population and facing the opposition of a united Christian front. The government was also anxious to avoid the formation of a Christian–Muslim coalition. It was much easier to deal with each community separately. Finally, the Israeli government bought or leased whatever land it could from the Christian community, exacerbating the already existent divisions. The land sales and leasing activities were a controversial issue, and the government used different carrot-and-stick measures to ensure that the Christian communities could not refuse their offers. Certain basic governmental services which the churches depended on, such as 'the issuing of visas, discretion over the imposition of taxation and the granting of planning permissions for new religious buildings were made contingent upon the churches' cooperation in selling property to the Israeli government.'[46]

After the 1967 war, relations between the Israeli government and the various Western churches, including the Vatican, improved significantly. There was a renewed sympathy for Israel, which was seen as the victim of Arab aggression, and a growing interest in Israel with respect to the fulfilment of biblical prophecies, especially as Jewish sovereignty extended once again to such biblical locales as Hebron and Bethlehem. However, the improved relationship with global Christianity overseas coincided with a deterioration of the relationship between the Israeli government and the local Christian population. The beginning of the settlement movement and especially the outbreak of the intifada drove many Palestinian Christians to undergo a process of Palestinization – i.e. consciously identifying as Palestinian and supporting the Palestinian cause – that further aggravated tensions.

The election of the Likud coalition in 1977 brought in a hawkish, national religious government that negatively affected the Palestinian Christian community. The coalition's main concern was the settlement of new Jewish immigrants and the establishment of Jewish dominance across the whole country, particularly in Jerusalem. The Israeli government showed 'less sensitivity to the churches' concerns and gradually began to override the more co-operative and consultative relationship previously established.'[47] These developments, along with the effects of the intifada and the growth of the settler movement, pushed the Palestinian Christian community and its leaders towards an ever more nationalist position. Even so, barring notable exceptions, the Palestinian Christian community generally chose to renounce violence as a means of resistance. This decision was stubbornly adhered to, despite the many provocations the community has endured from expansionist Israeli government policy and settlers, and the accusations of treason and collaboration from Palestinian Muslims throughout both intifadas and today.[48]

Another aspect that has had a significant impact on Palestinian Christian life, both in Israel and in Palestine, has been emigration. Since 1967, nearly 300,000 Palestinians have left the West Bank and Gaza, about 15.8 per cent of the overall population.[49] Among those that left, about 18,000 were Christians. This may seem like a small number, but it accounts for approximately 35 per cent of the entire Palestinian Christian population. The trend towards emigration has only increased since the failure of the Oslo peace process and the violence of the second intifada. While many factors contribute to the decision to emigrate, the Palestinian Christians' situation as a double minority, living between the Jewish and Muslim majorities, certainly plays a significant role as:

> It is clear that Palestinians leave because they do not have proper economic and occupational opportunities and prospects in their own land . . . Palestinians, including Christians, do not leave simply out of political or social frustration – they seem to have grown accustomed to these. They leave if they do not have opportunities to gain a livelihood, and in order to ensure some sense of stability in their own lives, and in those of their children.[50]

The result of massive emigration has been the uprooting of a community that has been in place for thousands of years. As many have warned for years, if the current trend continues, the Palestinian Christian community could soon almost completely disappear.

A Thematic Approach to Palestinian Christian Identity

Because of the importance of the Holy Land and the role holy sites play in Palestinian Christian identity, we will use the lens of four important cities in the Holy Land to explore Palestinian Christian identity – Bethlehem, Nazareth, Lyyda and Jerusalem. Each location represents and embodies particular aspects of the collective Palestinian Christian experience. Palestinian Christians say, 'while Christianity is spiritual, in practical terms, we must keep our feet on the ground – our ground.'[51] Because of both their history and their particular narrative, Palestinian Christian identity is best understood by reflecting on their life in the land.

Bethlehem's significance is paramount. For Palestinian Christians, Bethlehem represents the beginning of Christianity and is a source of pride because of its privileged position as the city where Christ was born. Mitri Raheb, a Lutheran pastor in Bethlehem, writes, 'I share my city with David and Jesus.'[52] The event of Christ's birth is commemorated in the Church of the Nativity, which has become a pilgrimage destination for people all over the world and an important landmark on the cultural plane of the Palestinian Christian community. It also represents the long historical continuity of the Palestinian Christian presence in the Holy Land. This presence has not been easy to maintain, but the Palestinian Christians are proud that they have endured: 'The [Arab] Christians of the Holy Land not only fought the Ottomans and rose up against them, but in earlier times fought foreign Latin Christians during the Crusader period, and the Romans before them.'[53] While others have come and gone, the Palestinian Christians are conscious of having remained rooted in the land and having faithfully preserved its holy sites.

Another aspect of Palestinian Christian identity represented by the city of Bethlehem is Palestinian nationalist aspirations. As noted, many of the leaders of Palestinian nationalism emerged from the Christian community, from the earliest stirrings of nationalist sentiment during the Ottoman period until today. While the rise of radical Islam has alienated some Palestinian Christians from the nationalist movement, many are still involved and serve as moderate leaders advocating for secular, pluralistic Palestinian autonomy. They boldly identify as Palestinian Christians, unwilling to sacrifice their identity as a Palestinian or as a Christian. Hanan Ashrawi, an Anglican Palestinian Christian and a prominent nationalist, states, 'I am a Palestinian Christian. I am a descendant of the first Christians in the world. Jesus Christ was born in my country and my land.'[54]

The next city is Nazareth, Jesus' home town for much of his life. A dominant feature of Nazareth's landscape, the Church of the Annunciation, celebrates the connection Jesus had to the city. Nazareth and the surrounding Galilee region represent Palestinian agricultural ties to the land, rooted in traditional Palestinian village life. The landscape in this region is home and the means of subsistence. Jesus' teaching ministry drew upon these themes, employing agricultural imagery to illumine his teachings about the kingdom of God. Elias Chacour, a Melkite archbishop from the Galilee, says that 'there are stories in the New Testament of people just like us who lived in the villages of Galilee.'[55] It is easy for Palestinian Christians in Nazareth and the surrounding villages to picture the stories from the New Testament and to imagine themselves as followers of Jesus. It is no accident, therefore, that one of Chacour's books is entitled *We Belong to the Land*, a sentiment shared by most Palestinian Christians, particularly those from the Galilee and Nazareth.

The city of Nazareth also represents the thin line walked by Palestinian Christians between the Palestinian Muslim and the Israeli Jewish societies in the state of Israel. Palestinian Christians are under extraordinary pressure from both sides; they often feel forced to integrate and separate simultaneously from both Israeli Jewish and Palestinian Muslim cultures. This dual process of Israelization and Palestinization has seen Palestinian Christians in Israel embrace their Palestinian identity, cultural heritage and history, while at the same time withdrawing from the radicalized segments of Palestinian society and moving towards secular, Jewish and Western cultural values. For example, many Palestinian Christians in Nazareth have begun to move to the Jewish neighbourhood of Nazareth Illit. The tension and strain between the Palestinian Christian and Palestinian Muslim communities is evident in the drama played out over the disputed construction of the Shihab al-Din mosque, situated directly in front of the Church of the Annunciation. The Israeli government prevented its construction because of its seemingly provocative placement near the church, a move that was supported by other international and ecclesial bodies. But the confrontation drastically raised the level of tension between these two neighbouring communities. Christian–Muslim relations in the city have suffered greatly as a result.

Like Nazareth, the city of Lyyda is located within the state of Israel and represents one of the most hurtful chapters of the conflict for Palestinian Christians. The Palestinian inhabitants of Lyyda, many of them Christian, were expelled from and then resettled back in Lyyda during the war in 1948. Their experience is not unique; many Palestinians throughout the country were likewise expelled and became refugees. However, in Lyyda and other Palestinian areas that came under Israel control, the near-total annihilation of the centuries-old Palestinian community was followed by decades of neglect, ambivalence, a concerted effort at erasing the Arab-Palestinian heritage through Israelization of buildings and places,[56] and finally rejection by the Israeli Jewish community. At the site of the Ben Gurion airport, scores of tourists and pilgrims pass through Lyyda, a location mostly ignored by them. Cut off from their cultural and religious heritage but still not accepted by mainstream Israeli society, the Palestinian Christians in places like Lyyda have suffered greatly, and collectively face an acute crisis of identity. In their volume on the history of the Palestinian people, Baruch Kimmerling and Joel Migdal entitled the chapter on Palestinian-Israelis 'Odd Man Out: Arabs in Israel' for good reason. Considered as outsiders among both Israelis and Palestinians, this segment of the Palestinian Christian community occupies a liminal space. Yet their marginal existence could facilitate reconciliation between the Israelis and Palestinians, because 'as the odd man out, the Palestinian citizens of Israel hold the promise of a new bridge to the future'.[57]

Naturally, the final representative city is Jerusalem, the city of Christianity's origins. Obviously, Jerusalem is important to all Christians, Jews and Muslims, but it is of special importance for Palestinian Christian identity. A letter jointly written by the Greek Orthodox, Latin and Armenian patriarchs states, 'The Church of Jerusalem has been nourished by the blood of Her martyrs, Patriarchs, Bishops, priests and lay people. Her spiritual heritage is deeply rooted in the Holy Land while She firmly abides in the hearts of Christian souls everywhere.'[58] Perhaps the most important site for Palestinian Christians is the Church of the Holy Sepulchre, 'an important symbol of Christian presence and custodianship in Jerusalem', and a 'symbolic anchor for Christians in Jerusalem.'[59]

The identity of the Palestinian Christian community is, in many ways, grounded in paradox, and the ancient Church of the Holy Sepulchre (called Church of the Resurrection by local Christians) embodies this sense of paradox, from its unique, almost hodgepodge architectural features and construction, to the crowds of faithful that gather underneath its roof. The church, like the Palestinian Christian community, stands between the opposite poles of the cross and the sword, humility and triumph, and stands as a testament to the history of Christianity in Jerusalem. In the minds of Orthodox Christians, the Holy Sepulchre encompasses the location of Christ's suffering and crucifixion,[60] and is thus inextricably linked to the cross, the ultimate symbol of God humbling himself and suffering for humanity's sins because of his great love for the world. Yet this church is also evidence of how the cross has been used and, indeed, abused by those who exerted a kind of politically and militarily powerful Christianity. These paradoxes influence Palestinian Christianity to this day.

Pilgrims have been making their way to Jerusalem and the Church of the Holy Sepulchre since at least 333 CE. Pilgrims continue to come, and in this way the church is timeless. But it has also been deeply affected by the many rulers and religions that have shaped Jerusalem. It has been built and destroyed, rebuilt, renovated, added to and taken away from, as well as divided and portioned out. Yet it stands, weathering the tests of time, not unlike the Palestinian Christian community itself.

As a minority living among and between the Jewish and Muslim majorities, the Palestinian Christian community is numerically small and militarily powerless. The power it does possess comes from the community's tradition and history, and from its connections to the global church. The building of the Holy Sepulchre mirrors this aspect of powerlessness. The fact that the key to the church is held by the Muslim community (because of internecine squabbles among the various churches within the Holy Sepulchre), coupled with the rundown state of the church and its disrepair, form a visual reminder of the lowly status of the Palestinian Christian community. On the other hand, each year at Sabt al-Nour (Saturday of the Holy Fire), the Holy Sepulchre is transformed into a public demonstration of the unity and strength of the Palestinian Christian community. This celebration of Christ's resurrection is also endowed with political meaning. Each year within the crowd there is a palatable hunger for political power, justice and vindication. This holy day has special significance for Palestinian Christians. They celebrate the resurrection of Christ to celebrate salvation as well as their hope for the future, a message that resonates strongly among those who perceive themselves as powerless. That self-perception and experience of powerlessness as a minority in the Holy Land stands in contradistinction to their membership in the larger, worldwide population of Christianity, which is, conversely, an indication of their power.

But their relationship with the rest of the church, especially the Western church, is complicated. Many Palestinian Christians have ambivalent feelings towards Western Christianity. Although they appreciate the help and support they receive from the West, they also resent the control that sometimes accompanies it. Palestinian

Christians feel dependent upon the West, but they also believe that the West is ignorant of their indebtedness to the Palestinian Christians for their faithful presence in the Holy Land. Consider, for example, the ambivalence with which Palestinian Christians reacted to the discovery of what became known as the Garden Tomb. From my observation, it seems some Palestinian Christians view the Garden as representative of the cultural effects of the Enlightenment and the power of Western Christianity, which arrived together with the colonial and imperial ambitions of European political powers in the Middle East. Major-General Charles George Gordon, a member of the British army, was one of the first to advocate for the Garden Tomb to be recognized as the tomb of Jesus.[61] Many Palestinian Christians have happily aligned themselves with Westernized Christianity, both Roman Catholicism and Protestantism, and have greatly benefited from it. The Protestant influence in the Holy Land brought with it an emphasis on education and a new approach to the Bible and individual spirituality that have added much to the Palestinian Christian religious experience.

Yet the close connection between political and religious power brought disappointment. Gordon's interest in the Holy Land was as much a reflection of British imperialism as it was of his own idiosyncratic religious beliefs. Western Christianity came to the East to change it, not to learn from it; Western Christians had little respect for the liturgy, spirituality and tradition of Eastern Christianity. Palestinian Christians sense that to embrace Westernized Christianity is to disconnect from their history and cultural identity.

Palestinian Christians are equally dismayed at the growth of Christian Zionism, which lacks theological space for Palestinian Christians in the Holy Land. Palestinian Christians find political support, though, from many mainline Protestant Christians in the West. This results in an odd theo-political marriage in which these generally liberal Protestant churches support the more conservative Palestinian churches, finding common ground in their mutual concern for justice. Many Palestinian Christians privately reject the liberal theology and ethics espoused by these Western Christians, even as they deeply value their political support. Furthermore, the arrival of Protestantism has had the unintended but negative affect of further fragmenting the already divided body of believers, deepening patterns of dependency for support from the outside.

Finally, the Palestinian Christian community, like the Church of the Holy Sepulchre, is caught between uniformity and diversity. The church is home to Roman Catholic, Greek Orthodox and Armenian Orthodox religious orders, with chapels for the Syriac Orthodox, Coptic Orthodox and Ethiopian Orthodox churches. Although they are divided in their customs, traditions, languages and even theology, they inhabit the same building and worship separately under one roof. The Palestinian Christian community tends to unify as a group in the face of persecution. Nevertheless, their divisions are apparent, particularly because the denominations tend to correspond to ethnic divisions as well. While it produces sporadic conflict, this diversity also adds flavour and serves as a living testament to the complex history of Palestinian Christians in the Holy Land.

5.

An Introduction to Israeli Messianic Jewish Identity

In order to begin to understand the complex nature of Messianic Jewish identity and specifically the *Israeli* Messianic identity, it is necessary to explore the backgrounds of this diverse population according to the three categories inherent in the term. In the second decade of the twenty-first century, this group constitutes an almost infinitesimal element within all three categories contained in the title. Israeli Messianic Jews are a clearly defined minority within the Jewish people, within the Christian/Messianic world, and in the land of Israel. As with many small but significant elements, it is not size that influences, but rather the nature of the element itself. Salt does not need to be a principal ingredient in a given recipe; yet its addition to any mix intensifies and enhances the surrounding substance.

Identity issues are multifaceted and complex. As the focus of this chapter is not identity studies, we will confine ourselves to a cursory discussion of the subject as it specifically relates to the general topic of this chapter: social identity. Several parameters are important to emphasize. One: Identity is fluid and affected by an extensive range of factors. Neither individual nor collective identity is fixed and immovable. Identity is not monolithic; it is layered and often opaque. Two: Identity consists of both personal and social elements that mutually shape each other. It is impossible to extract and separate one's personal identity from the social matrix in which one lives. Three: Identity is formed both by affirmation of what/who one is and by repudiation of who/what one is not. Further, identity is validated internally by the individual's sense of self as well as by recognition of the social group to which he or she belongs.[1]

The formation of social identity is through a series of mental processes – the first of which is categorization. Categorization is necessary in order to identify, understand and bring order. The second process is that of social identification in which group identity is assumed according to the identity of the category of the group one has chosen. This involves behaviour and has an emotional component. Group membership gives emotional significance to the one who identifies with the group, and one's sense of self-esteem is connected to membership status. The third process is social comparison. After categorization and identification, the remaining step is to compare one's own group with other groups. This is particularly important in understanding intergroup relations. Hostility and competition between groups is in part a function of competing identities.[2]

What Is 'Messianic'?

The identity of the Israeli Messianic Jew consists of at least three major components. Israeli can be understood as a civil or geographical designation; Messianic is a faith descriptor; and Jew can be a religious, ethnic or civil term. As this book is exploring issues of reconciliation in a faith-based context, the first component we want to look at is the faith element.

The key word in the title is 'Messianic', and as such it needs to be defined and elucidated. The astute reader will have noticed the linkage of the two terms Christian and Messianic 'Christian / Messianic' in the introduction. This is intentional, the purpose being to clearly establish an inseparable bond between the two words. Simply stated, 'Messianic' is the adjective form of the word 'Messiah'. The Hebrew word Messiah was translated to Greek as 'Christos'. The first use of the word 'Christian' to describe one who believes in Jesus is found in Acts 11.26 where we read that in Antioch the disciples (followers) of Jesus were first called Christians. It is debatable whether this term was complimentary or derogatory.

The movement that later became known as Christianity was birthed and formed in an entirely Jewish religious and social context during the Second Temple period. The New Testament documents comprise an important part of the literature of that period and they faithfully describe and represent that era. This was a time of great religious, social and political upheaval. Palestine was suffering under Roman rule, Hellenism was the reigning social influence in the Roman province of Palestine, and the prophetic voice to Israel had been silent for four hundred years. The religious life of the people of Israel was centred on temple worship with a number of Jewish sects functioning, each of which had a particular understanding of how to worship God. There was no single definitive Judaism in the Second Temple period. There were a number of 'Judaisms'. The Jesus movement became one of this number. Much of the controversy in the New Testament regarding the relationship between Jesus and the other forms of religious life was between his followers and the other sects, particularly as it related to matters of authority.[3]

Throughout Jesus' life and the lives of all the New Testament communities, the Jewish people were living under occupation. The fact of occupation of any people, whether ancient or contemporary, raises existential questions about the meaning and purpose of individual and corporate life. This context is conducive to the rise of new movements seeking social change. According to the New Testament, this was the 'fullness of time'[4] when conditions were fully in place for the coming of the promised Messiah deliverer of Israel. He came as a Jew, first to his people Israel who were the bearers of the covenants and promises of God. It is a matter of record that the first followers of Jesus were all Jews and had a strong connection with the Jerusalem temple.[5] Messianic Jews today often see themselves in a direct line of continuity with these first-century Jews who embraced Yeshua as Messiah and Lord. Therefore, it is against this background that today's Messianic Jew needs to be understood. The book of Acts chronicles the spread of the gospel in the Greco-Roman world and addresses some of the issues that emerged within the multi-ethnic body of believers in Jesus. In the early years of the spread of the gospel, increasing numbers of non-Jews were drawn to Jesus. The New Testament makes reference to the emerging problems of a mixed community, notably circumcision of non-Jews and dietary restrictions.[6]

As the community of Jesus-believing Jews grew, issues between the new community and the surrounding Jewish community grew. Tensions increased after the Bar Kochba revolt, a Jewish rebellion against Roman domination, in 132–5 CE. This rebellion was led by Simeon Bar Kosiba, who was seen as a Messianic figure and renamed Bar Kochva – 'son of the star' according to a reference in Numbers 24.17. Having embraced Jesus as Messiah, the Jewish believers in Jesus were not able to accept Bar Kochva as Messiah. This led to a breach in relationship with their fellow Jews who supported Bar Kochva. Because of their non-alignment with Bar Kochva, which was due to their faith, the Jesus-believing Jews were now perceived as being opposed to the mainstream Jewish community. This was a significant factor in determining an identity that contributed to an eventual clear separation from the Jewish community. Rome was the victor in this revolt and the Romans did not distinguish between the Jews who believed in Jesus and those who did not. All Jews, including those Jews who followed Jesus, were forbidden from entering Jerusalem and were uprooted from their mother community in Jerusalem. Prior to the revolt, all of the leaders of the early church were Jews. Eusebius lists fifteen bishops, beginning with James, as overseers of the Jerusalem church, all of whom were Jews.[7]

Following the Bar Kochva revolt, Jewish followers of Jesus became increasingly disenfranchised from Jewish people. Although there are other views concerning the significance of the Bar Kochva revolt for the relationship between Jesus-believing Jews and the rest of the Jewish community, this event has often been cited as a key turning point for the 'parting of the ways' between Judaism and Christianity.[8] During the same period as the Bar Kochva revolt, the Jesus-believing Jews' continued observance of Jewish tradition was rapidly becoming a problem for the growing numbers of non-Jews in the church. Already in the second century, the predominantly non-Jewish church began to institute liturgical elements that were in conflict with Jewish forms of worship. In the fourth century, the Council of Nicaea together with the earlier conversion of the Roman emperor Constantine to Christianity, provided the decisive framework for the church to become almost exclusively non-Jewish. Mass makes for dominance and creates new social space. The new non-Jewish 'Christians' influenced the culture of the church for generations in an anti-Jewish direction. Jewishness as an identity marker within the church gradually disappeared. Jews, however, did not. They remained a 'remnant' within the church,[9] maintaining a small but continuous presence.

Until the fourth century, there were communities of Jesus-believing Jews who continued to identify and live as Jews within the already predominantly non-Jewish church.[10] The shift from a body of believers who were all from the 'house of Israel' to a community where Jews were the minority took place over several centuries. The process culminated at the Council of Nicaea in 325 CE when the assembled representatives of the church adopted a calendar that decisively separated the date of the resurrection (Easter) from the date of the Jewish Passover.[11] This event served to denude the church of Jewish influence and set a course for the future that would effectively sever any Jew who believed in Jesus from his Jewish roots. The only choice for a Jew who believed in Jesus was to identify with the new culture of Christianity that had intentionally disassociated itself from the biblical heritage of the commonwealth of Israel.

The relationship between the church and the Jewish people continued to deteriorate throughout the period of the Middle Ages and beyond. Christian anti-Semitism emerged as the dominant mode of relationship between the church and the Jewish people, expressing itself in inquisitions, forced conversions, persecutions and pogroms against the Jewish people.[12] Over a period of several centuries, the Western church institutionalized anti-Jewishness in its official teaching.[13] The anti-Jewishness of European Christianity provided the background for the events that eventually climaxed in the Holocaust. Many professed Christians colluded with the Nazi government during the times of the Holocaust.

In the nineteenth century, after a hiatus of almost 2,000 years, significant numbers of Jews began to come to faith in Jesus and again identify themselves as Jews, many choosing to worship in Jewish-friendly forms, rather than assimilating into the dominant non-Jewish church culture. It was during this period, as issues of Jewish identity emerged, that Jesus-believing Jews began to call themselves Messianic rather than Christian. Prior to this, Jews who were Jesus believers and desired to maintain their Jewish identity were called Hebrew Christians.

Joseph Rabinowitz (1837–99) of Kishinev is generally credited as having been the first to use the term 'Messianic Jews' to refer to Jews who had come to faith in Jesus. He is also seen as the founder of the Messianic movement.[14] During the year 1882, Rabinowitz travelled to Palestine where, on the Mount of Olives, he had a revelation that Jesus was the Messiah and the elder brother of the Jewish people. Upon his return to Bessarabia (South Russia) he became active in reaching the Jewish people for their Messiah. By 1886 he had gathered large numbers of Jews who believed in Jesus. He called this new fellowship 'The Israelites of the New Covenant'. It is particularly noteworthy that the 'revival' Rabinowitz led happened without the influence of traditional missionary activity. It was an indigenous movement, shaped by Rabinowitz's vision of a distinctly Jewish expression of faith in Jesus. Today's Messianic Jews are indebted to the pioneering work of Rabinowitz. Although the movement he led died out after his death (1899), his work provided a foundation for later Jews who were to come to faith in Jesus.[15]

Messianic Jews are frequently asked, 'Why don't you just call yourselves Christians?' There are a number of answers to this question within the contexts of personal and social identity issues. In the earlier discussion of aspects of identity formation, one of the points was the way in which identity is formed in contrast to existing categories. For the Jewish people, the word 'Christian' or 'Christianity' has been at best a stumbling block preventing them from any real encounter with the substance of the faith, and at worst, an impenetrable wall of partition. For most Jewish people, the history of relations between the church and the Jews is written in Jewish blood. For all the multitude of definitions of what it means to be a Jew, there is one agreed-upon definition – a Jew is definitely *not* a Christian. 'Messianic' describes the faith commitment of the Israeli Messianic Jew with a term that is culturally appropriate and, at the same time, resonates with his or her sense of self as being part of the Jewish people. The essential content of a Messianic Jew's faith is in substantive agreement with the core beliefs of the evangelical Christian. Being a Jew in no way contributes to what it requires to come to faith in Jesus. How a Messianic Jew lives out his faith in Jewish social space does differ from how a Christian would express his faith while living in a Christian culture.

In the 1970s, the term 'Hebrew Christian' was largely abandoned in favour of the term 'Messianic Jew'. This name change was significant in that it embodies the continuity of Jewishness within the context of faith in Messiah Jesus. The term 'Hebrew Christian' suggests a lack of continuity with Jewish identity. For Jews, the term 'Christian' implies being 'not Jewish'. Jesus-believing Jews embrace their identity as part of the Jewish people. Their faith commitment is not to the organized religion of Christianity but rather to the person of Messiah Jesus.

What Is Jewishness?

The next element of the classification of Israeli Messianic Jewish identity to be considered is 'Jewish', together with the question 'What does it mean to be Jewish?' From antiquity, Jewishness was indeterminate and was variously defined in religious, ethnic and/ or geographical terms:

> Jewish identity in antiquity was elusive and uncertain for two simple reasons. First, there was no single or simple definition of Jew in antiquity. Indeed, the Greek word Ioudaios, usually translated as 'Jew', often is better translated as 'Judaean,' and the concepts 'Jew' and 'Judaean', in turn, need clarification. Second, there were few mechanisms in antiquity that would have provided empirical or 'objective' criteria by which to determine who was 'really' a Jew and who was not. Jewishness was a subjective identity, constructed by the individual him/herself, other Jews, other gentiles, and the state.[16]

The Jews (Judaeans) of antiquity were in fact a distinct ethnic group defined as living in a particular geographical area (including major communities in Alexandria and Babylon); having an understanding of their common origins, history and destiny; with a communal consciousness of their distinctiveness and sharing a number of unique characteristics. These elements combined constitute the definition of the Greek word *joudaismos*, translated as 'Judaism', but encompassing more than religion. Of the shared characteristics of Jews, the most distinctive had to do with the worship of their God, i.e. religion. A more comprehensive translation of the word *joudaismos* would be 'Jewishness' rather than 'Judaism'.[17]

In the centuries following antiquity, Jewishness as a descriptor for an ethno-religious group solidified and became monolithic so that only after the Enlightenment did the question of 'What is Jewishness?' begin again to arise. As a community living in dispersion, Jewish corporate religious life was the defining element of their identity. Jewishness was clear, unquestioned and largely self-evident. Since the Jewish Enlightenment (*Haskala*) at the beginning of the nineteenth century, definitions of Jewishness have expanded and become increasingly fluid. With the emergence of a more pluralistic Judaism, what it meant to be Jewish was differently defined by each stream within Judaism. One was Orthodox, conservative or reformed depending on one's view of Torah and *halacha* (religious observance). Modernity has made for blurred and permeable boundaries between what was once universally agreed upon and fixed. This is especially true regarding issues of identity, whether personal or collective.

The openness and questioning spirit of the Enlightenment saw new, more liberal forms of Judaism emerge in Europe and the United States. Identity for the Jew had largely been defined in terms of a social, communal construct. With the Enlightenment came an increased emphasis on the individual and individual identity and self-realization apart from the traditional bonds of peoplehood, and commonality of lifestyle and mentality. 'A Jew can be a Jew by nation, religion, ethnicity, biology, ideology, denomination – or any combination thereof. Yet scholars have often failed to reflect this complexity by relying on traditional categories of behavior, beliefs and belonging – rather than on the dynamic, sometimes contradictory, ways in which Jewish identity is actually understood and expressed.'[18] The religion of Judaism is no longer the decisive element in Jewish identity. Today there are 'Hinjews' and 'Jubus' – Jews who respectively embrace Hinduism and Buddhism yet retain their sense of Jewish identity.

In Israel today, for the purposes of the law of return that grants automatic citizenship to any Jew who requests it, a Jew is defined as one who is born of a Jewish mother and who has not converted to another religion.[19] This definition does not require that one adhere to Judaism. Jewishness in the twenty-first century is increasingly pluralistic with a growing number of Jews worldwide identifying themselves as secular. Secularism can be defined as 'the acceptance of a primary identity, unrelated to religion'. This category is multilayered as there are many forms of secularism. Felix Posen of the Posen Foundation suggests that secularism is becoming the unifying factor in Jewish identity. He points out that today the majority of Jews worldwide identify themselves as secular rather than religious and that secularism with its emphasis on culture could become the unifying force that would connect and bring together the majority, if not all of the different groups (religious and secular) that identify themselves as Jewish.[20]

For two thousand years, the Jewish people as an entity lived in a state of God-ordained exile from their homeland. While there were exceptions to this, with some Jews settling and maintaining vibrant communities in the Galilee and Jerusalem, the people never regained national sovereignty. The geographical, territorial dimension of identity had been inaccessible to them since the dispersion of 70 CE, and in fact Orthodox Judaism understood an eventual return to the land in terms of an eschatological hope that would only be realized by the Messiah who would himself restore Jewish hegemony in the ancient Promised Land. It has been stated that geography is but one element of identity; for the Jewish people and for 'Jewishness' (the sense of what it means to be a Jew), the element of the land of Israel was a powerful influence for the majority of Jews whose identity was bound up with a religious observance that continually reinforced the issue of diaspora with its hopes of spiritual renewal and return to the land. The longing for return had been kept alive in the daily prayers and yearly festivals of the Jewish people. Return to the fatherland, Israel, was a sleeping dream about to wake and further complicate answers to the question of what it means to be Jewish.

At the end of the nineteenth century, this dream came awake in the form of Zionism. Whereas Orthodox Judaism rejected physical efforts to return to the land from which they had been exiled, Zionism countered this understanding and encouraged the Jewish people to take control of their destiny and begin a return to the land of Israel. Zionism as a political ideology together with a short history of the movement is addressed in other chapters of this book. It is included here as an important subset of what it means to be Jewish in today's world.

Although the Jewish people had prayed for a return to Zion for centuries,[21] it was not the religious who were the pioneers of the Zionist movement. Early Zionism was secular in nature and provided the ideology for the founding of the state of Israel. Zionism as a political movement was largely formed in reaction to the ongoing anti-Semitism that was then prevalent in Russia and most of Eastern Europe. It was a Jewish nationalistic movement that aspired to self-determination and a continuation of Jewish history in the land of the ancestors. The Zionist narrative attempted to create continuity between the distant biblical past and the present that would legitimize a Jewish state in Palestine. Because Zionism stressed the connection between the Jewish people as Israel revived and the Israel of the Bible, the identity of modern Israel found itself inseparably bound to biblical Israel and hence to Judaism as a religious identity. Zionism's primary aim was to establish a state for and of Jews where they would be safe from the annihilation threatened by continued anti-Semitism and the brutal pogroms in Eastern Europe and Russia. Because of Zionism's early history and its continuing persuasive power, its influence for the Jew and for the meaning of Jewishness cannot be underestimated. It is all but impossible to construct an identity as a Jew without some reference to the Zionist ideology and agenda.[22]

It should be clear from this brief overview of what it means to be Jewish that there is no one single answer to the question. On the contrary, Jewishness is complex, difficult to define, and impossible to reduce to a formula or a single statement. 'Jewishness' is an admixture of ethnicity, religion, nationalism, biology, ideology, denomination, being, belonging and behaviour.

What Is 'Israeli'?

In the context of this chapter, it would be an oversimplification to dismiss the question with a reply that would posit the answer in solely geographical or nationalistic terms. While it would seem that this category is the most straightforward of the three descriptors in the chapter's title, this is not the case. Israel today is a predominantly secular state whose Jewish population consists of the native born and immigrants from many backgrounds. This cultural mix results in a pluralism that is unprecedented in Jewish life. There are almost as many answers to the question of what or who is an Israeli as there are to the parallel question of 'Who is a Jew?'

Following on from the previous section, we will continue the discussion of the importance of Zionism. Zionism not only impacts the issue of Jewishness; it also influences and shapes what it means to be an Israeli. Zionism remains the dominant ideological core paradigm for the existence of national Israel. Perhaps more than any other single factor, Zionism has determined what it means to be an Israeli. Zionism was envisioned as an ideology and world-view that places Jewish survival in the epicentre of its focus. An integral part of this ideology was the creation of a Jewish home-land, which later became a state for the Jews that would offer refuge to any and all Jews who wished to live in the land of Israel. As a direct result of this commitment, Israel was intended to be a land of immigrants with immense cultural diversity. Until today, this remains a strong element in all discussions of what it means to be Israeli.

After the Second World War, Palestine was seen as the only safe haven for Jews fleeing the Holocaust of Europe. A 'state of or for the Jews', a place where Jews would be safe from persecu-tion and anti-Semitism, was seen as essential if the Jewish people were to survive. Israel was established in 1948 to meet this need. However, the 'state for the Jews' quickly became a 'Jewish state'.[23] This is not merely a linguistic issue. There is a profound differ-ence between the two concepts. A 'state for the Jews' emphasizes the *state*. A state could have developed in a number of ways, including as a nation that equally embraced all peoples. However, a 'Jewish state' emphasizes the issue of *Jewishness*, signifying that Jewishness defines the nature of the state.[24] This is a critical differ-ence with serious implications for the Jews and for other peoples who would reside within the boundaries of the state of Israel. One result of this development was to link being Israeli with being Jewish. Boundaries between the two concepts became blurred, making definition difficult.

Issues of survival were and remain primary for an understanding of what it means to be an Israeli Jew. In the aftermath of the Holocaust, on 29 November 1947, the United Nations General Assembly passed Resolution 181 (the UN Partition Plan), calling for the creation of two independent states in Palestine. Israelis see this decision as giving international legitimacy to the new state of Israel. Revelation of the scope and extent of the Holocaust strongly influenced the international community as they voted for Israel to become a sovereign state in its ancient homeland. The threat of extinction of the Jewish people was a large factor in this decision. The new country quickly became strong and developed attitudes of self-reliance, independence and national pride. Israel declared independence in May of the following year. Israel's Declaration of Independence articulates many of the key elements that constitute a definition of what it means to be Israeli,[25] including the tenacious character of Jewish survival as an integral element of 'Israeliness'.

The shadow of the Holocaust continues to shape Israeli identity. The influence of the Holocaust is reinforced by continual threats to Israel's survival from an ongoing hostile political environment. This fact contributes to a strong stance of self-reliance that includes political autonomy and military prowess to respond quickly and efficiently to security threats.[26] In 1948, Israel's first prime minister, Ben-Gurion, stated, 'But we must not forget that our security depends on our own might'.[27] Over the years, other Israeli leaders have expressed similar sentiments. The principle of 'trust no one but yourself' is very much Israel's self-perception. Israelis are often noted for their extreme self-confidence and independence. While these qualities have a positive aspect, the downside is mistrust of others, including their motivations. Until today, Israel sees itself as David to the Goliath of the hostile nations surrounding it. The memory and impact of the Holocaust is further entrenched in the Israeli mentality by yearly memorials observed by every sector of society. Holocaust Day is marked by national events and wide media coverage. Children study the Holocaust as part of the regular curriculum from grammar school through high school.

Military conscription is mandatory for all Jewish citizens.[28] At age 18, young men and women alike are conscripted into the

Israeli Defence Forces to serve for three and two years respectively. Military presence is ubiquitous throughout the country. Military duty and a militaristic mindset characterize much of Israeli culture. The experience of military service often defines the worldview and sets the values of the individual for the rest of his life. Success in military life is coveted and there is much competition to get into elite intelligence and combat units. The essence of the military is to defend and protect the land and the people by whatever means are deemed necessary by the political leaders of the country. However one relates to the strong military presence, the existence of an active military is seen as essential to the survival of the nation and the people of Israel.

To grasp what it means to be Israeli, an understanding of the Israeli's attachment to the physical land of Israel is necessary. Jews were a stateless, wandering, persecuted people in dispersion for millennia. The land of Israel is both an enduring dream revived and a new vision for future survival in the ancient land of promise. It would be difficult to overestimate the significance of the land for what it means to be Israeli today. In an age of increasing globalization, there is a concurrent counter trend of intensified nationalism. Israel is at the same time widely cosmopolitan and narrowly sectarian. Some of the deep historical, psychological and social reasons for this have already been cited.

A recent study by the IDF Education Corps, published in the army journal *Maarachot*, showed that officers in the Israel Defence Forces tend to identify more as Israeli than as Jewish. Israeli military officers generally reflect a mid to high range of socio-economic levels. The survey also found that 94 per cent termed their Israeli identity very important. When asked about the components of Israeli identity, 62 per cent of respondents named service in the Israeli Defence Forces, 52 per cent said it meant being proud of the state, 42 per cent said it entailed actually living in Israel, and 44 per cent said it meant voting in Israeli elections.[29]

Another question the survey asked was which historical event the officers considered most important for themselves personally and for the Jewish people as a whole. The Holocaust was the highest-rated event in both categories. Twenty-five per cent of those surveyed believed this to be the most important event for them personally and 36 per cent for the Jewish people. The establishment of the state of Israel was in second place in both categories while third place was various Israeli wars – especially the Second Lebanon War of 2006.

Being Israeli is a complex issue. Israeli identity can be understood in many ways but it is certainly a national, political classification far more than a religious classification. The secular majority of Israelis holds varying degrees of anti-Orthodox sentiments. The clearest markers for the Israeli identity are Zionism, the land of Israel, the Holocaust, military service and extreme self-reliance.

What Shapes Israeli Messianic Jewish Identity?

To this point we have briefly examined the three components of this identity as individual elements. Now we will attempt to formulate a synthesis. Due to the complex, multifaceted nature of the individual elements, bringing them together is an almost unattainable objective. In her doctoral thesis on Israeli Messianic Jews, Keri Warshawsky states, 'Clearly, Israeli Messianic Jewish identity itself cannot be definitively mapped.'[30] To say that this identity is diverse would be to understate the case. However, the issues of God, the land, and the people of Israel are three significant, interwoven, communally held understandings that will help us navigate the subject.[31] In addition, a brief look at the history of Israeli Messianic Jews from 1948 to the present will provide background for understanding their current identity.

Early history of the Israeli Messianic Jewish community[32]

The community of Messianic Jews in Israel existed in seminal form from the period of the British Mandate in Palestine. In 1890–91 a 'Hebrew Christian Prayer Union' was functioning and led to the establishment in 1898 of the 'Jerusalem Hebrew Christian Association', which had approximately fifty members.[33] During the years 1925–9 there was a failed attempt to establish a Messianic Jewish congregation in Jerusalem. However, 'The Hebrew Christian Fellowship of Palestine' was established in 1931. It was the first regional grouping founded by Messianic Jews. Although the name was 'Hebrew Christian', it is significant that in their

Hebrew language documents the members referred to themselves as 'Messianic Jews'.

Prior to 1948, a number of small congregations were established in Haifa, Jerusalem and Jaffa. The Brethren denomination was responsible for the founding of these groups. The Messianic Assembly in Jerusalem was founded during this period by Ze'ev Kofsman, a French Jewish immigrant. In 1958, this congregation became the first Messianic congregation to be officially registered in Israel. Kofsman's vision was to return to the first-century expression of the early church as a faith model without reference to the later creeds of the church. He also strongly emphasized the use of Hebrew terminology based on the Hebrew translation of the New Testament.[34]

During the British Mandate period, the numbers of the community were estimated at approximately 120 persons. They were located in Jerusalem, Jaffa, Haifa, Safed and Tiberias and were connected with Protestant missionary organizations. Their desire was to express a distinct Jewish identity using Jewish terminology rather than Christian language, which they saw as foreign to Jewish life in Israel. This small, scattered community continued to struggle through the chaotic period of the Second World War and the events leading up to the establishment of the state of Israel.

To provide context for the issue of Israeli Messianic Jewish identity today, it is important to examine the roots of the phenomenon. This implies returning to those who embodied particular aspects of the newly forming identity. Two pioneers who sought to express their Jewishness in the context of their faith in Jesus were Bishop Michael Solomon Alexander and Rabbi Daniel Ben Zion. Bishop Michael Solomon Alexander (1799–1845) was a Jew of Prussian extraction who, after immigrating to Great Britain and attaining the status of rabbi, came to faith in Jesus through the efforts of the Anglican mission society, the 'London Society for the Promoting of Christianity Amongst the Jews'. He became an Anglican priest and was then made bishop. In 1842 he was sent to Jerusalem to establish the first Protestant bishopric in the Holy Land. Bishop Alexander began conducting services in Hebrew and was active in establishing a number of institutions for the Jesus-believing Jews, including a 'School of Industry' for training Jewish believers in basic trades, a book store, a Hebrew college, and in 1844 he established a modern hospital for the Jewish people.[35]

The second pioneer of Israeli Messianic Jewish identity is Rabbi Daniel Ben Zion (1883–1979) of Bulgaria. While praying and looking at the sunrise, Rabbi Daniel Zion had a vision of Yeshua. This vision was repeated three times. The third time, he began to speak with the figure who then identified himself as Yeshua. Rabbi Zion sought the help of the Greek Orthodox Archimandrite Stephan who advised him to concentrate on Yeshua himself and not to focus on Christianity. As a result, Rabbi Zion never officially 'converted' to Christianity. He believed in Yeshua and continued to serve as a rabbi while living a Torah-observant life. During the Nazi invasion of Bulgaria, Rabbi Zion wrote to the Bulgarian king interceding for the Jews of Bulgaria not to be delivered to the Nazis. He and his secretary personally delivered a letter to the king's secretary. The next day the king travelled to Germany to meet with Hitler himself. King Boris did not submit to Nazi demands to send the Jews of Sofia to the death camps of Germany and Poland. Ben Zion served as chief rabbi of Bulgaria until 1949 when he immigrated to Israel. He served on the rabbinical court of Jerusalem until rumours about his faith in Yeshua forced the chief rabbi of Israel to strip him of his title. Rabbi Ben Zion continued to serve as rabbi for Bulgarian Jews until 1973, often speaking from the New Testament parables of Yeshua and teaching about Yeshua and the New Testament from his home.[36]

The most prominent mission group operating in pre-Israeli Palestine was the Anglican mission, centred in Jerusalem with outposts in other parts of the country. The chapter in this book that relates the history of this period presents the difficult nature of the relationship during the Mandate period between the British and the local population, both Jewish and Arab. The Jewish leadership in Palestine was opposed to British rule and considered the British presence as inimical to the aspirations of the Jewish populace. Since many of the Jesus-believing Jews had connections with the Anglicans, there was a fear that the believers would also be seen as enemies of the incipient state. In fact, the fear was that Jesus-believing Jews would be seen as 'double enemies' because of their faith as well as their connection to the British presence in the land. Whether this fear was justified is a matter of historical debate.

Nonetheless, action was taken to protect the Jesus-believing Jews of Palestine. In what came to be known as 'Operation Mercy', an initiative was launched to evacuate all 'Hebrew Christians' who preferred not to remain within the anticipated new Jewish state. The operation transferred between seventy-five and ninety persons to Liverpool in England, leaving approximately twelve known Messianic Jews in Israel in 1948.[37]

This was to be a defining moment for Jesus-believing Jews in the Holy Land. While individuals and isolated families remained, Operation Mercy resulted in the extinction of the *community* of believers. The small local fellowships disintegrated and the influence of the Gentile missions receded, causing the remaining believers to distance themselves from the influence of foreign Gentile mission and align themselves with the fledgling nation of Israel as an integral part of their identity in the land. Out of this, local congregations would emerge with a strong Israeli identity expressed in clear allegiance to the state of Israel. Those who remained identified with the Zionist agenda of the new state. The tone was now set for the future of the Messianic movement and the new Israeli Messianic Jewish identity.

From 1950 to 2013

In the decades following 1950 to the present, the Messianic community[38] has continued to grow. During the 1950s and 1960s, there were massive waves of immigration from Europe to Israel. Numbers of Jesus-believing Jews immigrated along with non-believing Jews, many from Romania and other countries in Eastern Europe.

Before the Second World War, there had been active mission works among Jews in Romania and Hungary by Norwegian missionaries. With the wave of immigration to Israel, numbers of those who had been reached by the Norwegian missionaries immigrated to Israel. These new immigrants called out to their Norwegian friends to provide them with spiritual support. In response, in 1949, the Norwegian Lutherans sent pastors and began to establish bases in Israel that remain till today. During these years, many Protestant churches sent missionaries to Israel, many of whom established a presence in the country, purchased property and built institutions. For example, the Finnish School in Jerusalem was purchased in 1954 and the Baptist Village near Petach Tikva was established in 1955. Already from this time there were annual summer camps held for the children of believing families at both the Finnish School and the Baptist Village. During these years, there were small groups of Jesus-believing Jews who had been reached by the missionaries, and who were meeting and worshipping in mission premises. By 1967, there were an estimated 150 Messianic Jews in Israel.

Following Israel's overwhelming victory in the Six Day War in 1967 the small Israeli Messianic Jewish community interpreted the events as a highly significant 'sign of the times' that would lead to the second coming of Yeshua and the establishment of the Messianic kingdom on the earth. The reunification of Jerusalem under Jewish hegemony signified the end of the 'times of the Gentiles' when Jerusalem would no more be under the domination of occupying nations.[39] The Six Day War was viewed as the beginning of the final battle that would lead to Messiah's millennial reign over the world.

Partly as a result of these end-time speculations, some of the Messianic leaders taught that Messianic Jews, as good citizens, had an obligation to serve in the Israeli Defence Forces (IDF). Many believers fought in the Six Day War of 1967. Their theological Zionism was practically worked out and not only spiritually understood. The few who had remained in Israel in the wake of Operation Mercy were instrumental in raising a different generation of Israeli Messianic Jews who were strongly patriotic on the basis of their eschatological views. For the small Israeli Messianic Jewish community, despite accusations that Zionism was only a tool to legitimize themselves as Israelis, Zionism became a fundamental element of their theology, integral to their identity and way of life.

Within Christian circles outside Israel, there was much interest in Israeli affairs after its spectacular victory in 1967. Eschatological speculation was widespread and there was a revival of interest concerning Israel among Jesus-believing Jews worldwide, regardless of their level of Jewish identity or observance. In the following decade, numbers of Jewish believers immigrated to Israel. Many did so with the understanding that the end times were rapidly approaching the final stage.

The 1970s[40]

During this time period, two major events occurred that deeply influenced the growth of the Messianic community. One was the charismatic renewal, which impacted both the existing small groups of Messianic Jews and the missionary and expatriate community. By this time there were five or six congregations who held their meetings in Hebrew. In the mid 1970s the known number of Messianic Jews was estimated at about 300. The second event that impacted the Messianic community was an influx of believers, primarily from North America. These believers were happy to meet in homes and did not wish to affiliate with the existing mission works.

By the end of the 1970s there were approximately fifteen groups that were meeting in Hebrew. Congregations such as Grace and Truth in Rishon Letzion and Beit Asaph in Netanya were formed during these years. Other, older congregations that had been founded by mission societies began to take on a more indigenized expression of the faith. An example of this is the Beit Immanuel congregation in Tel Aviv, which began as an Anglican mission work but during this period started to attract numbers of young native-born Israelis. The general trend for the Messianic community at this time was to increasingly develop an indigenous identity differentiated from the earlier mission/church culture that had traditionally expressed itself in predominantly Gentile forms.

The 1980s

During this decade there was an increase in inter-congregational efforts. This was the era of the growth and development of para-church organizations although the national community was still relatively small (under a thousand). Events were organized that drew people from virtually all of the existing congregations and groups. In this period, annual Passover conferences began that attracted a large number of younger believers (those under 35). This era also saw the development of a Messianic hymnology. National music conferences were held where new Hebrew congregational music was presented. This new music was then reviewed and collated into songbooks on a yearly basis, providing a significant unifying factor for the young Messianic community.

A national quarterly pastor's fellowship was formed during this decade. This forum was open to all of the congregations. Pastors came together to share informally and pray with each other. Already at this stage, the congregations were functioning along differing theological lines. The older guard, the earliest congregations, was primarily non-charismatic and theologically conservative, whereas many of the newer congregations favoured a more charismatic expression. Issues of appropriate levels of Torah observance also began to become an issue.

One of the outgrowths of the National Pastors' Conferences was the formation of a National Evangelism Committee. This committee organized evangelism campaigns in the major cities of Israel, designing materials for street evangelism. Teams consisting of representatives from a wide variety of congregations took part in these outreaches. Particularly in the north of Israel, a number of the Arab Christian churches joined with these evangelism teams.

During the 1980s a national pro-life group was formed that became active in disseminating information about abortion throughout Israel. A national study centre was opened which became the basis for what is today the Israel College of the Bible. Other study initiatives also began at this time, including Caspari Center and the Messianic Midrasha in Jerusalem. Not all of these initiatives survived. In addition, two Messianic schools came into existence, one in the north of the country and one in Jerusalem.

The local congregations continued to grow and by the end of the 1980s there were approximately forty-five congregations and small groups meeting in Hebrew throughout Israel and no longer only in the large cities. Numbers were estimated at 2,500–3,000.

The 1990s

This was the decade of massive immigration from the former Soviet Union. From 1989 to 2005 Israel received 960,972 (almost one million) new Russian-speaking immigrants. When the number of Russian-speaking immigrants from earlier years is added to this number, we see that those with Russian background, language and culture account for about 33 per cent of the total Israeli population. This fact has had great significance for the Israeli Messianic congregations.

According to the only serious statistical research[41] that has been conducted on the Messianic congregations in Israel, the data shows that at the end of the 1990s Russian-background believers amounted to 42 per cent of the number of local believers. This data also showed that the community at the end of the 1990s consisted of approximately five thousand persons. They were organized in approximately eighty congregations, the majority of which were Hebrew-speaking fellowships.

Not all of the local congregations were able to absorb the new Russian-speaking immigrants who were also believers in Yeshua. This meant that entirely new congregations and fellowships were formed during this period. Alongside the Hebrew-speaking fellowships, a large number of Russian-speaking congregations formed. One such congregation has five affiliated groups with more than 450 persons who worship and meet in Russian. The Russian-speaking believers brought a new seriousness and openness to the existing local congregations. In the main, these believers were quick to share their faith with their extended families, and in their workplaces and neighbourhoods. This resulted in many coming to faith in the 1990s. Data from a personally conducted survey concerning the Russian believing community[42] shows that from 40 per cent to 60 per cent of the families cannot be defined as halachicly Jewish.[43] In addition to this, about 7 per cent of immigrants coming to Israel define themselves as followers of Orthodox Christianity.

All of the para-church organizations that had been formed in the 1980s continued to grow and develop. Musalaha, a ministry of reconciliation, which fosters relationship between Arab (both Israeli and Palestinian) and Jewish believers in Yeshua was founded during this time. As the congregations began to grow, the numbers of children also increased. This led to a strong emphasis on ministry among children and youth.

The twenty-first century – 2000–13
In this short period of a little more than a decade, the number of Messianic Jews and their congregations in Israel has proliferated to the extent that the number of Israelis believing in Yeshua and attending Messianic congregations is estimated at 10,000–15,000. This is a conservative estimate and numbers as high as 23,000 have been seen. It is difficult to give accurate numbers since no formal research has been conducted during this time.

Two major things characterize the Messianic community during this decade. The first is that theological streams are becoming more defined along lines of charismatic/non-charismatic expression and theology and also according to differing levels of Torah observance. This has engendered sharp theological debate, especially relating to issues of the deity of Yeshua and formations of Trinitarian statements of the Godhead. The second major characteristic of this period is the increasing number of younger people in the congregations. At this stage, there are second and even third-generation believers. Work among young adults, army-age believers and youth is increasing. The Messianic schools continue to grow and there are initiatives to form new such schools.

Together with this growth and emphasis, there is an increasing dissatisfaction with existing structures and growing disillusionment among those raised in Messianic homes. These young people are looking for alternative ways to express their faith. At the time of this writing, 2013, the best estimates show that there are approximately 150 congregations that meet in Hebrew, several Spanish-speaking groups, One Romanian-speaking group, between 30 and 50 groups that meet in Russian, and eight Ethiopian Amharic-speaking groups.

A number of the more forward-thinking leaders of congregations are seeing the need to fully disciple and train young believers. Some of the para-church organizations are endeavouring to meet this need. In addition, there are increasing numbers of conferences that focus on 'leadership' issues. However, the content seems to be Western in orientation and most of the focus is on models taken from the world of business and applied to the body of Messiah.

To a large degree, demographically, the Israeli Messianic Jewish community reflects the situation of the nation as a whole. As Israel is a land of culturally diverse immigrants, so too is the body of Messiah in Israel. The community is resistant to organized structures and is also resistant to being surveyed. For this reason, there are no recent reliable statistics as to its numbers or the breakdown of its cultural diversity. The only existent survey of the community (mentioned earlier in this chapter) was done in 1999, following the large wave of immigration from the former Soviet Union. This was reflected in the survey as it showed that 42 per cent of the community were from Russian-speaking backgrounds.

During the years since, the ratio of native Russian speakers has slightly declined as the community is now experiencing growth from within (second- and third-generation believers) and greater numbers of native-born Israelis are coming to faith.

Three Interwoven Themes: God, the Land and the Jewish People

Relationship with God

'The primary source of Jewish identity is the unique relationship of God to the Jewish people which has preserved them for nearly two millennia of Diaspora.'[44] This is particularly true for Messianic Jews who have returned to the God of their ancestors through their faith in Messiah Yeshua. This relationship is the core of their identity. Here the dual foci are 'returning' and the 'God of their ancestors'. When Israeli Messianic Jews describe themselves and their relationship with God, they invariably use biblical (Tenach)[45] terminology. The paradigms for understanding this relationship come from the narratives of the Old Testament scriptures. As much as Messianic Jews see themselves in continuity with first-century believers, they view them as embedded in the biblical context of the life of Israel. Hence, their own rootedness is in the life, the land and the narratives of Israel. Their models and heroes are the prophets and the patriarchs of ancient Israel.

The importance of the land of Israel

In spite of the fact that the majority of Israeli Messianic Jews were not born in Israel, their identification with the land of Israel is of supreme importance. Israeli Messianic Jews situate themselves in the land as a non-negotiable facet of their identity. Their self-understanding is intimately bound to the reality of Israel's sovereignty in its ancient Promised Land. In addition, living in the land is seen as an integral element of their faith journey.[46] The land is closely tied to their sense of having returned to the God of their ancestors. Whether immigrants or native born, Israeli Messianic Jews express a strong sense of identification with the land of

Israel. Even those Israeli born, for whom the issue of living in the land is self-evident, express a revitalized sense of connection to the land upon coming to faith in Jesus. For this community, faith in God and the living out of that faith are two sides of the same coin: minted and in circulation in the land of Israel.

Since Messianic Jews hold a high view of Scripture and, in the main, embrace a literalist interpretation of Scripture, they appropriate the scriptural promises to Israel for themselves as part of the restored Israel, living once again in the land of promise. In addition, the fact of residence in the holy Promised Land reinforces Israeli Messianic Jews' understanding of the continuing chosenness of the Jewish people and of their own role in the future promise of salvation for 'all Israel'. Living in the land intensifies their sense of personal significance and adds much to the experience of their faith as it is lived out against the background of, and in intimate relationship with, the biblical context of the land. Israeli Messianic Jews see themselves in continuity with the patriarchs, prophets, apostles and early followers of Jesus, all of whom lived in the land of Israel.

The Jewish people

The sense of belonging to a people, being part of something much larger than one's individual self, is an integral element in the identity of all Jews, including Messianic, Jesus-believing Jews. Peoplehood is more than an abstract concept; it is a living reality. A shared sense of community is a dominant element in the heritage of the Jewish people. As such, it is the common, universal experience of nearly all individual Jews, having been reinforced by family and the Jewish community throughout history. From the first, from the creation of the Jewish people, it was understood that each one was responsible for the other.[47] Family gatherings and communal celebrations of the festivals of Israel have contributed greatly to this sense of belonging to a community, being part of a people. The biblical feasts are the national holidays of Israel today. Passover, Pentecost (*Shavuot*), the Feast of Tabernacles (*Succot*), the Jewish New Year (*Rosh HaShanah*), the Day of Atonement (*Yom Kippur*) are all national holidays and observed by the large majority of the populace.

In the attempt to synthesize the elements that form Israeli Messianic Jewish identity, three themes have emerged. These three themes – God and relationship with him as a people, the land as the place to live out that relationship, and the Jewish people as the matrix of identity giving meaning to the individual – are deeply interwoven in the soul of the Israeli Messianic Jew. Together they help shape his identity.

Challenges Facing the Community[48]

The Israeli Messianic Jewish community faces many challenges as it struggles to define its identity and express itself in the multi-layered contexts of faith, nationality and ethnicity that constitute self-definition. The challenges can be broadly categorized as theological and practical. Understandably, these categories have a great deal of overlap. Theology is lived out in the practical, and the practical influences theology. In a sense, they are inseparable.

In general, there is little theological reflection and, where there are critical issues, they are frequently laid aside in deference to the practical. There are no forums or discussion groups meeting on an ongoing basis to reflect and discuss theological issues. The community is focused on activity and seems not to have time for, or not to see, the importance of long-term, reasoned theological reflection. Differences are not openly discussed and worked through, and the tendency is to fellowship with those who are most like you, to avoid groups with whom you may differ, and to indulge in polemic name-calling from a safe distance.

On the level of theology, there are several issues that pose immediate challenges to the Israeli Messianic Jewish community. Several of these have already been alluded to in this chapter. Since another chapter in this book will deal with the way in which Israeli Messianic Jews read Scripture, theological issues will be addressed in greater depth than is necessary in the context of this chapter.

The most prominent theological issue on the community's agenda is the question of 'Who is Yeshua?' and as a corollary 'How do we understand the persons of the Godhead and their interrelation'? While the vast majority of Messianic congregations and believers in Israel have come from evangelical traditions and their understanding of doctrine, there is a small, vocal minority who would see themselves as being more in continuity with traditional Judaism than in harmony with Protestant evangelical understanding. The issues of the Trinity and the deity of Yeshua regularly surface in the Messianic community and a minority position is increasingly being heard.

Because this issue is foundational in the life of the Messianic community, it has great power to divide. Feelings run high, as do accusations from each side towards the other. Those who do not believe that Yeshua is God accuse those who do of having abandoned a Jewish understanding of Scripture and having been influenced by Greek thought. Those who hold a strong view of the deity of Yeshua often accuse those with differing views of compromising on basic doctrine in order to be acceptable to the Jewish community. This is an important issue and the Messianic community is attempting to address it while endeavouring to maintain the unity of the body.

One of the theological issues that highlights the community's desire to connect with the Jewish side of their identity is Torah observance and its corollary – rabbinic authority. While the majority of the community embraces some form of traditional Jewish observance, a small but growing number of believers is embracing a Torah-observant lifestyle according to the model of rabbinic Judaism. Appropriate levels of Torah observance are increasingly discussed in Israeli Messianic circles today. This has caused tensions between the majority non-Torah-observant and the minority Torah-observant camp.

Another theological issue that is a constant undercurrent is the issue of the eschatological challenge of modern Israel. The majority of the Messianic community has immigrated to the country and, as such, they are ideologically and theologically motivated to see themselves as having a place in God's design to restore Israel. Modern Israel is for them the heir of biblical Israel and is undifferentiated from it. This understanding often leads to apathy when it comes to issues of justice, ethics and morality. How the prophetic scriptures are to be understood tends to be overlooked in the eschatological enthusiasm generated by this position. This view is rarely questioned and therefore the issue is not being faced.

A further, important issue that continues to be a concern is the question of identity: 'Who are we?' 'What is our true, primary identity?' This is a multifaceted issue, including theological, social and psychological aspects. The fact of living in a complex context of a Jewish majority, a Messianic minority and an Arab Christian faith community makes this matter a persistent, ongoing issue.

As the Messianic community grows in numbers so does the confidence and security of the individual within the community in relation to the social matrix in which he or she lives. The question of identity tends to be answered in relation to the social context rather than the point of reference being in the realm of biblical understanding. This is a subtle distinction since often it is the social context that influences the theology, and the community's corporate identity is formed in reaction to the society. Scripture is then used to bolster the confidence of the minority by justifying the faith community's position within the majority camp.

Given the ongoing Israeli–Palestinian conflict, it is understandable that the Messianic community should choose to identify itself as a part of the nation of Israel. The difficulty is that national identity can become confused with the principal spiritual identity of being members of the trans-national, trans-ethnic, trans-cultural body of Messiah of which there are also members from the 'enemy' community.

In the main, the Israeli Messianic community is apathetic regarding issues of injustice that are the daily fare of their Palestinian brothers and sisters. Messianic Jews' preoccupation with their own community and its issues tends to overshadow active engagement with the volatile issues of justice, human rights and peace that are vital for their Palestinian brothers and sisters. The predominant eschatological understandings of the Israeli Messianic Jew (referred to earlier) can preclude any realistic grappling with difficult issues such as inequality, corruption and oppression that are a constant backdrop in Israeli society and in the relationships between Israelis and Palestinians. The underlying fear is that to deal with these issues is to challenge the Israeli Messianic Jew's identity. Theologies of identity and ethnicity need to be worked out and articulated in the context of conflict in the land that is called 'holy'.

Practical implications of the theological understanding of identity have not been fully implemented. There are, however, small signs of hope. These are seen in a growing number of initiatives by individual Messianic congregations to relate to the Arab Christian communities and by the activities of Musalaha, which exists to bring together members of both communities in neutral settings so that the groups can become acquainted with one another and then move into more active relationship.

On the practical level, there are no fewer challenges than there are on the theological level. Marginalization is a major challenge for the Messianic community, particularly since it tends to be a closed community. Whereas in previous decades, it could have been said that the community resembled a ghetto, today it has become a subculture. However, there is much to be done before the community becomes integrated into the mainstream of society. On an individual basis, many believers are employed in the secular workplace. There is, however, very little social integration. There is a fine line between developing institutions, services and a distinctive culture as a subgroup and becoming a separated subculture that has little interface with the surrounding culture.

This issue is particularly relevant for the young generation. While work among the youth of the congregations has increased dramatically in recent times, much remains to be done in the interface between the life of the community of faith and the larger community. Young people seem to feel this tension more acutely than their elders, but it is the older generation who sets the standards and leads the way. In the main, this issue is not on the agenda of the community.

Israel is a mixed secular and religious society. Historically the Messianic community has found its place within secular Israel and has had little to do with the religious community. The Orthodox sector, however, is the fastest-growing segment of Israeli society and there is no indication that this trend will diminish. Generally speaking, the Messianic community neither understands nor relates to the religious community. The general attitude is one of fear bordering on hostility. The Messianic community tends to see the religious community as their enemy. This is in part due to levels of harassment and persecution coming from small Orthodox 'anti-mission' groups who see Messianic Jews as dangerous enemies.

There are a small number of believers who are themselves committed to a Torah-observant lifestyle and they sometimes try to find their place within and relate to the religious sector of Israel. However, congregations as bodies have not tried to seriously understand the religious community by learning about their value system and how this community thinks and acts. Since this community will continue to grow in numbers and influence in Israel, the Messianic community needs to recognize and address this challenge.

This short section regarding the challenges faced by the Israeli Messianic Jewish community is by no means exhaustive. Many other issues could have been cited. In this brief overview, we have looked at some of the most significant issues. The Israeli Messianic community is in process. It is attempting to find its place, negotiate its identity and fulfil its destiny in a context of conflict, misunderstanding and marginalization as a minority in every category. Despite the uncertainties of life in a context of conflict, Israeli Messianic Jews remain confident in their sense of having returned to their God, their land and their people – with all the ambiguity, uncertainty and complexity that this statement implies.

6.

Reading Scripture as a Palestinian Christian

What does a reader bring to a text? And how does he or she interpret it? These questions, which have occupied philosophers, literary theorists and theologians alike, are questions of hermeneutics. Although there are many different ways of defining 'hermeneutics', and even more theories as to the relationship between a reader and a text, a person's hermeneutic may be first imagined as the lens through which he or she perceives and receives the meaning of a text. Perception relates to expectations of what a text (or texts in general) may be or do; reception relates to the individual's cognitive response to the text as perceived. These are inevitably influenced by the context in which the reader reads, as well as their individual presuppositions and inherited cultural norms.

For Christians, reading the Bible is not like reading any other text. As believers, we understand it to be the Word of God, and the realization that a reader brings something to a reading may cause a measure of anxiety among some Christians. Does acknowledging this hermeneutical lens in some ways 'pollute' the revealed Word? Some may say, 'I don't bring anything to the text – I just read it literally.' Indeed, our assertion that the reader brings presuppositions and cultural norms to the text may be misunderstood to mean that the text is *merely* subject to a person's presuppositions and norms, limiting Scripture's transformative, chastening power, or that somehow Scripture lacks authority and truth outside a reader's perception and reception of it as authoritative and truthful.

Nothing could be further from the truth or from our position. For a Christian to take account of hermeneutics is not to rob the text of its authority or transforming power – far from it! Instead, it is to recognize that this power is realized within and extends throughout human history and civilizations, through constant engagement with Scripture. As an extreme example, a Dutch Reformed Church reader in apartheid South Africa, thoroughly convinced of the rightness of the fundamental differences between races, would find in specific passages biblical endorsement for racial separation, both because they expect to find this in Scripture and because there are verses in the Bible that can be interpreted in line with this expectation.[1] More mundanely, readers of Scripture in suburban America may quickly grasp the existential isolation of Psalm 13 while finding the expression of infanticidal rage at the end of Psalm 137 almost impossible to incorporate into their interpretative system. Any kind of biblical engagement is informed, to some extent, by a person's specific social, political, economic, cultural, psychological and historical place in time and space. Even within churches whose congregations are largely culturally uniform, some people will encounter one text as problematic, in need of interpretation in the light of another 'unproblematic' text, while other readers will invert the relationship. This depends to some extent on the place and time of their reading, and upon the specific cultural, ethnic, political, social, psychological and even gender of respective readers. Again, acknowledging this hermeneutical lens is not to diminish Scripture or its truth in any respect. Rather, it reflects a robust confidence that the Bible is God's word in all places and at all times.

Palestinian Christians, as much as anyone else, read the Bible within history. In this section we will also show that Palestinian Christian interpretation of Scripture is influenced by four major factors: 1) a sense of special inheritance due to dwelling in the land of the incarnation; 2) the arrival and continued influence of Islam; 3) relationships between Palestinian churches and institutional centres elsewhere, primarily in Europe; and 4) the emergence and success of Zionism with its Jewish and Christian theological justifications. These common factors shape Palestinian Christian perception and reception of Scripture, regardless of denominational affiliation or theological tradition.

Before we continue, it is important to note that our reconciliation encounters have focused primarily on evangelical Palestinian Christians and Messianic Jews. Yet, as many Palestinian evangelicals come from Catholic or Orthodox backgrounds, these traditions influence their approach to Scripture. Consequently, some Catholic and Orthodox ideas are overviewed in this section.

When we discuss Palestinian evangelicals specifically, there are two primary influences on their ideology and theology. British Brethren teaching impacted the Christian communities in Jordan and the Galilee, and accordingly, there are Palestinian evangelicals in these areas who hold to classic dispensationalism. As dispensationalism became a more prominent theological expression with political influence, it became more Zionist in nature. The Zionist aspect of dispensationalism is a later expression of this theology, and is largely absent from the theology and ideology of most Palestinian evangelicals. The Brethren teaching influenced Palestinian evangelicals in the following areas: a literal reading of Scripture, the size of the church, the role of the elders, the place of women, and conservative lifestyles.

A second important influence on Palestinian evangelicals came from the Southern Baptist Church and the Assembly of God in the United States. Compared to other Protestant denominations, these two focused on spreading the gospel through evangelism and countering other religions (here, primarily Islam) through apologetics. After the first intifada, an apologetic theology began developing among Palestinian Christian evangelicals to challenge the state of Israeli and Christian Zionism, as well as Palestinian liberation theology. While many Palestinian evangelicals agree with the questions raised by Palestinian liberation theology, they differ when it comes to the authority of Scripture (primarily the Old Testament, which Palestinian liberation theology downplays). Furthermore, Palestinian evangelicals sought theological and ministry training in evangelical schools, although after the 1980s and 1990s, they began to study in reform and covenant theological schools that influenced a new approach in their theological reactions here in the land. They returned home and began to address Palestinian issues from within the Palestinian tradition, while maintaining a high view of Scripture. While Palestinian liberation theology fails to sufficiently address Islam and the mandate of evangelism, Palestinian evangelicals have written a number of important works on Islam and witness to Muslims using a contextual approach.

Inheritance

Palestinian Christian hermeneutics are thoroughly informed by a unique sense of physical and historical proximity to Jesus of Nazareth. As Kenneth Bailey has shown, to read Scripture as a Palestinian whose roots go deep into the soil upon which Jesus walked is to hear Jesus' parables acutely, to feel the incarnation as a profound and immediate reality, and to carry a powerful endowment of inheritance in the journey of faith. This sense is not merely imaginative or figurative. One may hear a Palestinian Christian today in Bethlehem or the Galilee region wonder whether a particularly ancient olive tree, tended and harvested as in biblical times, ever shaded the incarnate Word himself.[2]

Palestinian Christians understand themselves to be descendants of the first apostolic-era believers and to embody a faithful testimony to the events of the Bible.[3] This self-perception is not primarily understood as a racial inheritance but a communal one. Indeed, to extrapolate the DNA of one group from another in the Holy Land would be a futile exercise; the Holy Land is one of the most historically cosmopolitan areas in the world. But throughout the rise and fall of empires and myriad conquests, the multi-ethnic church in Palestine has endured, including Jews, Arabs, Phoenicians, Greeks and others. As members of this community, Palestinian Christians retain a sense of deeply rooted custodianship of the land.

To try to reduce this sense of attachment to a political sentiment is to fail to see the way in which a person's theology is profoundly affected by living in the land. Here, the church was born, the first fruits of resurrection hope tasted. The inhabitants of Jerusalem witnessed the very beginning of the church family. Attachment to the land of the Bible and the narrative of Scripture, both in retelling these events and in its continued liturgical use, contributes to Palestinian Christians' profound sense of inheritance. Michael Prior frames this attachment to the land in the language of 'textual sacredness', which is to say that the language of the biblical texts is given life and dynamism in the physicality of the land. When writing on the experiences of Gregory of Nyssa as a pilgrim to the land, Prior comments:

Gregory insisted that Christianity was not the matter of the mind only, but invited participating in sacramental practices and symbols. The terrain of the holy places 'received the footprints of life itself' and serve to remind one that God once walked on the earth. As if by way of some osmosis the pilgrim absorbs some of the holiness of the place. This is strikingly true of Jerusalem . . . That portion of the cosmos, at least, is charged with the grandeur of God.[4]

We may imagine this to be a sentimentalism that prevails only in the traditional churches, but the continued arrival of evangelical Protestant Christians in the Holy Land, who seek to walk where Jesus walked, demonstrates the importance of place even in more self-consciously scripturalist forms of Christianity. In any case, while many Western evangelical churches attach less importance to the administration of the sacraments, liturgical and ecclesiastical traditions, and the sacredness of the holy sites, these remain at the heart of faith for many Palestinian Christians. Most Palestinian evangelicals worship in a non-liturgical, more contemporary-church fashion (following Western evangelical churches), and they are divided as to the importance of the ecclesial and liturgical traditions of the local Orthodox and Catholic churches. Some embrace it as part of their spiritual heritage and choose to marry in the traditional churches, while others adamantly reject this as incompatible with their evangelical faith. As inheritors of the testimony of their forebears, the Palestinian Christian community continues to live out that testimony in its worship and life. This kind of embodied witness in the Holy Land, therefore, has a universal message for the whole world: Jesus was a real person who lived, died and rose again, and he did it here, among us.

It is worth noting at the outset that this sense of living witness brings to the fore certain aspects of Scripture that can be more easily ignored outside the land. For example, the historicity of Scripture itself is harder to overlook or dispute. The continued 'performance' of Scripture – the process of continually giving voice to Scripture in settings of worship – is part of the social and cultural milieu, which in turn influences the reading or interpretation of Scripture. For example, Christmas and Easter are celebrated in the towns and sites where the incarnation and resurrection took place, namely at the location that each respective denomination recognizes as the site of the event. For the traditional churches, this is the Basilica of the Annunciation in Nazareth, the Church of the Nativity in Bethlehem and the Church of the Holy Sepulchre in Jerusalem. Many Palestinian evangelicals also visit these sites, although some choose to celebrate the resurrection at the Protestant location of the resurrection, the Garden Tomb. And for many, as we shall see, the priority is not settling upon a decisive interpretation of the Bible but upon encountering and worshipping God through it. As more traditional Christians would put it, biblical interpretation – the kind of biblical engagement dominant in modern Protestantism – proceeds from human reason, whereas 'Scripture performance' is incarnational and proceeds from God himself. In short, for most Palestinian Christians, interpretation of Scripture cannot be separated from worship through Scripture.

The Influence of Islam

While the establishment of Israel in 1948 significantly influenced Palestinian Christian biblical interpretation, this event was by no means the first decisive rupture in the political-cultural-social context in which Palestinian Christians read the Bible. Palestinian Christians today have a 'double minority' status, as a Christian minority living among Jewish and Muslim majorities.[5] Palestinian Christians have lived under Muslim rulers for most of their history. Of course, Palestinian Christians have drawn on resources from patristic theology and their Western co-religionists, but a significant intellectual influence derives from distinctively Arabic thinking. Jørgen S. Nielsen writes that Arabic as a vernacular language was well established in most parts of Syria and Mesopotamia by the beginning of the seventh century, before the arrival of Muslim armies from Arabia. With the introduction of Islam, Arabic became a literary language of significance as the role of the once dominant liturgical languages of Greek and Syriac waned.[6]

With the decline of the Byzantine Empire, the region underwent a process of Islamization and Arabization. The growing use of Arabic as both a vernacular and written language meant that the development of Christian literary Arabic was directed by the internal needs of the community as well as its external polemic with Islam.[7]

The Christian population under Arab-Islamic rule depended upon its scholars and priests to help navigate them through this new Muslim world. Nielsen is careful to describe how, at the popular level, Christian heritage and identity were preserved despite the intellectual and political priorities of their rulers.[8]

With the coming of Islam, Arab Christian theologians quickly saw the need to address Islam's religious claims. As early as the mid seventh to early eighth centuries, Arab Christians were writing systematic theology and trying to make sense of this new, fast-growing religion. John of Damascus argues that Islamic theology was a distortion of Christian apocryphal works, and he also addresses other theological topics, among them predestination and icons. Other early Arab Christian theologians during the early years of Islam are Theodore Abu Qurrah, 'Ammar Al-Basri, Habib ibn Hidmah Abu Ra'itah Al-Takriti and Severus ibn al-Muqaffa'.[9] Unlike Byzantine Christian theologians who engaged in an apologetic of distinction, seeing Arab culture and Islam as inferior to their culture and religion, Arab Christian theologians engaged in an apologetic of affinity, emphasizing the common culture and language they shared with Arab Muslims, while rejecting Islam. Their theological approach was influenced by Arab culture, which they were a part of and affirmed. One important document on the incarnation states that God chose to honour humanity through the incarnation. This focus on God *honouring* humanity reflects the concept of honour in Arab culture.[10]

Meanwhile, as Heleen Murre-van den Burg notes, the formation of Arabic-Islamic intellectual culture grew out of close dialogue with Christian elites. She writes, 'It was especially after the Abbasid Caliphs took over the leadership of the Islamic empire and the centre of the empire moved from Damascus to Baghdad (749) that the Syriac Christians entered a period of relative prosperity and had considerable cultural influence'.[11] This dialogue between Islam and Christianity, with their distinct systems of thought, persists to this day, mediated by the common vernacular of the Arabic language. Palestinian Christian hermeneutics have been influenced by Islamic tradition and heritage, much as contemporary American hermeneutics draw upon the intellectual culture of the Enlightenment, particularly with regard to the relationship between the reader and a text.

Contemporary Palestinian Christian hermeneutics in a globalized world has to respond to the growth of fundamentalist Islam which asserts a view of holy texts that, ironically, draws heavily on a predominantly Western heritage of texts as 'fixed signifiers' of immutable meaning. This interpretive posture contrasts with the 'traditional' approach that texts must be uttered to be fully realized, an assumption still embraced within the Arabic-speaking world;[12] that was, incidentally, the assumption at the time when the patristic writers were writing their treatises.[13] Rather than emphasizing oration (or, the embodiment of the text), Islamic reform movements with a fundamentalist orientation have adopted certain assumptions about the sufficiency of a written text removed from embodiment, an idea with modern, European lineage.[14] This rise in fundamentalism has led to an increased marginalization of the Christian minority and inter-religious hostilities within Arab society.

Naturally, Palestinian Christians have sought to make sense of the contemporary relationship between Christianity and Islam. These include Palestinian evangelical dispensationalists Anis Shorrosh and Imad Shehadeh, both of whom critically engage Islam, emphasizing the differences between Christian and Islamic doctrine, and raising the issue of Christian evangelism in a Muslim context. Their impact is curtailed, however, because they overlook what one Palestinian Christian theologian terms 'the important relational mentality that dominates many Middle Eastern minds'.[15] Their confrontational style, coupled with their self-consciously Western theological approach, makes their positions problematic for many Palestinian Christians and complicates dialogue with Palestinian Muslims.

In contrast to this approach towards Muslims, a number of Palestinian Christian evangelicals have attempted to create a set of vocabulary that would help Muslims understand the gospel message without taking away from the content of the message. One example is the *New Creation Book for Muslims*, a book co-authored by Salim Munayer and Phillip E. Goble, in which the gospel is presented in a culturally sensitive manner through contextualized language.[16] The authors intend to reduce the number of cultural or linguistic obstacles Muslims may encounter in order to make hermeneutical space for them to encounter the scandalous and gracious truth of the cross.

A third approach emphasizes historical and contemporary cooperation between Christians and Muslims. This approach of Palestinian Christian hermeneutics is evident in the work of the Catholic Al-Liqa' Center for Religious and Heritage Studies in the Holy Land. Based in Bethlehem, the Al-Liqa' Center gathers scholars together for interfaith dialogue and to develop contextualized Palestinian Christian theology. To this end, Al-Liqa' hosts numerous conferences and lectures and publishes various books and an important quarterly journal. As a Greek Catholic associated with Al-Liqa', Geries Khoury focuses on these issues and especially on the need for developing a contextualized Palestinian theology.[17] His book, *Arab Christians: Rootedness, Presence, Openness*, is indicative of his theology and the central concepts within a contextualized Palestinian Christian theology. Khoury draws the parallel between the Palestinian political scenes of Jesus' time and those of today, chiefly in the shared experience of occupation by a foreign authority. According to Khoury, in this context of apparent powerlessness, Palestinian Christians are called to incarnate the gospel in the Holy Land as living testimonies to Jesus' death and resurrection. Khoury's contextualized theology seeks to fight against discrimination and oppression, drawing heavily on historic Arab Christian theology and emphasizing Arab Christianity's uniqueness. Acknowledging the Greek influence, he describes how Christianity in the West developed differently, especially since it eventually became the official religion of the empire. Imperial Christianity began early in Western Christianity, which he argues was vastly different from the experience of the church in the East.[18]

Khoury also highlights the gains made within Arab Christianity during Muslim rule, particularly the 'golden era' between the ninth and thirteenth centuries. While many consider Islam and Christianity to be religiously and culturally incompatible, Khoury shows that the historical record says otherwise. Although Arab Christianity grew more apologetic with the advent of Islam, Khoury demonstrates that Christians were still able, as Christians, to articulate a theology that was culturally coherent to Muslims. Civil and political life benefited from this cultural openness. Pointing to history as evidence that coexistence is possible, Khoury calls for Palestinian Christians today to engage the challenges they face both from the

Jewish and Muslim majorities, and for openness to other religions and cultures.

Other Palestinian Christians have reached out to Muslims in a spirit of reconciliation. 'Sulha', Palestinian Christian evangelical Yohanna Katanacho explains, 'is the Arabic cultural way of conflict management and of advocating peaceful coexistence through societal reconciliation and compromise'.[19] A number of Palestinian Christians, such as Anglican Bishop Riah Abu El-Assal and Lutheran Bishop Munib Younan, have adopted this traditional method of conflict management and attempted to apply it to Christian–Muslim relations in the Palestinian context. These theologians seek peaceful relations with their Muslim neighbours, as well as common theological ground with Islam. Abu El-Assal writes, 'My studies taught me that Islam supports our faith in nearly every doctrine',[20] and Younan writes that Christian–Muslim coexistence should be a priority, even if it means avoiding discussion of 'the nature of the Triune God, the divinity of Christ, or his salvific work through the cross'.[21] While this approach has helped to build bridges between the Christian and Muslim communities, easing some of the existing tensions, Katanacho argues that this approach has 'paid an unnecessarily high price. What does Christianity have to offer if it does not discuss Trinity, Christology, and atonement; or if it agrees with Islam in nearly every doctrine?'[22] By carefully avoiding any Christian teaching that might give offence, these theologians have essentially capitulated to the Muslim majority. But, Katanacho says, an overly concessionary approach cannot be properly called true reconciliation. This approach also makes the mistake of assuming that doctrinal disagreement with Muslims will inescapably lead to conflict, when this is not necessarily the case.

In recent years Musalaha and Salim Munayer have integrated the eight moral values of Brian Cox's approach to Christian–Muslim relations in their work. These principles are derived from Romans 12.18, where Paul calls on followers of Christ to 'live peaceably with all'. Munayer argues that there are limits to the effectiveness of established patterns of 'interfaith dialogue', no matter how well intentioned they may be. Munayer and Cox propose a grass-roots initiative that brings together Christian and Muslim Palestinians to emphasize Abrahamic values. This

'Abrahamic model of reconciliation' has proven effective in the way it integrates respect for religion and religious values with the principles of conflict resolution and reconciliation.[23]

Looking elsewhere

By generalizing aspects of Palestinian Christian encounters with Scripture, it is worth pausing to note that just as Palestinian Christian identity is differentiated, so too are Palestinian hermeneutics. The Palestinian Christian community is comprised of diverse ecclesiastical and theological traditions, including the Eastern and Oriental Orthodox churches, churches affiliated with Roman Catholicism, and various Protestant denominations and evangelical non-denominational churches. Ironically, bearing in mind the importance of place and land to Palestinian Christians, it is also true that many belong to traditions and ecclesial institutions that 'look elsewhere', drawing their support and guidance from entities largely based outside the Holy Land. Each of these ecclesial bodies – none of which has its institutional centre within the Holy Land – makes differing ways of encountering the text of the Bible available to its Palestinian members.

Let us then take into account what each tradition may contribute from its own history of interpretation. We are suspicious of the tendency to place the 'traditional' churches (i.e. Roman Catholic and Orthodox) and the Protestant churches on opposing sides of an interpretative chasm. In an overview such as this, oversimplification is unavoidable. Our goal is not to be representative but to demonstrate something of the range of engagements with Scripture within Palestinian Christianity. When discussing the diversity of tradition in Palestinian Christianity, the words of Michel Sabbah, a former Latin Patriarch of Jerusalem, speak to this tension. Sabbah urges sensitivity and tolerance towards the numerous denominational communities found in the Holy Land, each one born from a particular liturgical tradition. Each has its own way of expressing, receiving, meditating on, and celebrating the gospel message that is particular to their historical and cultural context.[24] Sabbah believes that this diversity is of great value for the church, which must continually seek a deeper, richer expression of the inexhaustible mystery of God. To speak of a single Palestinian biblical hermeneutic would be misleading and artificial, as well as impoverish believers of the wealth of theological tradition available to them.

Given the importance of Greek literacy among Western theologians in the study of the New Testament since the Protestant Reformation, there has been surprisingly scant attention given to the theology of the Greek Church. The Greek Orthodox Church is the largest single denomination in Israel and Palestine. The relationship between the Greek centre and the Palestinian periphery is a complicated one. Since the sixteenth-century reforms of Germanius, the relationship between Palestinian Christians and the Greek hierarchy has been problematic at times. Nevertheless, Palestinian Orthodox Christians have adopted and adapted significant elements of Greek theology and, most relevant here, Greek Orthodox hermeneutics.

Central to all Orthodox theology is Scripture's role in testifying to Christ above all. This does not imply a disregard for the text. On the contrary, Paul Tarazi, a Palestinian professor at St Vladimir's Orthodox Theological Seminary, responds to a Protestant Bible translation that adapts the language of the biblical text to make it more inclusive, by stressing the importance of preserving the integrity of the text, 'a pure text unburdened with interpretations that may well prove to be wrong'.[25] Interpretation will certainly occur, but this, he says, should take place in preaching so that it is open to criticism and correction, and not in the text itself. The problem, he writes, is that the Reformation elevated Scripture above all: 'The Reformation de facto exchanged the Roman Catholic Church Pope and *magisterium* for Scripture as a sure source of authority'.[26] From Tarazi's perspective, both Roman Catholicism and Protestantism made the same mistake in that when 'they looked for a tangible source of authority, they looked for a tangible source of security. They simply forgot that there cannot be any other such source for us Christians except Jesus and his only vicar: his Spirit'.[27]

Tarazi has also written *Land and Covenant*, which deals with the issues of land in the Israeli–Palestinian conflict from a scholarly and biblical perspective.[28] Tellingly, in this book he presents an Orthodox view of Scripture as witness to the person of Jesus, the ultimate source of authority for the Christian, and the posture of the church to the words of Scripture:

Scripture does not have a 'canon' assigned to it by an outside authority, but is itself the 'canon' by which we have to abide. We do not
judge scripture; it judges us. The scriptural canon is not created by us
believers; it is rather received and accepted as we hear it in the [words
of the] *Synodikon* we recite every year on the first Sunday of Lent,
known as Sunday of Orthodoxy: 'As the prophets have seen, as the
apostles have taught, *as the Church has received'*.[29]

Note here the parallels between the Orthodox inheritance of
Scripture and the sense among Palestinians of inheritance of
Scripture's land. Both belong firstly to God and are not subject
to temporal authority, but to God's will. In the same book, Tarazi's chapter 'Scripture: History of the Jewish People or Word of
God?'[30] addresses some of the issues that face Arab and Palestinian Christians in their encounter with the Bible. To the question posed in the title, Tarazi answers that 'the biblical story is
in no way the story of Israel – let alone its history. It is the story
of God'. In saying so, Tarazi is not discounting the importance
of Israel; rather, he is magnifying God as the story's protagonist,
shepherding, if you will, a people and a narrative around himself.
With sensitive cultural insight, Tarazi elucidates:

> Whoever has witnessed the activity of shepherds in the Near East will
> have noticed . . . the flock is not an agglomeration of sheep, but rather
> a creation of the shepherd. Without him the sheep would scatter and
> ultimately perish. The existence of the individual sheep is literally
> bound to the reality we call a flock, and there is a flock only where
> there is a shepherd who walks ahead of the sheep that recognize the
> sounds emitted by him and thus 'follow his voice'.[31]

There are other Orthodox churches in the Holy Land whose litur-
gies and institutions are closely connected to another vital centre
of early Christianity: Syria. These churches mostly comprise those
who rejected the christological formulation of the Council of Chalcedon in 451 CE, including the Coptic, Ethiopian, Armenian, and
Syriac Orthodox churches. While differing from the Chalcedonian
Orthodox church family rooted in Greece on matters of language
and Christology, they share an emphasis on the embodied Word
of God in Christ and then in the body of Christ as the church.

As with Greek Orthodoxy, non-Chalcedonian Orthodox Christians do not view themselves as having a 'lower' view of Scripture. Indeed, among Syriac Orthodox Christians in Bethlehem, church leaders emphasize the importance of Bible teaching especially in the face of perceived threats such as fundamentalism and emigration.[32] But these Christians approach Bible study in a way quite distinct from that of evangelical Protestants; Scripture is encountered first through the worship of God, mediated through the wisdom of the church, and 'performed' by the church under the inspiration of the Holy Spirit.

As well as the Holy Land's demographics, Western Christianity has also significantly shaped the hermeneutical encounter of Palestinians with the Bible. As a result of the Crusades, missions and the work of the Franciscan Custody of the Holy Land, the Catholic Church is the second largest ecclesial body among Palestinian Christians. In addition, there are a number of smaller churches with Greek, Syriac or Armenian rites that are in communion with Rome.

Catholic theologians have significantly influenced a Palestinian Christian approach to the Bible. These have arguably asserted a more distinctively Palestinian-Arab heritage when compared with the Greek Orthodox Church. Perhaps part of this relates to a eucharistic theology that is more open to local expressions of Christianity within global Roman Catholicism, and less bound up with the replication of the liturgy in exactly the same form. Speaking on behalf of the Palestinian Catholic community, Michel Sabbah writes, 'God's people have never separated the sacred book from the oral tradition, i.e. from its living liturgical, cultural, or historical interpretation.' For Sabbah a hermeneutical approach must be grounded in the community of God's people expressed through the traditions of the church. He states that 'for us [Palestinian Christians], too, the Word of God is inseparable from the life of the people which received it. We also must follow the same path as we try to understand this Word. Today, we can develop a true understanding of Scripture only in communion with the Church, in the light of Tradition, through the living liturgy and progress in Biblical studies'.[33] The ecclesial community is vital to the hermeneutical task:

> It is not easy to read and understand the Bible. It is a task that requires a particular effort on our part and a special grace from God.

It is, therefore, of prime importance to know how to read the Bible in order to discern the authentic Word of God in it. This cannot be done by one's own strength alone. Only together, in community, in the Church, in the light and strength of the Holy Spirit can such a task be undertaken.[34]

Protestant missionary activity in Palestine, then under Ottoman control, accelerated in the nineteenth century, alongside British and Prussian imperial ambitions. Some missionaries, but by no means all, were motivated by a kind of proto-Zionism or 'Restorationism'. It is worth bearing in mind something of the intellectual history of Protestant and evangelical Christianity, especially as some of the most significant writing on Palestinian contextual theology today is emerging from this section of the church. Institutions such as Bethlehem Bible College ground themselves in a Western hermeneutic tradition of evangelical Protestantism, while increasingly taking account of textual heritages closer to home. Paradigmatically, Protestantism emphasizes the principle of Sola Scriptura – 'Scripture alone' – over and against church tradition as the final arbiter of truth. But the equally Protestant principle of the 'priesthood of all believers' is also at work in Protestant hermeneutical engagement. Protestant interpreters approach the biblical text with an expectation that God speaks clearly to individuals through the Bible. Scripture's immediate relevance to life is a fundamental aspect of Protestant biblical interpretation. Intriguingly, early Protestant activity in Palestine accompanied a period of rapid and ongoing change in the region, not unlike the dynamics at play today. The intense territorial conflict in the Middle East means that the approach of Palestinian Protestant Christians to reading and interpreting the Bible will necessarily involve asking how the Bible addresses the political and religious conflict in Israel-Palestine.

Zionism and Its Effects

Before the establishment of the state of Israel in 1948, the term 'Palestinians' referred to all Muslims, Christians and Jews who permanently resided in the land of Palestine. During the waning days of Ottoman rule, Palestinian Christians were a part of the original Arab national movement, which developed new expressions in opposition to the colonial enterprises as well as to the Zionist movement. There were a variety of ideological approaches within the intellectual movement itself. On the whole, though, Palestinian Christians tended to favour secular-nationalist political visions rather than religious ones. In the last thirty years Palestinian Christians have observed the growing political strength of predominantly American Christian Zionists and the acceleration of US governmental support for Israeli expansion during the Reagan years; the rise of the Islamic movement as an appealing alternative to Palestinian secular nationalism; the flourishing of liberation theology in the struggle against apartheid in South Africa; and, most recently, the re-emergence of an American evangelical movement passionately engaged with social justice issues. These have all played a part in prompting Palestinian Christians, particularly theologians and thinkers, to respond to theological strains they find problematic and combative and to communicate about the Palestinian situation to new audiences.

An important recent work is *Challenging Empire: God, Faithfulness and Resistance*, a compilation of papers presented at Sabeel, an ecumenical liberation theology centre in Jerusalem, at their 2011 international conference. Expressions of empire are markedly felt by Palestinians today, and the papers in this book examine empire's role on various aspects of life, and present a challenge that we should view empire and its effects in light of Jesus' teachings. It also offers suggestions for peaceful and non- violent resistance. One chapter by Professor Richard Horsley aptly discusses this subject as related to Jesus' first-century context. Empire is often legitimized through culture and religion. To see Jesus in his true context, we must see beyond the lens of Western individualism that portrays him as an individualistic Saviour and political figure speaking timeless truths. On the contrary, he was leading a community renewal movement that clashed with the Roman imperial order and the leading Jewish classes that colluded with the Romans. Jesus' message was not only for the house of Israel, but for non-Jews as well, emphasizing that God's renewal of his people was not bound to an exclusive ethnicity.[35] Palestinian Christians, evangelical and non-evangelical, are adopting the rhetoric of countering empire in their theological writings.[36]

Palestinian Protestants are producing much of the recent literature on Palestinian Christianity and often write for a Western audience. As one of the more prominent evangelical voices, Palestinian theologian Yohanna Katanacho has surveyed the different positions among Palestinian Protestants and divided these into four categories: biographies, apologies, liberation theologies and reconciliation theologies.[37] Most of the works surveyed here have been written by Anglicans, Lutherans, and evangelicals from a variety of denominational affiliations, addressing Protestant readers.

The biographers Katanacho researched include Elias Chacour, Anis Shorrosh, Audeh Rantisi and Mitri Raheb, who consider the Israeli–Palestinian conflict and its related theological disagreements in their personal stories.[38] Alex Awad has also recently published a book in this genre that, like the others, includes significant personal family history, a more general presentation of the Palestinian Christian historical narrative, and a challenge to Christian Zionist theology. Each biographer makes mention of his experience of discrimination and abuse, along with a confirmed dedication to non-violent resistance, reconciliation, justice and forgiveness. As biographies, these texts do not provide rigorous academic analyses of the social and political situation or biblical research. Their function is to raise questions of justice and meaning through the telling of personal narratives, which are frequently undervalued in theological and political discourse.[39] By writing these stories in a distinctly Palestinian Christian voice, these authors implicitly and explicitly challenge prevailing historical narratives and theological assumptions about Palestinians and the Palestinian experience within Western churches.

As the most prominent Palestinian liberation theologian, Naim Ateek and his christologically grounded liberation theology offer a uniquely theological response to the Palestinian experience of dispossession by the state of Israel and perceived abandonment in that dispossession by many global Christians. In *Justice, and Only Justice*, Ateek articulates the key elements of Palestinian liberation theology within a particular christological hermeneutic.[40] This hermeneutic provides the foundation upon which Ateek then constructs his theology and reinterprets his political and religious context. Echoing Orthodox christological readings of the

Bible, Ateek affirms that the person of Christ is at the heart of the experience of God and of what one knows about God's will and purposes for the world. For Ateek, the character of Jesus revealed in the New Testament is a lens through which Scripture should be read and interpreted. This hermeneutic, then, serves as a benchmark for discerning moral criteria. An action or situation is biblical and ethical only so far as it conforms to what we know about Christ as revealed in the gospels, and therefore, interpretively supersedes any divergent moral criteria that may operate within the biblical canon.

Using this particular reading, Ateek asserts that it is possible to trace a progressive historical and theological development throughout the Scriptures. The biblical narrative moves from a nationalistic God in the earliest parts of the narrative, one whose only moral concerns are for his chosen people, to a universal God in the latter part of the narrative, one whose concerns are for humanity. Therefore, a fiercely territorial God eventually emerges as God of the entire cosmos. That is, God himself does not change, but the human narrative reveals the progressive understanding of God and his will that is refined over time and in community. According to Ateek, a hermeneutical application of, for instance, Old Testament conquest narratives to the contemporary political situation is anachronistic. But more critically, this kind of biblical reflection produces false theological knowledge and morally dubious analysis. The key to interpreting the Bible appropriately is through his christological hermeneutic.

Ateek's hermeneutic raises questions about the nature of the biblical canon, especially of the Old Testament, something that Lebanese evangelical Riad Kassis addresses in an Arabic-language book, *Why Don't We Read the Book that Jesus Read?*[41] Kassis gives four main reasons why Palestinian Christians avoid the Old Testament. First, they view it as immoral; the narratives that depict divine sanction of genocide in the conquest of Canaan, for instance, invite a kind of instinctive moral opprobrium among many Palestinian Christians. It is easy to see why, especially when these passages are used as proof-texts to justify injustices perpetrated against Palestinians. Naturally (and Kassis' second reason), Palestinian Christians avoid reading the Old Testament because of their political situation. The Old Testament seems to justify a Zionist position. Third, they avoid the Old Testament because it is difficult to understand and seems removed from daily life; Jesus provides all the moral guidance one needs. And finally, Kassis says, they avoid it because of the suspicion that the Old Testament does not have a firm historical or scientific basis; it is all based on myth.[42] Psychological obstacles also keep Palestinian Christians from reading the Old Testament, particularly created by the belief among some Western Christians that the Old Testament is primarily *about* the Jews and even the Jewish state, by which many of their compatriots have been dispossessed.[43]

Kassis offers Palestinian and Arab Christians a few helpful hermeneutical tips for reading the Old Testament.[44] He notes that the Old Testament must be viewed as a divine book with a very human element. Its problematic aspects are a result of the latter, not the former. One must also understand the historical, cultural and linguistic context of the Old Testament; these are key to understanding the true meaning of the text. Understanding the moral and ethical context of the Old Testament is also crucial, especially in comparison to other biblical and ancient texts. Finally, and perhaps most importantly, Kassis advises that we approach the Old Testament with humility and an open spirit, willing to learn and grow.

Another important theological response recently developed within the Palestinian community is the Kairos Palestine document.[45] Formulated by leaders of various ecclesial bodies and Christian denominations in Jerusalem, the document encourages global Christians to avoid supporting injustice and dispossession against the Palestinian people and, as a collaborative effort, represents a significant step towards unity within an often-fractured community. It also represents a unique moment in the community's history, for not only did it bring together Palestinian Christians from various traditions; it has also publicly stated the biblical and spiritual issues for Palestinians to a wide audience. It gives perspective on the theological reasoning taking place within the Palestinian church and calls upon Christians around the world to acknowledge and respond to a distinctly Palestinian biblical hermeneutic and theological approach. While addressing the unique strengths of Palestinian Christianity, the document is notable for also raising the community's weaknesses, such as the failure among Palestinian Christians to address Jewish religious and historical attachment to the land they claim as their own.

It is hard to overstate how deeply pained Palestinian Christians are over biblical fundamentalism and especially the ideological tenets of Christian Zionism. The Kairos Palestine document gives voice to that pain and challenges its source:

> It is unacceptable to transform the Word of God into letters of stone that pervert the love of God and His providence in the life of both peoples and individuals. This is precisely the error in fundamentalist Biblical interpretation that brings us death and destruction when the word of God is petrified and transmitted from generation to generation as a dead letter. This dead letter is used as a weapon in our present history in order to deprive us of our rights in our own land.[46]

Those involved in writing the Kairos Palestine document confront the biblical hermeneutics of Christian Zionists, not just their stated political vision. It is their contention that these approaches often attempt to appropriate biblical language into contemporary discourse with little meaningful reflection on its context or other issues that may affect its interpretation. Palestinian theologians point to the misuse of Scripture in the justification of the African slave trade, noting parallels to this hermeneutical approach in the social issues of their situation. Overly literal readings of certain biblical passages among slaveholders seemed to provide support for what many people would now describe as a catastrophic moral failure.[47] Palestinian Christians argue that the ways in which many have interpreted Scripture on behalf of the state of Israel, and the resulting deleterious effects upon Palestinian life, are worth serious re-examination.[48]

Paradoxically, some Palestinian Christians have embraced a narrowly literalist reading of the Old Testament, which 'accepts the ancestral connections of Arabs to Ishmael and Jews to Isaac and that predetermines the nature and future of these two groups based on a literal interpretation of the Abrahamic promises'.[49] This position has led some of the 'Apologists' to adopt a view that is 'theologically supportive of a national Jewish state and find it difficult to find a theological justification for a Palestinian one'.[50] As a Lebanese Bible teacher strongly influenced by dispensationalist teaching, Tony Maalouf, as noted earlier, connects the narrative of Ishmael with the Arab people. In his exegesis of the story of Ishmael, Maalouf counters many of the negative views of the Arab people that have developed among Christians over the centuries. And yet, the enduring mythical connection of Ishmael to the Arabic-speaking peoples and Isaac to the Jewish people raises more questions about ethnicity and historicity and presents significant interpretive challenges for many biblical scholars.

One more newly established venue in which these kinds of biblical and political questions are addressed is Bethlehem Bible College's 'Christ at the Checkpoint' conference. Many presenters grapple with the conundrums of particular strains of biblical interpretation, as well as the perceived outsized influence of Christian Zionism and politicized dispensationalism. The conference draws together local and international Christians to discuss these and other issues. Although the number of Palestinian Christians who self-identify as 'evangelical' number no more than a few thousand, their ability to speak in intelligible terms to Western evangelicals is politically important.

Another approach Palestinian Christians have taken is to develop a theology of reconciliation that will engage Israeli Messianic Jews. For example, Hanna Massad, a Palestinian Baptist pastor from Gaza, makes the cross central to his theological attempt at reconciliation. He writes, 'The cross of Christ for us is not only the place of salvation where our sins are forgiven, or where we are to be reconciled to the Father, but it is also the place where we can experience healing of wounds which we have inflicted on one another'.[51] While the cross is indispensable to the process of reconciliation, Massad's theological approach does not address some key issues. He does not deal with the issues of land or chosenness, for example, and for the sake of reconciliation he seems willing to sacrifice justice, writing, 'Let us pursue not justice but a community of love. We will never reach perfect justice, but let us pursue confession, repentance, forgiveness, and love, which will prepare us to embrace one another as members of one body and will allow us to experience reconciliation.'[52] One must ask if this is an overly narrow understanding of biblical justice. As Katanacho writes, 'Biblical justice is at the core of confession, repentance, forgiveness, and love. The cross is equally a sign of God's love and of his justice. Without the latter, there is no true reconciliation either with God or with people'.[53] It is a critical debate among Palestinian Christians as to whether God asks his people to abandon their claims to justice. Indeed, the Bible seems to place a high value on social justice and its interdependence with righteousness before God, but what shape that takes and how it relates to the current political situation are still very much in debate among Palestinian Christians. Rediscovering this prophetic call to justice in the Old Testament may help to re-engage Palestinian Christians to encounter the full witness of the Bible.

Palestinian Christians are also uniquely situated to provide cultural insight into the Bible and especially the Old Testament. Because they read the Bible from a Middle Eastern perspective, in some ways they are able to understand immediately and intuitively what those from a Western perspective must study to learn.[54] All of this represents a growing trend and overall effort to reclaim the Old Testament and affirm its importance within the biblical canon and in the lives of Palestinian Christians. One recent sign of Palestinian rapprochement with the Old Testament is the growing number of Palestinian Christian theologians who have received training in various ancient and especially ancient Jewish source material. For example, Yohanna Katanacho's word study on Psalm 87 and Salim J. Munayer's commentary on Hosea both make extensive use of biblical Hebrew and other ancient texts.[55] Another Palestinian theologian, Munther Isaac, tackles one of the most complex and divisive passages for Palestinian Christians in the whole biblical canon – the Israelite conquest narrative of Joshua 6.[56] Concerning Joshua, Isaac writes:

> The difficulties in the passage are numerous. In this chapter we encounter the Holy War and ban (the *herem*) principle, a woman prostitute traitor/heroine, miraculously fallen walls, a curse on a town, and (most shockingly), the approval of God for all these things. No wonder some Christians view this story as an embarrassment, problematic, awkward, offensive, and others have gone as far as describing the events in the story using terms such as genocide and ethnic cleansing.[57]

Isaac speaks about the difficulties many Palestinian Christians have when reading this passage and others from the Old Testament. They often see themselves as the enemies of the Israelites. Without doing any real study of the biblical text, this would seem to be a logical conclusion to reach. How are Palestinian Christians from Jericho today supposed to feel and think when they read Joshua 6? Is one supposed to identify with the people inside or outside the city walls? Isaac shows that instead of abandoning the Old Testament, Palestinian Christians should claim it as their own. As the people of God, they are the offspring of God's chosen people. 'We – the community of believers in God's Son, Israel's Messiah – are God's people today and in the OT. The OT is our story. Joshua is not simply my hero. He is my forefather. The Patriarchs are our ancestors. Israel's victory in the OT is our victory as a community of faith today'.[58] A similar reply is echoed by Lutheran pastor Mitri Raheb, who asserts how essential it is for Palestinian Christians to persist in using the whole canon even when one is not able to decisively interpret it, embrace it or even accept it.[59] It is their inheritance. The re-emergence of this kind of accepting and engaging posture for the whole biblical canon is hopeful, especially in finding common ground with Christians with radically different approaches to biblical interpretation.

Conclusions with New Questions

Palestinian biblical hermeneutics tend towards high contextualization and have developed much of their distinctiveness in reaction to other theologies that, for good or for ill, find political or social resonance in historic Palestine – Israel and the Palestinian territories.[60] How Palestinian Christians read the Bible is shaped by and continues to shape their identity as a minority group living between Jewish and Muslim majorities. Palestinian Christian theologians face significant, even burdensome tasks, including how to make sense of the biblical narrative for daily life, how to understand the Bible as a source of comfort and a tool for peace and reconciliation, and what the Bible has to say concerning their contemporary political situation. This survey is admittedly limited and does not take into account the growing number of Palestinian Christian women, such as Cedar Duaybis, who contribute to the discussion. What we have tried to show is the continued need for Palestinian Christians to develop theologies that will address the unique set of challenges they face as a community, and the attempts some have already made to do this.

As a Christian minority living subject to Jewish sovereignty, Palestinian Christians inhabit a unique moment in history. For much of their history Arab Christians have had to make sense of Christian life within a Muslim context. However, being a Christian minority among a Jewish majority, and a minority whose members perceive themselves as largely abandoned by other Christians (including Messianic Jews), raises questions like, 'Who are the people of God?' and 'How do we approach fellowship?' The difficulty here is twofold. First, on a practical level, Palestinian Christians have had to make significant accommodations to Jewish social and religious practices, especially to establish fellowship with their Messianic brothers and sisters. As Messianic Jews assert their identity as Jewish and explore that identity, they often take interest in rabbinical Judaism, the contours of which can present a challenge to fellowship. For example, how should they approach Halaka (Jewish religious law, customs and tradition), or the Sabbath and the Jewish holidays? These questions affect not only their religious lives, but their social lives as well, particularly as the Jewishness of the state of Israel is emphasized.

Second, most in the Messianic Jewish community associate Palestinian Christians with the traditional churches and do not seriously relate to Palestinian Christian heritage and history. Rather, they tend to view Palestinian Christians only through their own hermeneutical lens of eschatology. Palestinian Christians think that Messianic Jews do not hear or appreciate the full extent of their suffering. Palestinians Christians think that Messianic Jews are, at times, wilfully ignorant or negligent about Israeli policies that directly affect Palestinian life. Theologically, Palestinian Christians take offence at the notion that, according to certain extreme rabbinical attitudes, Messianic Jews and others sometimes regard them as strangers in the land. Palestinian Christians, who find this notion threatening and inaccurate, are themselves in the odd position of having to provide a theological and hermeneutical defence and justification for their presence in their homeland; that is, for their very existence. Yet the coin can be reversed. The lack of any space for Palestinian Christians and their distinctive witness within most articulations of a Messianic Jewish theology is to some extent mirrored in Palestinian Christian theology concerning Israeli Messianic Jews. For example, many Palestinian Christians reject Christian Zionism, which most

Messianic Jews perceive as a rejection of their own theology.[61] These factors are the source of much misunderstanding and hurt, which makes reconciliation difficult, and for many, nearly impossible to countenance.

Reflecting on the importance and difficulty of hermeneutics, Michel Sabbah writes, 'Reading the Bible, the Word of God, is a difficult, sensitive and delicate task, since the matters to be tackled are related to our daily life'.[62] Nowhere is this clearer than in the land of Jesus. Indeed, Sabbah reminds Palestinian Christians that to fulfil their calling to remain faithful in the land is to face the possibility of martyrdom. Christians have persisted despite mass killings associated with Roman, Persian, Islamic, Mongol and of course other Christian empires. According to Sabbah, these losses and this persistence constitute their cruciform witness. As with the crucified Christ, theirs is not a posture of passive acceptance of injustice but one of solidarity with those most hurt by sin; indeed, chiefly, by identification with Jesus himself, who 'for our sake [was made] to be sin who knew no sin, so that in him we might become the righteousness of God' (2 Cor. 5:21).

A hopeful sign within Palestinian Christian theology, the Kairos Palestine document was written and endorsed by theologians and clerics from the full range of ecclesiastical expressions found among Palestinian Christians. The historic relationship between these churches has not always been a happy one and has often, regrettably, failed to embody Christian love among its members. However, faced with a pressing need to articulate a series of theological and hermeneutic principles that are at once robustly Christian without being exclusively Catholic, Orthodox or evangelical, the Kairos group has managed to incorporate the irreducible premises of diverse hermeneutics with remarkable fluency. The capacity of this document to embrace both evangelical scripturalism and Orthodox christocentricism in terms acceptable to the other provides a model for a hermeneutic of reconciliation. It is a work of intellectual hospitality that could provide a starting point for a further engagement with Christians from different sides of a serious hermeneutic or theological divide. What made this possible is the sense of urgency. It is our belief that reconciliation between Palestinian Christians and Messianic Jews is just as urgent.[63]

7.

Reading Scripture as an Israeli Messianic Jew

Israeli Messianic Jews come from a wide variety of theological backgrounds and persuasions, all of which influence their reading of Scripture. Since the community is in no way homogeneous, many differences exist. However, for the Jesus-believing Jew, the Scriptures are not only read, but are also experienced as an integral part of his or her history and heritage. For centuries, the meaning of Jewishness has been tied to the Scriptures. Jews are the quintessential 'people of the book'. The books of the *Tenach* (Old Testament) and the later codified commentaries found in the Talmud have shaped the identity and the destiny of the Jewish people in ways that are unique to them.

According to ancient Jewish tradition, on Sinai, Moses was not only given what was to become the written Torah; he was also given an 'Oral Torah' whose purpose was to interpret the written Torah. Jewish tradition has it that the development of codified interpretation began when the Jews were in exile in Babylon. It was here, in exile and without a temple, that Ezra the scribe began a process that continued through the end of biblical times and culminated with the development of Mishnah and Talmud. This process took place over a seven-hundred-year period from 220 BCE to 500 CE.[1] With the destruction of the second temple in 70 CE, the religion of the Jews, which was pluralistic and embraced 'many Judaisms', fundamentally changed from being a religion based on events to being a text-based religion. The presence of God in the midst of the people shifted from God acting in history to God being present in the Torah. The rabbinic tradition that began in Babylon was now institutionalized in the Talmud.[2]

While Israeli Messianic Jews hold diverse theological views and understandings of Scripture, there is substantial agreement on a number of key issues. The first is the issue of who God is. He is the God of Abraham, Isaac and Jacob. He is the God of Israel; the only God; and he is the God of all the nations.[3] Second, the Land of Israel is the covenant inheritance of the Jewish people and their return to the land is God's everlasting, unconditional promise to them. Third, the Jewish people remain the covenant people of God together with those from among the nations who have been 'grafted in' to them and, finally, the Torah has ongoing significance for the Jesus-believing Jew.[4]

The fact of living in the land of their ancestors causes the words of Scripture to resonate powerfully with Israeli Messianic Jews. For them, the Torah, the prophets, and the history of the people of Israel are not only history; they are a present reality. This chapter will explore this community's reading of Scripture in the framework of several critical issues that permeate the community's understanding of biblical texts. These issues are heritage, land and promise, and Torah. These three themes are each in themselves multilayered. Together they are interrelated and cannot easily be separated. They therefore need to be viewed in terms of a fluid and dynamic interrelationship.

It is vital to recognize the various hermeneutical lenses through which Scripture is viewed. Although Messianic Jews come from diverse backgrounds, in matters of interpretation of Scripture their views have been shaped by Western Evangelical Christianity and Judaism in a variety of admixtures. In addition to the issues of heritage, land and Torah, the predominant hermeneutical approaches that are typical of the community will be explored. Since hermeneutical viewpoint in large part determines theological positions and conclusions, this is where we will begin.

Hermeneutical Viewpoint

Hermeneutics and exegesis are the tools through which meaning is extracted. They are the base from which understanding and interpretation are derived. Regarding the Scriptures, hermeneutics is the art of understanding and the theory of interpretation;

whereas exegesis is the practice of interpretation of the biblical text. For our discussion of the subject, hermeneutical viewpoint includes both the theory and the practice of interpretation.

Hermeneutics is not only about determining the meaning of the text. More important is ascertaining how it applies to you and your situation at this particular time in history. The multiple contexts of the text itself, the human author and the interpreter, together produce numerous interpretations of the same text. Biblical backgrounds, linguistic analysis, historical context and literary studies are some of the relevant areas that need to be in place in order to seriously approach the task of interpretation. The text is essential; however, what one does with the text is what ultimately determines its contemporary relevance. No one comes to the text of Scripture objectively. Many factors affect understanding, not the least of which is identity. In the Israeli/Palestinian context, the social, political and spiritual location of the interpreter are the factors that determine the meaning of the text far more than is generally recognized.[5]

In the context of the Holy Land, hermeneutical and exegetical questions are much more than abstract concerns. The very life of the believer in Jesus, whether Israeli or Palestinian, is centered in the Scriptures, and the individual's hermeneutical viewpoint influences how he or she lives and interacts in the world. The theological dimension of the Israeli/Palestinian conflict is considerable and largely underestimated. Ultimately, one's theology is determined by one's hermeneutic:

> The question of hermeneutical viewpoint is thus the key issue in life and is not to be thought of solely as the science that informs the interpretation and application of Scripture . . . The scope of hermeneutics is all-embracing and serves to disclose the inner patterns of meaning and intention that identify each human being and determine the presuppositions one brings to the interpretation of Scripture.[6]

Sadly, there are few theologians and little theological discourse within the Israeli Messianic community. Neither is there significant theological engagement with the key issues that divide the Messianic community from their Palestinian Christian brothers and sisters. One of the aims of this book is to begin to rectify that situation and to put forward an attempt at a joint theology of reconciliation that will engage with the theologically divisive issues.

Much of the theological impetus in Messianic circles comes from abroad and often from Messianic Jews living outside of Israel. In addition, many of the current Israeli Messianic leaders received their theological training in the West. In recent times, Mark Kinzer has become one of the leading theologians of the Messianic movement. His influence tends to be most evident among Messianic immigrants from the West. Although based in the United States, the influence of his theology is growing in Israel. He articulates the situation of most Messianic Jews on the question of interpretation and offers a critique of the prevailing view:

> Many Messianic Jews consider the message of the Bible as clear and indisputable, a fact independent of external interpretation. The individual who reads the text with faith and an open heart will understand what it says . . . [However,] All attempts at a purely biblical perspective are destined to fail. One never reads the biblical text apart from preconceptions drawn from one's own particular historical setting and from some stream of interpretive tradition. That setting and tradition will shape the questions we address to the text, the concepts and terms we use to answer those questions and our selection of the portions of the text that speak most directly to our questions and therefore seem to be of the greatest importance . . .[7]

Kinzer does not hold to the reformation view of Sola Scriptura. For him, as well as for growing numbers of Israeli Messianic Jews, the understanding that God continues to act in and through history mandates that history must be taken seriously. While this view is not unique to Kinzer, he sees an ongoing interaction between the text of the Scriptures and the events of history, including recent events such as the Holocaust and the return of the Jewish people to the land of Israel. The lessons of history of necessity affect the reading of Scripture.[8] One of Kinzer's greatest contributions to the developing theology of the Messianic community is in the way he rephrases issues and questions the underlying presuppositions that are generally brought to the text.

Echoing Kinzer, the majority of Israeli Messianic Jews hold to a literal, or plain sense, hermeneutic. The Scriptures, particularly those related to Israel, are to be understood literally. David Stern, a prominent Israeli Messianic Jew and author of *The Jewish Bible*, states the case for a literal hermeneutic when he discusses the issue of the land.[9] Stern views the Torah as the starting place for Messianic Jewish theology, which should then progress to the New Testament and 'move forward to new Torah discoveries that would not have been found without the New Testament.'[10]

Arnold Fruchtenbaum is another Diaspora Messianic Jew whose view further emphasizes the pervasive nature of the literal hermeneutic. His views are influential in the Israeli Messianic context. In an article entitled 'Eschatology and Messianic Jews: A Theological Perspective', Fruchtenbaum writes, 'In dealing with this issue, sound hermeneutical principles have been applied. First, there is the principle of literal interpretation of Scripture. The normal plain sense is assumed rather than assuming a figurative, spiritual or allegorical meaning – unless the text itself indicates otherwise.'[11]

A voice from Israel is Joseph Shulam who supports what he calls a 'First Century Jewish Way of Understanding the Scriptures'.[12] He distances himself from traditional Western evangelical hermeneutical methodology, instead basing his interpretation[13] of Scripture on rabbinic methods. Shulam advocates a multifaceted approach to interpretation and cites the rabbinic Pardes[14] approach together with principles derived from Hillel and Rabbi Ishmael.[15] Shulam, together with Hilary de Cornu, has produced commentaries on the books of Acts, Romans and Galatians. These works utilize rabbinic hermeneutics and rely heavily on rabbinic source material from the Talmud and Mishnah.

Jewish hermeneutics is based on the statement that the Torah has seventy faces. This understanding makes for diverse methodology, including word and grammatical studies, and allegorical and mystical interpretations. Evangelical Christianity has traditionally embraced a grammatical-historical method that sought to uncover the original meaning of the text as it would have been understood by its first audience.[16] However, since the 1970s, there have been striking changes in the field of evangelical hermeneutics. Conflicting definitions were introduced for what had been standard terms, and influences from disciplines such as philosophy, anthropology and even business have strongly impacted standard evangelical hermeneutics. Today, new guidelines for interpretation exist alongside the traditional ones.

Understanding the Jewish backgrounds of the New Testament and of the Messianic faith is a fast-developing discipline. These studies are not confined to Messianic Jews, but they contribute much to this field. While it is impossible to return to the first century, there is much that can be gained from an understanding of the linguistic, socio-historical milieu of that period. All of the theological voices coming from within the Israeli Messianic community would agree on the importance of understanding the first-century context of their faith.

Gershon Nerel, an Israeli Messianic Jew, is a strong proponent of the view that there is clear continuity between the first-century Jesus-believing Jews and contemporary Israeli Messianic Jews. This continuity is expressed in the matter of spiritual authority. Nerel's view is that Israeli Messianic Jewish leaders have the same spiritual authority to interpret the Scriptures as did the first-century Jewish disciples of Yeshua.[17] In addition to the issue of spiritual authority, Nerel prioritizes the significance of biblical texts. The words of Yeshua take precedence over all other scriptural texts. Nerel does not reject the applicability of Paul's letters, but if there is (or appears to be) a contradiction between what Paul says and what Yeshua says, Yeshua's words trump Paul's.[18] The importance of the original Hebrew language for the understanding and interpretation of the Scriptures is another pillar in Nerel's hermeneutical viewpoint.

Richard Harvey is a British Messianic Jew with strong ties to Israel. His book, *Mapping Messianic Jewish Theology*, is a seminal treatment of the current state of Messianic theology which discusses the contours of Messianic Jewish thought according to the following categories: 1) the doctrine of God; 2) Yeshua the Messiah; 3) Torah in theory; 4) Torah in practice; and 5) the future of Israel.[19] Although he does not treat the issue of hermeneutical viewpoint directly, he says much concerning the type of thinking that informs the various resulting theologies.

Harvey identifies eight types of Messianic Jewish theology and classifies them as corresponding to the following theological streams: Jewish Christianity, Christocentric and Reformed; Dispensationalist Hebrew Christianity; Israeli National and

Restorationist; New Testament Halacha,[20] Charismatic and Evangelical; Traditional Judaism and the Messiah; Post-Missionary Messianic Judaism; Rabbinic Halacha in the Light of the New Testament; and Messianic Rabbinic Orthodoxy.[21] Harvey locates these theologies along a spectrum moving from Protestant evangelicalism to Orthodox Judaism. To understand how the Israeli Messianic Jewish community reads Scripture, it is helpful to have a grasp of the theological streams that are the source and the matrix for the many conflicting, strongly held views coming from within this community. Harvey recognizes the need and proposes a way forward to continue the development of Messianic Jewish theology. At one point he cites the context of the Israeli/Palestinian conflict as the arena where issues of Jewish/Christian relations, ecumenism, and interfaith dialogue need to be addressed.[22]

This brief overview of the various hermeneutical viewpoints and theological streams represented in the Israeli Messianic Jewish community demonstrates its rich theological diversity. Our concern here is specifically the Israeli Messianic Jewish community that unquestionably identifies with Israel and the Jewish people. The context of conflict, together with the range of theological positions, combines to marginalize any quest for an authentic theology of reconciliation. It is the conviction of the authors of this book that this quest is essential and must become a priority for both Israeli Messianic Jews and Palestinian Christians.

Heritage

Until the period of the Enlightenment, the Hebrew Scriptures, together with their Talmudic interpretations, shaped the life experience of all Jews. Secular Jews simply did not exist. The only kind of Jew was a religious Jew, whose life was based on and regulated by rabbinic (Talmudic) interpretations of the Scriptures, primarily concerning Torah. It is impossible to underestimate the influence of such a heritage. All discussions that would look at the place of Scripture for the Messianic Jew today must seriously reckon with this venerable, yet still living, tradition. Today's Israeli Messianic Jew, while not always consciously aware of this heritage, is nonetheless deeply influenced by it.

In the main, the Israeli Messianic Jew identifies more with secularism than with the Orthodox Judaism that is the dominant religious expression in Israel today. However, Jesus-believing Jews in Israel understand themselves as children of their father Abraham by birth and by faith. As Jews, they are rooted in a tradition that stretches back to Abraham who was called the first 'Hebrew'. For millennia, the Jewish people have prayed to the God of Abraham, Isaac and Jacob and have been held together by observance of traditions stemming from their corporate understanding of Scripture. To minimize the relevance of this religious, cultural and social heritage on account of the recent appearance of secularism would be to misunderstand the connectedness that most Jews, including Israeli Messianic Jews, have with the Bible. It is the experience of many Messianic Jews that their connection with their Jewish heritage, rather than decreasing, significantly increased when they came to faith in Jesus as their Jewish Messiah.[23]

In recent years in the secular sector in Israel, interest in the Bible and Jewish texts has been growing. This interest, however, was not a part of the early secular Zionist movement:

> The secular return to the Bible is also linked to a different trend that represents a broader secular interest in Jewish tradition. Of late, a growing sense of loss among secular Israelis has led them to look for ways to reconnect with Jewish tradition as part of a cultural, rather than religious, heritage. Departing from the earlier view that saw the Bible as a sacred national canon associated with antiquity and regarded the Talmud as a religious text associated with Jewish life in exile, the current trend articulates secular Israelis' desire to get reacquainted with both canonic texts without such distinctions.[24]

Although Israeli Messianic Jews' view of the Bible differs from this, they are impacted by the same cultural trends.

When their heritage is described in exclusively religious terms, Israeli Messianic Jews find themselves in conflict, as they do not inevitably identify themselves with the agenda of rabbinic Judaism. Judaism is most frequently seen as a rabbinic reinterpretation and a corruption of true biblical Judaism of which Messianic Jews feel themselves to be the legitimate heirs. This view holds that rabbinic Judaism is a human invention and represents a deviant religious system at odds with the 'true' way.[25] Authority and its source then become dominant issues. For the majority of Israeli Messianic Jews, rabbinic interpretation and tradition are in no way authoritative. Rabbinic tradition can be helpful in providing background and understanding of social customs and the historical, linguistic and cultural setting of Scripture.

Jewish heritage includes the reality of the Diaspora experience. The Jew has historically been characterized as the 'wandering Jew'. Exile and all that it implies is intrinsic to Jewish consciousness; included is the ongoing context of anti-Semitism and its legacy in the Jewish soul. As exiles, the Jewish people developed a strong sense of cohesion around issues of persecution, rejection and suffering. To this day, the experiences of crusades, pogroms and the Holocaust are matters of almost daily conversation for a large percentage of Israeli Jews. Diaspora experience factors strongly into the interpretation of Scripture. The self-understanding of a wandering, homeless, persecuted people is experienced and read into the text, often becoming the dominant narrative that gives the text its meaning.

As an important element of their heritage, Israeli Messianic Jews have adopted the biblical calendar along with the scriptural commands to observe the yearly festivals. The biblical festival cycle also has a strong agricultural component that serves to tie the Messianic Jew more fully to the land of Israel and to the Torah. The connecting link to previous generations is thus lived out in the contemporary context. This makes the relationship with the biblical text an existential reality experienced as a deep bond and a sense of continuity with the Jewish people throughout the centuries. The adoption of the biblical festivals is generally accompanied by a rejection of 'Christian' holidays, which are seen as being unbiblical and heavily influenced by paganism and anti-Judaism. In addition, many Messianic Jews do not identify with cultural Christianity and do not wish to be perceived as 'closet Christians' by other Jews. The Israeli Messianic Jew sees deep Messianic significance and a relationship to events in the life of Yeshua in the content and the cyclical nature of the biblical festivals. The festivals of Israel are also prophetic in the sense that the life, death, and resurrection of Yeshua are prefigured. Keri Warshawsky claims that 'the layering of Messianic significance and New Covenant

events upon Hebrew biblical holidays is a challenge of the hermeneutical hegemony of the Jewish establishment and a clarion call
to face the Messianic claims of Yeshua in their Jewish context, and
the subsequent Jewish identity claims of his followers.'[26]

The Messianic Jew sees particular Messianic significance in
the festival of Passover. Virtually all Israeli Messianic Jews will
celebrate this feast using some form of the Passover Haggadah[27]
in their observance of the festival. There is rich symbolism in the
celebration, and the Messianic Jew identifies with a double deliverance – deliverance as a people from the slavery of Egypt and
deliverance from the bondage of sin through the death of the Passover lamb – Yeshua.

Shaye Cohen portrays a history of Jewishness, describing a
progression whose steps represent the heritage of Jews. His depic-
tion begins with 'membership in a people, to citizenship in a state,
to adherence to a religion, and finally, as evidenced in rabbinic
texts, to membership in an ethno-religion.'[28] Heritage, like identity, is multifaceted. To speak of heritage at all mandates a sense
of collective experience. In Cohen's taxonomy, membership in a
people is foundational, and upon this foundation other elements
are built. 'Ethno-religion' is his term for the final stage of Jewish
history, identity and heritage. Due to the added religious dimension of their already multifaceted identity, the Israeli Messianic
Jew is in this mix in a more complex way than are Jews who are
non-Messianic. The heritage of Israeli Messianic Jews is endur-
ingly linked to the Scriptures, both the Old and the New Testament. Without them, their Jewish identity becomes meaningless
and corporate heritage is supplanted by individuality.

Torah

There is no one factor more central than Torah for the life of the
Jewish people. It is also the Jew's lasting legacy to the world.
Jewish life has been framed, and given cohesion and meaning by
Torah. One's view of Torah determines how many other essen-
tial issues such as God, land, people and promise are understood.
Messianic Jews today wrestle much with Torah and its implica-
tions for their lives. Perhaps more than any other issue, this is the

central controversial point around which Messianic Jews frame
their reading of Scripture.

For the Messianic Jew, the issue of authority is part of any
discussion of Torah. In evangelical Christianity, authority resides
in the full canon of Scripture. This is also the case for a large
percentage of the Messianic community in Israel. In addition,
some Messianic Jews are uncomfortable with ceding authority to
the historical church and they reject or only marginally recognize
the church's authority. They are, however, not representative of
most Messianic Jews, who do acknowledge the authority of the
historic church and its creeds. Nonetheless, they would distance
themselves from submission to 'church' rules or governing bodies.
They do not see themselves as obligated by church creeds, which
they would see as being merely cultural expressions rather than
universal binding statements of faith. Often it is the linguistic,
cultural form rather than the theological content of the creedal
statements that is objectionable. Within the Israeli Messianic
Jewish community, there is a minority that would, alongside the
canon of Scripture, also recognize authority in the Jewish rabbinical tradition of Torah interpretation and the Jewish canon that
includes Talmud and Mishnah.

The view that Torah has ongoing significance for the Jew who
believes in Jesus enjoys a high degree of agreement among Messianic Jews. Immediately, however, questions of definition arise.
What is Torah and how is its significance expressed are the two
core questions. Torah as a term literally means 'instruction' and
can be used to mean the Pentateuch, the whole of Jewish tradition,
the 'Oral Torah' including Mishnah and Talmud, or the Hebrew
Scriptures. The rabbinic tradition understands Torah to be far
more than the original, first words coming from God at Mt Sinai.
Rabbinical Torah is the entire interpretive tradition of the Jewish
people from Sinai until now. This expansion of Torah emerged
from the study of Torah over centuries.[29] The common factor in all
uses of the word is that 'Torah' refers to God's unique revelation
to the people of Israel. Israeli Messianic Jews locate themselves
along a continuum that ranges from being free in Messiah with no
obligation to Torah observance (a Torah-negative stance) to full
obligation to Torah according to rabbinic tradition (a Torah-positive stance).

As with all the issues being discussed in this chapter, Israeli Messianic Jews occupy a variety of positions along a wide spectrum of opinions. Richard Harvey surveys the situation in the Messianic community on the issue of Torah according to Torah in theory and Torah in practice. His typology of Messianic Jewish theology also provides an approximate framework within which to situate the variety of views on Torah. For the majority of the eight types of theology identified by Harvey, there is an accompanying understanding of Torah. For our discussion we will make partial use of Harvey's categories and frame the discussion in terms of Torah-positive and Torah-negative approaches.

One end of Harvey's theological continuum is occupied by Arnold Fruchtenbaum whose theology can best be categorized as dispensationalist Hebrew Christianity. Israeli Messianic Jews from a number of the older, more conservative congregations that were influenced by the Plymouth Brethren resonate with Fructenbaum's views. He has a 'Torah negative' approach based on his dispensational understanding that the dispensation of law has been superseded by the dispensation of grace. The death of Yeshua has made the law of Moses inoperative and consequently there is no longer any obligation to observe Mosaic law or Jewish tradition.[30] The key word here is obligation. In Fruchtenbaum's understanding, the Jewish believer in Jesus is free to observe aspects of the law if they are in harmony with New Testament principles, but is under no obligation to do so.[31]

Another 'Torah negative' view is held by Baruch Maoz, an Israeli, whose theology can be categorized as Jewish Christianity, Christocentric and Reformed. Maoz, recently retired from the pastorate of Grace and Truth Assembly, identifies himself as a Hebrew or Jewish Christian rather than as a Messianic Jew.[32] His theology is Protestant and Reformed. He articulates and expresses his Jewish identity in exclusively national, ethnic and cultural terms. The Torah has been superseded by the coming of the Messiah. The New Testament values of freedom in Messiah are primary and the ideal of obligatory Torah observance is seen in terms of legalism, which the New Testament condemns. Maoz therefore sees no religious requirement or ongoing place for Torah observance. For him, any observance of Jewish tradition must be severed from religious obligation and engaged in only if it is on the grounds of cultural or national reasons.[33]

The third 'Torah negative' theology is Israeli National and Restorationist. Dr Gershon Nerel is the main proponent of this view. Nerel is a historian who writes on the history of Jewish believers in Yeshua, attempting to bridge the historical gap from the first century to the modern resurgence of Jewish believers in Yeshua in the nineteenth and twentieth centuries. Nerel's agenda is to restore ecclesial hegemony and halachic authority to the Israeli Messianic Jew as the natural successor of the first-century Jewish believer in Yeshua. Although not a theologian, he has written on Torah and Torah observance.[34] Nerel accepts the ongoing validity of Torah but distances himself from rabbinic tradition. His Torah observance is tied to the locus of Messianic life – the land of Israel. On that basis, he makes a strong distinction between diasporic tradition that he labels 'Yiddishkeit' and biblical land-based tradition.[35] For Nerel, how Yeshua related to Torah, his words and actions, is the ultimate authority for the Jesus-believing Jew today.

The 'Torah positive' expressions coming from within the Israeli Messianic community range from centrist to the margin of Messianic rabbinic Orthodoxy. In Israel, the centrist expression is becoming the majority view. David Stern and Dan Juster are the key voices espousing a nuanced observance of Torah within the frame of a New Testament charismatic and evangelical theological position. Juster is a theologian whose views of Torah are seen through the lens of covenant. He has written widely on this subject.[36] Writing for the newsletter of his organization, Juster states:

> Our view of the rabbinic heritage is that **we must be discerning – approving what is good and rejecting that which is not good or not in accord with the letter and the spirit of the Bible.** In addition, our adoption of any tradition not commanded in the Bible, even if it is good, should only be embraced as we are so led by the Spirit; there is to be no rule beyond that.[37]

The 'letter and the spirit of the Bible' reflects Juster's evangelical heritage, while being 'led by the Spirit' expresses his charismatic conviction. Both traditions influence Juster's view of rabbinic tradition and Torah observance.

Referring to an ancient Jewish tradition that when Messiah comes he will both explain and change the Torah, David Stern situates his conclusions regarding Torah observance in the context of the Messiah Yeshua's Torah. Following a lengthy discussion of definitions, and the meaning and place of Torah, Stern concludes, '"observing" the Torah of the Messiah means accepting the guidance of New Testament *Halakhah* for our lives, while remaining sensitive to the Holy Spirit.'[38] Yeshua has not abrogated the Torah; rather he has been given the authority to interpret it.

Compared to the literature related to centrist and Torah-negative perspectives, the literature coming from the Israeli Messianic Jewish community on the remaining Torah-positive views is sparse. There are three principal voices espousing strongly Torah positive views: Zvi Sadan, Joseph Shulam and Ariel Berkowitz. Although there are a number of other Israeli Messianic Jewish leaders who hold these positions, they have yet to express themselves in writing. Diaspora voices dominate the Torah-positive theological discourse.[39]

Israeli Messianic Jew Zvi Sadan situates his Torah-positive view within a clear commitment to Yeshua and the New Testament scriptures. For Sadan, how one interprets Paul and his view of Torah is a central issue:

> my unambiguous conclusion is that the new Testament does not teach us to abandon Torah, nor the tradition of the fathers (at least that which was known during that period). Consequently, however we understand Paul's epistles, the guiding exegetical principle for interpreting his letters must be that he remained an "observant Jew" to the end of his life . . .[40]

In Sadan's understanding, the oral law is integrally a part of the New Testament and of Yeshua's teachings and life. Rabbinic tradition is that which has preserved the Jewish people and maintained their identity throughout history. It is therefore authoritative and to be accepted by Jews who believe in Yeshua. Sadan is clear that if there is a conflict between the words of Yeshua and rabbinic halacha then it is the words of Yeshua that are authoritative.[41] 'The new Testament gives no one the authority to reject Yeshua's explicit statements that his disciples, in principle, should observe halakah as long as it is not opposed to him, his teaching, or that of the apostles.'

Joseph Shulam is the spiritual leader of the most orthopraxic Messianic congregation in Israel. He also has the distinction of being the only Israeli Messianic Jew to have gone through the complete process of Jewish Orthodox rabbinical training.[42] He is known for his outspoken Torah-positive approach. Basing his approach on Matthew 23.1–4, Shulam promotes a form of observance that is founded on rabbinic tradition. His unequivocal position is that Messianic Jews should study, internalize and observe halacha that is as much as possible based on rabbinic interpretation.[43] While recognizing the difficulties inherent in such a task, he both sees a need for and advances development of 'Messianic halacha'.[44]

A variant of the Torah-positive approach is advocated by Ariel Berkowitz. He defines Torah narrowly in the sense of Pentateuch and sees no authoritative place for 'Oral Torah' (rabbinical interpretation).[45] Berkowitz views Torah as an everlasting covenant between God and the Jewish people, involving mutually binding obligations.[46] Torah was given to the people of Israel as a way of life to act as protector, reminder and source of blessing for God's people. A biblically oriented Torah lifestyle is God's chosen way for the Jewish people to live.[47] Torah is in no way salvific but it is God's mandated way for his people to live under his blessing.

The voices within the Israeli Messianic Jewish community that see Torah as obligatory for the Jesus-believing Jew are still relatively few. The majority of those who view Torah in any form as binding are Diaspora based. Mark Kinzer is the best known of those who espouse this view. Since this chapter is concerned with the Israeli Messianic Jewish community, Diaspora views are less represented. It should be noted that the Diaspora views are not without adherents in Israel. At this time, however, they represent a minority opinion and are at the outer edge of Harvey's theological spectrum.

The question could be asked as to the reason for this lengthy section on Torah as a major theme through which Israeli Messianic Jews read the Scriptures. While this section has been largely theological, the implications of the theology described are lived out in practice by the Messianic community. Both individual and communal life is shaped by how Torah is viewed. Life cycle events, holidays and daily activities are all affected by how one views Torah. These lifestyle issues have the power to interfere and even damage relationships outside of the home community context. How Israeli Messianic Jews and their Palestinian brothers and sisters relate to one another can be deeply influenced by this seemingly 'Jewish' issue.

Land and Promise

The Israeli Messianic Jew has chosen to live in a context of conflict that is essentially land based. Whether born in the land or having immigrated to it, the decision to remain in the land guarantees an ongoing necessity to grapple with the difficult questions of the meaning of the land. Israel/Palestine is simultaneously a place of conflict and a place of promise. Complicating the way Israeli Messianic Jews view the land is the fact that living in the land of Israel is an integral element of their identity. They see themselves in continuity with their people, the Jewish people, who have returned in their generation to the ancient land given as a part of God's covenant promise[48] to the Jewish people in perpetuity.[49] For the Israeli Messianic Jew, the land of Israel is the space where the Jewish people will fulfil their final destiny. The land of Israel is thus permanently linked with promise. It is the locus of their eschatological hope.

This perspective is not new; it was a part of the consciousness of Messianic Jews prior to the foundation of the modern state of Israel. Numbers of Messianic Jews, or Hebrew Christians as they termed themselves in that era, were involved in political Zionist movements in Europe. Their involvement was based on their reading of the prophetic scriptures concerning the return of Israel to Zion. 'Those Hebrew Christians who enthusiastically expressed Zionist aspirations, in word or in deed, did so from an inherent belief rooted in their understanding of biblical prophecy. In fact, their Zionism, which often integrated political and spiritual aspects, should be understood as a *condicio sine qua non* of their individual and national identity.'[50] Zionism has profoundly influenced Israeli Messianic Jews and, with few

exceptions, it remains the prevailing paradigm for their attachment to the land.

Messianic Jews base their understanding of their permanent
status as God's elect on Romans 9 – 11. This passage is a keystone
in their sense of being doubly chosen – as ethnic Israel, having
never been rejected by God, and as having come to Messiah and
been spiritually incorporated into God's universal family. A literal
reading of the text definitively classifies Jesus-believing Jews as
being in the 'remnant' of Israel that would return to the God of
their ancestors. In the mind of the majority of Israeli Messianic
Jews, returning to God is integrally connected with a return to
the land of Israel. This passage, Romans 9 – 11, is crucial for the
self-understanding of Messianic Jews and their place and role
in history. As events unfold, Israeli Messianic Jews today firmly
situate themselves within the Israel of the Scriptures that has been
reconstituted today in its ancient land. Richard Harvey surveys
the eschatology of the Messianic movement and draws the conclusion that 'Messianic Jews see themselves as part *of* Israel, and their
understanding of prophecy impacts them personally as part of the
Remnant (Rom. 9 – 11)'.[51] Addressing this issue, Israeli Messianic
Jew David Stern writes. 'Isaiah 51:10 says that "the redeemed of
the Lord shall return and come with singing unto Zion and everlasting joy shall be upon their head." If these "redeemed of the
Lord" are not the Messianic Jews now living in the Land, then
who are they?'[52]

An important aspect of Israeli Messianic Jews' connection to
the land of Israel is their understanding of covenant. The promise
of land as the inheritance of Israel is an integral element of the
covenant promise given to Abraham. It is irrevocable and unconditional.[53] The question that arises is: how can this actually be
realized? Considering the hiatus of a two-thousand-year absence
of Jewish hegemony in Israel, how is this eternal promise to be
realized in the twenty-first century?

This understanding of the relevance of the land of Israel is not
unique to Messianic Jews. They are in continuity with the rich
tradition of Judaism. The difference is that in traditional rabbinic
understanding, the link between Jews and the land of Israel would
only be fully realized in the eschaton; whereas the contemporary
understanding of both religious Zionists and Messianic Jews is

that eschatology is *now* realized in the return of the Jewish people and their settlement in the land of promise. Within Judaism, what was once an otherworldly aspiration for the 'world to come' is today a reality as Jews are again in the land, having reclaimed their inheritance. From a philosophical perspective, Abraham Joshua Heschel writes:

> There is a unique association between the people and the land of Israel. Even before Israel becomes a people the land is preordained for it. What we have witnessed in our own days is a reminder of the power of God's mysterious promise to Abraham . . . The Jew in whose heart the love of Zion dies is doomed to lose his faith in the God of Abraham who gave the land as an earnest of the redemption of all men.[54]

Heschel articulates a twofold understanding that the land of Israel is both a place of promise and a proleptic assurance of redemption for all humanity. The land is a sign of God's covenant with Abraham and a promise for all people. This view is consistent with the traditional Jewish view that the land is an integral part of Israel's eschatological hope. This Jewish view both anticipates and resonates with Paul's doxology at the end of Romans 11. In addition, the language of 'earnest' is reminiscent of Paul's use of the same word in reference to the Holy Spirit as a downpayment or earnest of the inheritance of the believer in Jesus.[55]

Jewish tradition has long associated Israel's everlasting possession of the land of Israel with the Creation narratives. David Hartman quotes Rashi's[56] commentary on Genesis 1:1, concluding, 'The reason the Bible begins with the narrative of Creation is to justify the legitimacy of Israel's claim to the Land of Canaan. The Lord of Creation can allocate the lands of the earth according to His preferences.'[57] From the perspective of a biblical worldview, it is God who has chosen Israel, given them a land, and set them apart from the other nations of the world. Israel has a divine destiny that will only finally be realized in the ancient land of promise. God will work in history to see his purposes fulfilled, regardless of Israel's repeated unfaithfulness; he will be faithful. Anything less than this would impugn God's character.

Ian Lustick identifies seven basic beliefs that embody the worldview of religious Zionist fundamentalism. These are: 1) the uniqueness of the Jewish people among the nations of the world; 2) the meaning of Arab opposition to Israel; 3) Israel's international isolation as proof of Jewish chosenness; 4) the impossibility of arriving at a negotiated peace; 5) the cardinal importance of the land of Israel; 6) current history as the unfolding of the redemption process; and 7) faith and ideological dedication of the Jews as a decisive factor in national redemption and the establishment of the Messianic kingdom.[58] In varying degrees, the majority of Israeli Messianic Jews would concur with this worldview, basing each belief on their reading of Scripture. In this picture of Zionist fundamentalism, the importance of the land of Israel is axiomatic. The same holds true for any Israeli Messianic Jew who bases the legitimacy of their claims to the land on their view of Scripture. It is somewhat startling to realize the near-complete accord between the fundamentalism of religious Zionism and the Zionism of the Israeli Messianic Jew.

Secular Zionism, contrary to religious Zionism, whether of the Christian or the Jewish variety, views the land of Israel through the lens of Jewish survival. The nation is the means by which the Jewish people will survive as a community. Faith in God or adherence to a Torah lifestyle is no longer the matrix of Jewish life; nor is faith any longer a necessary component of Jewish identity. 'Loyalty to Jewish history does not entail loyalty to the god of Israel, the Jewish tradition or the authority of Halakhah. The state thus provides a frame of reference for Jewish membership and community consciousness independent of specific religious content'.[59]

Israeli Messianic Jews' attachment to the land of Israel is founded on both religious and secular foundations. Their unqualified commitment to what they see as God's agenda for the land often results in an un-nuanced patriotism, thereby relegating issues of justice, ethics and human rights (for anyone other than their own community) to secondary considerations. There are very few conscientious objectors and even fewer pacifists in the Israeli Messianic community. The established practice is for Israeli Messianic Jews to serve in the military and to seek to excel in their service to the extent that there is some degree of pressure to request service in elite military units. While Israeli Messianic Jews highly value the biblical view of the place of the land, they are nonetheless influenced by secular Zionism. For them, the logical outworking of their position is to fully embrace the modern, secular, political entity of Israel, frequently identifying themselves with a strongly nationalistic, even fundamentalist agenda.

Notwithstanding the context of intractable conflict, with land rights occupying the focal point of the conflict, Israeli Messianic Jews have been hesitant to express their views in writing. Two surveys, done fifteen years apart, touched on how Messianic Jews view issues of land and peace. In 1997, Bodil Skjøtt surveyed a representative sampling of the Israeli Messianic community on a number of issues including how they understood biblical teaching on the land of Israel, the place of the Jewish people, the significance of the return of Jews to the land of Israel, the borders of Israel, their relationship with Palestinian Christians, and Palestinian demands for a sovereign state. The survey results were not surprising. Ninety-five per cent believed the Bible promised the land of Israel to the Jewish people permanently and unconditionally. The majority saw the return of Jews to the land of Israel as a fulfilment of divine promise and 76 per cent placed Judea and Samaria within the boundaries of Israel.[60]

The second survey was undertaken by Richard Harvey in 2012.[61] Harvey's survey sought to assess views from within the broader Israeli and the Diaspora Messianic community. His focus was towards a theology of reconciliation with emphasis on possibilities of peace building. Harvey did not specifically ask questions about the 'land', but what is important for our discussion is the result that 71 per cent of the respondents were pessimistic about the possibility for peace between Israelis and Palestinians. Another 18 per cent classified themselves as realistic, very slightly optimistic, or pessimistically optimistic. Only 7 per cent were clearly optimistic. Numbers of the respondents cited their scriptural views of the land as reasons for their responses.[62]

Philip Ben-Shmuel is a new voice coming from the Israeli Messianic Jewish community. Ben-Shmuel advocates an incarnational hermeneutic that he defines as a contextualized literal approach, having a Christ-centred contemporary application, with Yeshua (his life and words)[63] as the 'Archimedean point' around which the Scriptures need to be understood.[64] This hermeneutic places the land promises to Israel in a broader, globalized understanding of land and places holiness, justice and peace as themes by which the land is understood. Ben-Shmuel identifies himself as a new breed, or an alternative kind of Zionist. His definition of Zionism is not limited to 'particular Zionism' for the Jewish people liberated to serve God in the land of Israel, but is expanded to include a 'general Zionism' that embraces the redemption of the world.[65] As the body of Messiah in Israel, the Messianic Jewish community is called to bring holiness, justice and peace to the land.[66] The land is ultimately meant to bring blessing to all the nations of the earth. Ben-Shmuel's vision is for a Messianic Zionism that would 'seek to bring the Jewish and the Palestinian peoples to a covenantal relationship with the land.'[66] The land as a place of justice features strongly in Ben-Shmuel's views.

Conclusion and Challenge

How Israeli Messianic Jews read the Scriptures has far-reaching implications for how they live their lives. Given the context of this book, the subject is particularly relevant for how they relate to Palestinian Christians living together with them in the land. The issues chosen for this chapter reflect some of the unique factors that are primary concerns for Israeli Messianic Jews as they read Scripture. This is not to say that other issues such as Christology and eschatology are inconsequential. However, due to space considerations, the most broadly characteristic issues were the focus of the chapter.

The Israeli Messianic Jewish community needs to explore new avenues of communication with their Palestinian brothers and sisters who are also committed to Jesus and hold the Scriptures as their rule for life and faith. All faith communities elicit different understandings from the same biblical texts and they apply those texts differently according to their particular hermeneutic, their individual and collective history, and their social context. It is therefore important to be aware of our own presuppositions, our historical and social location, and the various lenses through which we view Scripture. Our view is never the 'only right view'. Any approach to Scripture must be with an attitude of humility and openness to hear how others read the same texts. Our different backgrounds and social locations can be enriching rather than oppositional. Approaching the Scriptures, and one another, with a spirit of love and respect can protect us from the theological arrogance that assumes our view to be the 'right' one. One of our aims in this book is to hear the Lord together through his living word, spoken into our different contexts.

8.

Theological Disagreements

We will now explore a few of the theological issues that can, and often do, create spiritual and political division between Palestinian Christians and Israeli Messianic Jews.

Defining the Issues

Sadly, the prevailing cultures within our believing communities often impede even fledgling attempts at reconciliation. One of the biggest obstacles to the process of reconciliation between Israeli Messianic Jews and Palestinian Christians is theology, specifically the theological differences that separate them. It should be no surprise that exclusive theological positions have developed on both sides. These positions inform the way Israeli and Palestinian believers view each other and the political conflict in which they are enmeshed. While many leaders on both sides claim that reconciliation is a high spiritual priority, these same leaders too often fail to engage with those on the other side who present significant challenges to their theological positions. They do not truly engage their 'theological enemy'. True reconciliation faces and does not run from the hard cases.

Palestinian Christians and Israeli Messianic Jews have many political and even a good number of theological reasons for avoiding each other, so the need to develop a theology of reconciliation that fosters genuine fellowship is great. The animating vision for this book is to develop a theological basis for our coming together and to restore relationships that have been deeply damaged by the political situation and by theologies that have cultivated animosity and maintained distance between the two communities. For this reason, we must take stock of the issues that divide us. We need to talk about the hard cases – the theological 'minefields' – and begin to put them in perspective for the greater good of mutually embracing one another in Messiah.

The theological aspects of the Israeli–Palestinian conflict make it unique among other global conflicts and particularly problematic for peacemaking. The religious and historical narratives of the three Abrahamic faiths – Judaism, Christianity and Islam – are rooted in the Holy Land. All claim territory according to their respective sacred texts. Jews, Muslims and Christians who live in Israel-Palestine clearly feel a strong personal connection to the homeland of their faith. The theological conflict in the Holy Land is further intensified by the vested interests of people of faith from around the world. There are few conflicts that capture the imagination and emotions of the world in the way the Israeli–Palestinian does.

We will now explore four theological concepts that consistently emerge in theological dialogue and create spiritual and political division between Palestinian Christians and Israeli Messianic Jews. These concepts are: 1) chosen people; 2) land; 3) covenant; and 4) justice. The discussion for each concept is not meant to be exhaustive but serves to give a sample of how each group approaches and frames the concepts in the context of the conflict. The discussion will also illustrate some of the theological challenges. As Israeli and Palestinian believers, it is our hope that by understanding how each side thinks and feels about these issues; we will begin to reject the fear that our differences create, build trust as we dialogue together, and by so doing take steps to fulfil our biblical calling to dwell together in unity.

Identity in terms of chosen people

A Palestinian Christian view

Palestinian Christians find themselves on the theological defensive, having to respond polemically to counter Christian Zionist arguments. This defensive posture hardly represents the full picture of Palestinian theological views, but it is a significant aspect of their current theological reflection. Beyond polemics,

Palestinian Christians would represent their views as *basic Christianity*.

Whether from an Orthodox, Roman Catholic, mainline Protestant or evangelical Protestant perspective, Palestinian Christians affirm the biblical idea of a chosen people, set apart by God and for God. While at one time God chose the Israelites to be his consecrated people, the advent of Jesus Christ formed a new kind of kingdom, new ways of being, and new birth in the Holy Spirit who now calls his chosen people from the four corners of the earth. As followers of Jesus Christ, as members of his body through the church, Palestinian Christians see themselves as among these chosen people; not because they are Palestinian inhabitants of the Holy Land, but because they are Christians. Yet, as Palestinians, they take seriously their inheritance and unique calling as the Christians of the Holy Land. This view corresponds closely to a kind of national 'chosenness'.

With Messianic Jews, Palestinian Christians understand the concept 'chosen people' as an expression of God's sovereignty. Beyond that, the groups disagree. For Palestinians, generally, one's chosenness in God is publicly expressed through the sacrament of baptism. In baptism one is given to God and gives oneself to God as an act of responsive faith. Election, being chosen, finds its theological *basis* in God's nature and his call upon a person's and a people's life. Election is not a state of being that is conferred by ethnicity or nationality. The Palestinian Christian community believes that all believers receive and are confirmed in this elected identity in the sacrament of baptism. They then confirm it in life through obedience to Jesus' commands to love God and to love one's neighbour as oneself. Anticipating the multi-ethnic plurality of the kingdom of God, the baptismal covenant draws together those whom God has chosen in Jesus Christ, and it also sends them out into God's creation to share his love with all.

Palestinian Christians do not see God's choice of the people of Israel in the Old Testament as a kind of immutable natural law defining what it means to be Jewish, although it does point to what it means to be chosen. Countering the perception of claims that election is bound to ethnicity, Paul Tarazi, an Orthodox Palestinian theologian, notes that what is unique in the experience of ancient Israel is their dealing with a personal deity who reveals himself as 'I AM'. As Tarazi sees it, God – not Israel – is the subject of the history in the Old Testament. Apart from his initiative to form the Jews as a people and sustain them in his love, biblical Israel would have remained one among many petty tribes, destined for self-destruction.

The stories of Isaac and Ishmael, and Jacob and Esau, serve to illustrate this movement away from ethnicity towards the primacy of God's sovereign choice in his setting people apart. Hailing from the same family and tribe, it is God's sovereign choice alone of Isaac and Jacob that is the basis of their election. Beginning with God's election of Abraham, Tarazi discovers that chosenness is a remarkable statement about the nature of God and not about the nature of those whom he chooses.

That assumption regularly creeps into the intuitions of the faithful, both among those whose lives are chronicled in the Scriptures as well as those living today. If the covenant is presented as having been given to a purely national/ethnic community, it is, finally, a function of Jewish national identity. If that be the case, Tarazi argues, non-Jews are necessarily excluded from the community. Yet Tarazi maintains that, throughout the Scriptures, ethnic belonging *alone* did not define Jewish identity and was not the deciding factor in determining the body of 'Israel'. The lines between those who were 'inside' and those who were 'outside' were more fluid than ethnic categories or national boundaries suggest:

> The inclusion of outsiders into the community of Israel should remind us that renewing Israel has the connotation of creating Israel: the people of God are those who are saved by God. Concepts such as nationhood or statehood, which may be central to the idea of peoplehood at the level of human understanding, are not basic to the understanding of the peoplehood of the Israel of God.[1]

In the Old Testament, all who were called to join the community of faith did indeed join ethnic Jewish Israel and were initiated into the law that constituted what it meant to be Israel. With the coming of Jesus, however, the elect were those who were called to recognize the embodiment of God's love of Israel in Jesus, God's first chosen. Those who join the community of the chosen are now identified by their embrace of Jesus. In *Jesus and Israel: One Covenant or Two?*, New Testament theologian David Holwerda writes:

> In essence Israel is, and has always been, the people who were called into existence by God's love and who continue to live from his love. Promise, call, gift and love are the actions of God embracing and sustaining Israel, and Israel must always respond with a faithful acceptance of that which God promises and gives. If Israel forgets its essential nature, if Israel tries to establish another basis for its existence, then it lives outside the promise and gifts of God.[2]

Despite the people of Israel's repeated attempts to ground their identity in something other than him, God remained faithful to his covenant with them; the climactic satisfaction of which is his victory in the life, death and resurrection of Jesus Christ. As Tarazi notes, nothing about God's election of Israel is theirs, as if his election becomes *their* possession of his gifts, an entitlement they are owed by God. Rather, by his loving kindness and patient mercy, they are sustained as a people and are preserved. Without God's care for Israel, they would have destroyed themselves. The story of Israel is, finally, the story of God and his actions on behalf of his creation.

As we noted earlier in the section on Palestinian biblical hermeneutics, Tarazi paints a powerful word picture of a Middle Eastern shepherd with his sheep. It is worth repeating. The entity that is the flock depends entirely upon its shepherd. Those who follow the shepherd are those who belong to his flock, who listen to and obey his voice; the shepherd forms the flock and sustains it.[3] Palestinian Christians say that, in *Christ*, the Good Shepherd of the sheep, the covenant blessings to Abraham and his children now extend throughout the earth (Gen. 12). The story of Israel tells the story of God. Just as that history has everything to do with God's loving sustenance as opposed to something that was guaranteed to Israel, the same is true concerning history's future. God's sovereign election of his people, called together from the four corners of the earth, is preserved as his gift. The chosen people are those who follow the Shepherd and obey him as members of his flock.

An Israeli Messianic Jewish view

The chosenness of the Jewish people is an integral, unquestioned element in Israeli Messianic Jews' understanding of their relationship with God. The idea of chosenness, or divine election, is a primary assumption upon which much of Jewish and Messianic theology is founded. Contrary to much of Christianity, Israeli Messianic Jews see no abrogation of the chosenness of the Jewish people resulting from the incarnation of Yeshua and the formation of a multi-ethnic body of Messiah. The Jewish people within the body of Messiah retain their status of chosenness. This doctrine is developed on the basis of Torah and continues through the Tenach into the New Testament. From Abraham to Paul, Israel's chosenness is repeatedly stated. God's promises to Abraham, Isaac and Jacob form the foundation of this understanding.[4]

Deuteronomy 7.6 is the fundamental passage that sets the trajectory for all future discussions of the issue. 'For you are a people holy to the LORD your God; the LORD your God has chosen you out of all the peoples on earth to be his people, his treasured possession'. This is a sovereign act of an unchanging God who has freely chosen the people of Israel to bear witness to him and to be the instrument of his salvific will for the nations of the world.

His choice and his promises are irrevocable as they are based on God himself rather than any intrinsic merit on the part of Israel. 'It was not because you were more numerous than any other people that the LORD set his heart on you and chose you – for you were the fewest of all peoples' (Deut. 7.7). God's choosing of Israel is an act of eternal, unconditional love; a love that does not discard the beloved when they have 'served their purpose'. Indeed this love is rooted in a covenant that remains in effect through New Testament times and beyond (Rom. 11.28).

Concerning the issue of chosenness, the problem is not who is chosen, but rather who is *not* chosen. The prevailing human tendency is to categorize according to a dualistic standard. Chosen is good; not chosen is bad or at least not as good as being chosen. One is preferred over the other and this automatically relegates the 'non chosen' to an inferior position. This understanding is flawed and reflects a simplistic, either–or mentality that is inconsistent with the character of God – the one who is the chooser. He is infinite and is not confined to the narrow categories of human reasoning. In God's economy, chosen does not mean better or having more rights than the non-chosen. God is eminently relational. He brings a rich and multifaceted diversity of encounter to his relationships within the human family. Michael Wyschogrod expresses it well:

> The consolation of the Gentiles is the knowledge that God also stands in relationship with them in recognition and affirmation of their uniqueness. The choice, after all, is between a lofty divine love equally distributed to all without recognition of uniqueness and real encounter, which necessarily involves favorites, but in which each is unique and addressed as such. If Abraham was especially loved by God, it is because God is a father who does not stand in a legal relationship to his children, which by its nature requires impartiality and objectivity. As a father, God loves his children and knows each one as who he is, with his strengths and weaknesses, his virtues and vices. Because a father is not an impartial judge but a loving parent and because a human father is a human being with his own personality, it is inevitable that he will find himself more compatible with some of his children than others . . . And it is also true that a father loves all his children, so that they all know of and feel the love they receive, recognizing that to substitute an impartial judge for a loving father would eliminate the preference for the specially favored but would also deprive all of them of a father. The mystery of Israel's election thus turns out to be the guarantee of the fatherhood of God toward all peoples, elect and nonelect, Jew and gentile . . . When we grasp that the election of Israel flows from the fatherhood that extends to all created in God's image, we find ourselves tied to all men in brotherhood.[5]

To fully understand the concept of chosenness is to value all people for their unique individuality, and all ethnicities for their distinctiveness. Uniqueness implies difference. Difference in no way implies inferiority. Our God, who is relational, has sovereignly elected to choose Israel. Since he is a faithful, covenant-keeping God, his choice is never revoked. It is natural, yet regrettable, that to be 'not chosen' is experienced humanly as hurtful, rejectionist and demeaning. Those who are spiritual, however, endeavour to look beyond themselves and see into the heart of God who has chosen to be in a unique, personal, individual relationship with all of humankind.

The New Testament reaffirms the understanding that Israel remains chosen. The relationship of chosenness has not been rescinded by the coming of Messiah and the birth of the multi-ethnic *ecclesia*. Jesus and Paul were both noted for first going, but not exclusively, to the house of Israel during their respective ministries.[6] Romans 9.4 supports this assertion by stating in the present tense, regarding ethnic Israel, 'They are Israelites, and to them belong the adoption, the glory, the covenants, the giving of the law, the worship, and the promises'. Romans 11.28 clearly addresses the issue of the election of Israel in the following words: 'as regards election they are beloved, for the sake of their ancestors'.

This issue has been a source of much misunderstanding and difficulty between Messianic Jews and Christians, not the least of whom are the Palestinian Christians with whom Israeli Messianic Jews find themselves in conflict on a wide variety of theological, political and cultural issues. It has also been the source of much anti-Judaism, anti-Semitism and theological supersessionism. Here, it is important to affirm the relational aspect of chosenness and unchosenness by stating unequivocally that Messianic Jews (because of their chosenness) are in no way superior to Gentile Christians. All Christians are in one respect chosen, whereas Messianic Jews are in a position of being doubly chosen. Election, or chosenness, is always a matter of grace, never of works or on account of merit.[7] God's lack of revocation concerning his choice of Israel testifies to his faithfulness and is the basis upon which he can be embraced as trustworthy by those from among the nations whom he has chosen to be members of the multi-ethnic body of Messiah. Ultimately, chosenness is about God and not about human beings.

The land[8]

A Palestinian Christian view

For Palestinian Christians, the legitimacy of their belonging to the land is one of the most important aspects of their identity. They see their presence in the land where Jesus was born, lived, died and was resurrected as a testimony of God's faithfulness to the world. That sense of belonging is as non-controversial as any other people's sense of belonging to a homeland. Additionally, as Christians with a long historical presence in the region, Palestinian Christians see themselves as the guardians of the holy sites and as those who have remained faithful to God in Christ throughout centuries of persecution and oppression.

However, in their theology of the land, Palestinian Christians have consciously developed theological positions in reaction to Messianic Jewish and Christian Zionist claims that God promised the land of Israel-Palestine to the Jewish people exclusively. For the most part, Palestinian Christians believe that this is false and that God's promise to Abraham is not limited either to the Jewish people or to the land of Canaan. It was and remains a promise for all God's children and for the whole earth.

Canon Naim Ateek, one of the most prominent Palestinian theological voices, argues that the land is no longer important since the coming of Christ. As Christ is the climax and culmination of the Old Testament promises, Christians should view history through the progressive revelation of God's will in the Old and New Testaments, and in effect, read the Old Testament through the lens of Christ's coming and purpose. He argues that many parts of the Old Testament are exclusive, Zionist and racist, and can result in 'fanatical actions by fanatical people'.[9] The value of the Old Testament is that it pointed to Christ, but it is not sufficient or relevant as a stand-alone text. He continues that Jesus was not interested in land, but in the kingdom of God. Jesus offered an inclusive message to counter the exclusive, primitive and discriminatory claims of the Old Testament. In light of our present conflict, Ateek says that, as both Palestinians and Jews live on the land today, they must learn to share it and take care of it together. Only once justice is met can peace and security be achieved.[10]

In Yohanna Katanacho's article 'Christ is the Owner of Haaretz [the Land]', he seeks to counter popular theologies (namely dispensationalism) that advocate Israel's ownership of Haaretz. Exploring the various territorial dimensions of Haaretz within the Old Testament, he surveys a number of studies that demonstrate the fluidity of borders, and the multiple meanings of the term *Haaretz*. The giving of Haaretz, according to the biblical text, is conditional on obedience, justice and righteousness. He adds an original perspective by arguing that Haaretz should be seen in light of God's redemption of the world, and that the true inheritor of Haaretz is Christ himself. The biblical requirements for right living are best embodied in the person and ownership of Christ, and he argues that God's plan for a particular location is in fact a plan for holiness, justice and righteousness that should encompass the whole world.[11]

In his exploration of the biblical text surrounding the issue of land, co-author Salim J. Munayer concludes that the land is vitally important. It is a gift that was given in covenant, and as such it comes with responsibility, meaning it is not an unconditional promise. Our moral choices are linked with the health of the land. When exploring the meaning of 'Promised Land', a common literary device termed *spatial merism*[12] is often employed, designating the boundaries as being 'from . . . to . . .' Various borders are discussed in this 'from . . . to . . .' formula, indicating that the Promised Land was not just a territory, but an idea that was universal in scope. The territory of the Promised Land specified boundaries from the sea, wilderness and mountains. Similar to other Ancient Near Eastern literature, the use of spatial merism indicates the cosmic borders of the Promised Land. Instead of a small Middle Eastern strip of land, it extends the scope of the blessing and promise to the ends of the earth. God's promises were made available to the whole world and to all of humanity through the coming of Jesus. From the time of the fall, when sin entered the world, God sought to restore relationships and bless the whole world and its inhabitants. His promises for the land were universalized.

While God's promises were extended in scope, land does not lose its importance. In fact, it is all the more important. We cannot spiritualize 'the process of salvation away from the land' as the 'centrality of the land has merely shifted in God's redemptive work'.[13] The process of restoration that God envisions for us entails reconciliation, and land is the gift, the place, where this is enacted. The reconciliation between humanity and God, and people and their neighbours, must occur on land, as it was on the land that sin entered the world and humanity rebelled against God. This reconciliation is possible through the person of Jesus. The Holy Land is important as it is a symbol for the whole earth, and if peace and reconciliation are possible here, it is a witness and testimony that it is possible for the rest of the world.[14]

Clearly, Palestinian Christians have a different understanding of the biblical land promises than most Messianic Jews. Palestinian evangelical theologians are examining the Old Testament texts instead of focusing primarily on the New Testament to shed light on the Old. Palestinian Christians do not see the land promises as a kind of eternal property deed for Jews. The coming of Jesus casts all biblical revelation in a new light, not as an abrupt departure from what God began with Israel, but as an expanded fulfilment of his purposes for all those whom he calls his people.

The same is true concerning the priority of land in God's story. Until the time of Jesus, anyone who wanted to worship the God of Abraham, Isaac and Jacob had to come to the temple in Jerusalem. Yet not all who sought to worship God journeyed to Jerusalem. The Samaritans and the Jews considered each other as enemies and disagreed over the location of God's true temple. However, in a well-known conversation at a local well with a Samaritan woman who queries him on this contentious point; Jesus seems to simultaneously de-emphasize the essential centrality of Jerusalem even as he expands the notion of holy ground. He does not necessarily lessen the importance of the land, but rather paints a picture of a time in which *true worship* of the Father is in the *Spirit* – 'a time [that] is coming and has now come' (John 4.23 NIV) is the central focus, not land. Neither the mountain of the Samaritans nor Jerusalem delimits the location of this worship. More importantly, the location is not what makes the worship 'true'. Instead, the whole earth is the scene for the unfolding of a kingdom made up of 'true worshippers' (John 4.24). Jesus uses a similar universalizing device when he tells his disciples that they are to be his witnesses 'in Jerusalem, in all Judea and Samaria, and to the ends of the earth' (Acts 1.8).

The Kairos Palestine document sums up well how Palestinian Christians think theologically about the land:

> We believe that our land has a universal mission. In this universality, the meaning of the promises, of the land, of the election, of the people of God open up to include all of humanity, starting from all the peoples of this land. In light of the teachings of the Holy Bible, the promise of the land has never been a political programme, but rather the prelude to complete universal salvation. It was the initiation of the fulfillment of the Kingdom of God on earth.[15]

Palestinian Christians also see the land as a kind of witness to the events of the Scriptures as the setting God chose to make his name known through the Israelites and ultimately in the person of Jesus Christ. Many Palestinian Christians, as well as Messianic Jews, believe it is where Jesus will one day return. But the land itself is not the central character of the story. The writer of Hebrews praises Abraham's faith for dwelling in tents in the Promised Land, and yet the patriarch 'looked forward to the city that has foundations, whose architect and builder is God' (Heb. 11.9–10). For Abraham, the Promised Land was *not* the ultimate destination.

An Israeli Messianic Jewish view
Concerning the land of Israel, Israeli Messianic Jews situate themselves within the long and venerable tradition of their people. From the dispersion and exile in Second Temple times, Jewish people have continued to long for a return to the land of promise. As noted in the previous chapter on how Israeli Messianic Jews read the Scriptures, land is a key issue. The hope of the Jewish people was firstly eschatological, but not exclusively. The theme of return has always been present in Jewish liturgy and as such was a continual reminder that exile from the land was a temporary state of affairs. Jews, including Messianic Jews, deeply identify with this longing to return to the place of promise in the ancient land of the ancestors. This hope and longing is not merely emotion detached from reason or reality. God's promises to Abraham, Isaac and Jacob are experienced as truth for this day and are the theological underpinnings of the Israeli Messianic Jew's attachment to the land.

This was not always the case. During the two thousand years of exile, there were times when Jews assimilated and became comfortable in their host countries. Many assimilated Jews since the Enlightenment invested thoroughly in the life of their host countries, having accepted diasporic life as the norm. Orthodox and ultra-Orthodox Jews place themselves in juxtaposition to secular, assimilated Jews regarding their views of the land. Some groups of Orthodox Jews view the land as their home only when Messiah returns and Israel turns back to God. Others see it as their divine destiny to possess and 'redeem' the land today since it has been unconditionally given to the Jewish people. Zionism, both the religious and secular versions, has provided a contemporary rationale for the right of the Jewish people to claim the land as their own. While religious Zionism looks to the covenants and promises of God as the basis for their possession of the land, secular Zionism sees the land as a political necessity to ensure survival and human rights for the Jewish people. Israel Messianic Jews understand Zionism both as a nationalistic political movement and as a divine act in which God is bringing about the fulfilment of his covenant promises concerning return from exile and possession of the land.

Israeli Messianic Jews understand that the 'earth and its fullness'[16] are God's possession to do with what he wills. God is the ultimate owner of the land. He, being sovereign, has chosen to grant the land of Israel to the Jewish people, just as he has set boundaries for the other nations of the earth.[17] Today many Israelis, including most Messianic Jews, believe the land of Israel has been given by God to the Jewish people in perpetuity. Israel is the homeland. There is, however, no single Israeli view on the theological status of the land. Living in the land for the Israeli Messianic Jew is conceived in terms of destiny and prophetic fulfilment and has eschatological significance.[18]

A number of Israeli Messianic Jews have expressed themselves on the issue of the land of Israel. Messianic Jewish author David Stern writes, 'God promises the Land of Israel to the Jews. This promise has not been revoked, and, like all of God's promises, it will be fulfilled through our blessed Jewish Messiah'.[19] This unambiguous statement is representative of the understanding of the clear majority of the Israeli Messianic Jewish community.

Baruch Maoz is more nuanced in his approach to the land as he emphasizes the importance of the theme of land in the Hebrew Bible. For example, he notes that 'man and the earth are evidently so closely related that the latter partakes of the moral consequences of the former. When man sins, the earth becomes "corrupt"'.[20] He sees the biblical principles connected with land as being worked out in the history of Israel. Israel was meant to be an example from which the other nations of the world could learn. Israel was meant to always keep in mind that the land was the stage of its service to God. Yet, Maoz stresses, the land was a gift of God's grace as Deuteronomy 9.4–6 states, and he notes that when Israel was in

Egypt and not serving God, his gracious gift of the land was none-theless part of his plan for them. God's graciousness is also seen in Israel's lack of any inherent quality that merited God's grace (Deut. 7.7). Living in the land, Maoz states, implies obedience.[21] This view is held in varying degrees by a significant number of Messianic Jews.

Maoz notes that from the time of Israel's journey to the land, the people became so bound up with it that the two were often indeed indistinguishable. Furthermore, Maoz sees the New Testament as building on these foundations and never superseding the religion of the Old Testament, neither does he see Jesus as coming to annul it, but rather to fulfil it (Matt. 5.17). The implication of this for Maoz is that Israel remains 'a distinct nation in the purposes of God and [is] still to be a blessing in the world'.[22]

Maoz analyzes the relationship of the land and the covenantal expectations for living in it.[23] He argues that possession of the land has always been inextricably part of righteous living for Israel. There is no so-called 'right to the land' outside of the joyful constraints of covenant living. *How* Israel possesses the land is of great concern to God, and Israel's obstinate disobedience has resulted in the people's expulsion and exile from the land. Yet even God's discipline of Israel is an expression of his love. For the sake of his name among the nations, God longs for his people to return from exile to him. 'Any view of the present or future that assures Israel of possession of the land in spite of its sin misses the true burden of biblical prophecy. The prophets were concerned, as we should be, that the land should be filled with justice.'[24]

As a result, Maoz believes that partition of the land and terri-torial compromise are the way to ensure a lasting peace agree-ment for Israel-Palestine. This is in keeping with biblical accounts that rarely suggest that the people of Israel ever possessed what is now termed 'Greater Israel', stretching from the Nile to the Euphrates. Neither should territorial compromise be understood as a religious transgression, as is understood by some of the more extreme religious Zionists. This view allows Maoz to hold together some of his more characteristically Zionist theology which asserts that the land remains a divine promise to the Jews and that the land will yet play an intrinsic role as a vehicle of salvation for the nations. This is combined with the moral imperatives that are bound to that possession of the land. He is emphatic in stating that divine promises cannot and should not serve as a basis for a nationalist agenda. God alone brings what he has ordained into fruition.[25] Maoz's view concerning moral imperatives as a factor in Israel's possession of the land is not the majority view within the Messianic community. Maoz's understanding is seen as conditioning possession upon obedience, whereas the majority view sees the promises of Israel's ownership and possession of the land as unconditional. This issue needs to be more fully explored since ownership and possession are not equivalent concepts.

Covenants

A Palestinian Christian View

When Palestinian Christians address the issue of covenant, they often do so in reaction to Christian Zionism (and its approaches to the issues of the land and election) and their historical experience with Islam and Islam's understanding of law. Addressing various themes within covenant without looking at it as a whole concept, Palestinian theologians are wary of the implications of this topic. As we have a long history of living as a minority *dhimmi* population under Islamic autocratic regimes that use and misuse religious power for their own ends, we often approach this with caution and with an eye towards its implications. As a result, much Palestinian theological work on this subject focuses on the New Testament, emphasizing the centrality and importance of the cross instead of focusing on aspects of covenant in the Old Testament. Two evangelical theologians who have addressed this topic from different perspectives are Salim Munayer and Munther Isaac.

In Munayer's commentary on the book of Hosea, he looks at the narrative presented as a sign act or drama in which God discusses marriage as covenant. Faithfulness is a key issue of the covenant, and violation of faithfulness violates the covenant, calling for a new framework of relationship. Throughout the biblical text, we find that God chose to enter into a marriage covenant with the people of Israel and he remained a faithful husband in spite of Israel's infidelity. As a symbolic act that mirrored God's relationship with Israel, Hosea was instructed to marry a harlot, while knowing that this wife would be unfaithful. Despite the ensuing infidelity of Hosea's wife (and Israel), God and Hosea sought reconciliation. While it was his right to put Israel aside, God chose to remain committed and loving to Israel, demanding repentance in return. Yet the unfaithfulness of Israel and Hosea's wife had lasting consequences. Hosea's task was to live out God's love and calling with his adulterous wife, summoning Israel back into right relationship with God. With the people's repentance, God welcomes Israel into a new covenant of faithfulness and in this context renews his marriage commitment.[26]

Isaac examines the two concepts of covenant found in the Old Testament and its Ancient Near Eastern context, namely a covenant of grant, and a treaty, both of which are between a master and servant. God's covenants with Abraham and David are generally labeled covenants of grant, where a master makes a promise to his servant, obligating himself to a certain action. In contrast, God's covenant with Israel at Sinai as well as the framework of Deuteronomy indicate a treaty covenant, where a master imposes an obligation upon his servant. At Sinai, the obligation imposed on Israel is the law given to Moses.[27]

Isaac surveys positions regarding unconditionality and conditionality in terms of covenant, including the *dashna* concept in the Ancient Near Eastern context where a gift could be taken back by a benefactor. He argues that there is an element of this in the Davidic covenant (a grant), where what was previously viewed as unconditional was later qualified within the biblical text (for example, see 1 Kgs 2.3–4). Likewise, when God established covenants in terms of 'forever', it did not necessarily indicate that a covenant was unconditional. In 1 Samuel 2.30, God seemingly made an eternal promise to Eli, but then revoked it. Isaac argues that this should be understood as an emphatic statement and promise for an express purpose and task that has terms and conditions.[28]

Jesus' sacrifice in the New Covenant is central to understanding Palestinian Christians' views on the covenants. At the last supper, Jesus pours a cup of wine and says, 'This cup is the new covenant in my blood' (1 Cor. 11.25), which directs us to Jeremiah 31.31–33 and the prophet's discussion of a new covenant.

The writer of Hebrews quotes this passage and frames the quotations in asserting that 'in speaking of "a new covenant", he has made the first one obsolete' (Heb. 8.13). This new covenant involves the law dwelling within people's hearts and minds, and will, like the previous covenant, constitute a people. Like all the previous covenants, this new covenant is also an act of grace that requires a faithful response from all who hear its message. The salvation accomplished on the cross is both a radical new work of God and, at the same time, a coherent fulfilment of all that has gone before, bringing the covenants to completion. The Mosaic covenant is not abandoned nor made redundant; rather, Jesus brings the law to its full and proper consummation. In Jesus' own words, 'Do not think that I have come to abolish the law or the prophets; I have come not to abolish but to fulfil' (Matt. 5.17). Participation in this covenant is open to Jews and Gentiles alike, but it is through Christ alone, through his body and his blood of the new covenant.

An Israeli Messianic Jewish view

Historically, Judaism has seen the place of covenant as a central focus around which the relationship between God and Israel revolves. God's promises to the Jewish people are covenantal in nature. This implies a level of formal commitment by both parties; the first being the commitments made by the initiator of the covenant. In this case, we are referring to God himself who instituted the covenants with Israel. Covenants need to be understood in the context of the ancient Middle East. Much of what happened in terms of intergroup relationships was based on treaty or covenant between parties where one was the conquering power.

Judaism understands covenant as a metaphor for a relationship, with Torah as its essence, yet Torah is secondary to covenant. Covenant implies divine favour, collective human responsibility and vocation, and defines spiritual identity. All Israelites, regardless of gender or social status, are in a covenantal relationship with God that transcends intra-Jewish doctrinal differences. Covenant implies mission and has a visionary, eschatological dimension.[29] Although the view articulated above is taken from Jewish sources, it is the view held by the majority of Messianic Jews.

The issue of covenant is rightly seen as a subset of chosenness or divine election. God made covenants with those he chose to be his people, thereby confirming their divine election. He made no less than five covenants with Israel, including the new covenant, made with the house of Israel and the house of Judah, promised in Jeremiah 31.[30] The book of Hebrews (particularly Heb. 8.13) relates to the issue of covenant in the context of that 'new covenant', stating that the new has made the old obsolete. This statement needs to be seen in the wider New Testament context. Jesus lived a covenant-faithful life. He stated that he did not come to annul the Torah but to fulfil it (Matt. 5.17–20). Torah and covenant are inextricably linked since Torah was the God-ordained way for his people to live out the covenant. Obsolescence does not necessarily imply abolition. Fulfilment and completion retain the original, but in an expanded sense.

The new covenant of Jeremiah 31 is key in the understanding of Messianic Jews. The 'new' covenant could easily be translated as the 'renewed' covenant since there is no word in biblical Hebrew that distinguishes between new and renewed. Jesus' inauguration of the new covenant in his blood was a reaffirmation of the covenants of promise made with Israel. The covenants of promise were not replaced or abolished, but they were expanded to include non-Jews. Paul makes a distinction between '"covenants of promise" and covenants with commandments, but suggests the unconditional covenant made with Abraham and his offspring is the master covenant incorporating all the others (Eph 2.12–15; Gal 3.15–18)'.[31]

Messianic author David Stern's viewpoint is that all five biblical covenants remain in force today. This view is generally representative of many non-dispensationalist Messianic Jews. He points out that the Abrahamic covenant (Gen. 12 – 13; 15; 17) is an unconditional covenant 'except for the requirement of circumcision'.[32] Stern acknowledges that the New Testament teaching – which, according to Acts 15, sets forth more minimal conditions for the acceptance of Gentiles into the body of the Messiah – parallels the Noahide laws, with the definitive new covenant addition of faith in God through Jesus.

Stern sees this covenant as applying to Jews and Gentiles (in terms of God's vehicle of blessing the world) according to Romans 4 and Galatians 3: 'The Jewish people will one day bless the world in unprecedented ways.'[33] This covenantal expectation is also seen in Zechariah 8.23 where the prophet declares, 'Thus says the LORD of hosts: In those days ten men from nations of every language shall take hold of a Jew, grasping his garment and saying, "Let us go with you, for we have heard that God is with you."'

The Mosaic covenant, however, is conditional from the Jewish side, but not from God's side, 'for God is faithful even when his people are not' (Rom. 3.2–3).[34] Stern acknowledges that the Jewish people have broken that covenant (Jer. 31.31–32) and are currently the recipients of its curses, not its blessings (Deut. 28). When Jews are obedient to the covenant, God will bless them as a nation. Stern stresses, however, that the Torah 'supplied under this covenant was given forever and never abolished, and that Torah is still in force'.[35] Stern sees God's covenant with David (2 Sam. 7) as having been fulfilled in Yeshua as the Son of David and the one who will ascend the throne 'in the Father's good time' (Acts 1.6–7; Rev. 20.2–6).[36] Lastly, God's new covenant with the house of Israel and the house of Judah (Jer. 31.30–34) is seen as complementing the earlier covenants rather than annulling them (Gal. 3).[37]

For the most part, Israeli Messianic Jews agree with Stern's basic understanding of the continued validity and effectiveness of all five of the biblical covenants, even if some disagree on varying details. The issue of Torah observance as a sign of Jewish covenantal faithfulness is less prevalent among Israeli Messianic Jews than among their Diaspora brethren. There is, however, a growing movement among numbers of Israeli Messianic Jews toward a theology that affirms their Jewish religious identity as well as their national Israeli identity.

Dan Juster analyzes the covenants, concluding that they should be seen as exhibiting an essential unity as covenants of grace.[38] He affirms the ongoing validity of covenant for Israel and the Messianic Jew today. Following an examination of covenant and dispensationalist theologies and their biblical rationales, he proposes:

> a Messianic theology that expresses itself in the unity of the covenants of grace. It is a theology that recognizes the Jewish context of the whole Bible . . . that reaffirms the call of the nation of Israel as God's chosen nation along with God's call of the universal people of God within the New Covenant . . . Fulfillment does not eliminate the past.[39]

Messianic Jews, both Israeli and diasporic, unanimously affirm an understanding of the continuing context of covenant as the basis of their relationship with the God of their ancestors in the person of Jesus. However, in Messianic circles today, the place of Torah as expressing this relationship in covenantal faithfulness remains a hotly debated issue.

Justice

Biblical justice
'Justice' is a core issue in the conflict between Palestinian Christians and Israeli Messianic Jews. We will first look at justice from a biblical perspective. Following this, we will discuss some aspects of justice and lastly we will briefly look at the subject from the perspective of both communities.

There is no one Hebrew word that can be directly translated as 'justice'. The concept is larger than any single word. For this reason, the Old Testament uses two words to describe justice: *tsedeq* and *mishpat*. *Tsedeq* is generally translated 'righteousness', but the concept it represents is nuanced to include vindication, judgement, justice and justification. *Mishpat* is generally translated 'judgement' or 'justice', but it also represents a broad concept including vindication of the oppressed, requital, vengeance, or the retributive justice of God.[40] Together, these words indicate righteous judgement, which in effect is equivalent to the English word 'justice'. *Tsedeq* and *mishpat* are both crucial to and support healthy human relationships within community. Both concepts are important to a vision of *shalom* (peace). They are necessary for the relationship between people and God and for the just structuring of society. These concepts of justice were precisely what God's covenant with his people sought to establish. Additionally, covenant envisions justice inextricably connected to *hesed* (mercy). Mercy and justice are usually perceived as antithetical concepts. However, the Scriptures often bring the two concepts together in order to highlight the close relationship between the two.[41] With these three aspects of justice – *tsedeq/mishpat, hesed*, leading to *shalom* – we gain a richer picture of what the Bible conceives of as right communal ordering: 'Generally, the righteous person in Israel is the one who preserves the peace and wholeness of the community by fulfilling the demands of communal living.'[42]

God has always been concerned for justice, both for the individual and for the community at large. The Scriptures, both Old and New Testaments, express a vision of justice in which God calls his people to live justly and to administer social justice. The social aspect is reflected throughout the Scripture as the God-ordained, necessary framework in which the community can live together in harmony and stability. Justice was such a primary concern that God's people were expected to represent his character as they administered his justice. It was not a light or peripheral issue. Those who dispensed God's judgement and executed his justice were standing in his place before the people. 'You should also look for able men among all the people, men who fear God, are trustworthy, and hate dishonest gain' (Exod. 18.21a). They were also expected to be impartial as they administered justice. 'I charged your judges at that time: "Give the members of your community a fair hearing, and judge rightly between one person and another, whether citizen or resident alien. You must not be partial in judging: hear out the small and the great alike; you shall not be intimidated by anyone, for the judgement is God's"' (Deut. 1.16–17a). The teachings of Jesus and Paul both emphasize the importance of godly character (holiness) as a requisite for harmonious life together. While reflecting on the Sermon on the Mount, Richard Hayes, in his opus *The Moral Vision of the New Testament*, concludes that its teachings 'specify the character of a community that seeks to embody the eschatological vision of God's righteousness.'[43]

God's justice is always redemptive. The primary motivation for his justice is to bring about redemption or restoration. Sin has ravaged the relationships between God and humanity, and between human beings. Those broken relationships need God's action to be restored or healed. God is ultimately a redeemer who, at great cost, takes that which was broken, restores it and brings it back to a state of wholeness. God's purposes are based in love. It is important to state this as axiomatic before we proceed to a discussion of specific aspects of biblical justice. The Old Testament's vision of justice involves many facets of meaning and function; we will explore several of these.

When God executes judgement (*mishpat*) on behalf of the oppressed and against the oppressor, he extends saving help to both. When 'God executes judgment in order to call Israel to return to him . . . *mishpat* as judgment is the precursor to repentance . . . In this sense, judgment is also an act of hope . . . God both strikes and heals, and strikes in order to heal.'[44] God's judgement exposes sin as sin and upholds the right against the wrong. A choice is then extended to the one judged, giving opportunity to either continue in sin or change and accept God's healing, and his agency on the part of the judged. Divine justice always condemns sin. An example of this is the exodus narrative that shows God's judgement of Egypt and the liberation of the children of Israel. God used Israel's liberation to hold them accountable for future action. When they entered the land of Canaan they were to obey God's command to care for the alien, the poor, the widow and the orphan among them. They were to remember their marginalized status and bondage in Egypt.

Biblical justice involves mercy[45] as well as retribution, vengeance, punishment and judgement. While mercy is extended to the guilty, it never obscures the *rightness* of righteousness. There is no moral equivocation or ambivalence within the economy of God's justice. God's mercy towards the unjust preserves clear moral standards and does not preclude punishment.

Biblical justice includes *restitution and repayment*. Exodus 22 outlines the particular 'laws of restitution' for various offences. Isaiah 59.17–18 portrays a righteous God who repays (*shalem*) the unjust with his wrath. *Shalem* is also used in Joel 2.23–25, but to describe God repaying his people with mercy after the damage caused by his punishment. As Keith Regehr puts it, 'In an act of mercy for the offender, peace (*shalom*) is the repayment (*shillum*) that God offers.'[46] In Psalm 62.12, *shalem* suggests repayment for any behaviour, whether good or evil: 'For you repay (*shalem*) to all according to their work.' Repayment therefore can be an expression of God's judgement but also of his mercy and faithfulness to the covenant.

Biblical justice also encompasses *vindication and vengeance*. In numerous examples, God takes vengeance against oppressors on behalf of the oppressed, in much the same way as he acts against the Egyptians on Israel's behalf after their long enslavement. In so doing, God vindicates the oppressed, giving testimony to their innocence, and demonstrating the oppressors' guilt. Vindication and vengeance are distinct from vindictiveness. Vindication is an act of judgement that upholds the innocence of the victim in contrast to the guilt of the oppressor. Divine vengeance is a form of justice-inspired harm caused to the offender, with the intention of bringing about a change and re-establishing justice. Vindictiveness, on the other hand, is the desire to cause harm for the sake of harm, without a vision of restoration. God's justice is never vindictive.

Biblical justice includes *retribution and punishment*, in which offenders receive what they deserve. The 'eye for eye' calculations of Exodus 21 indicate the exact punishments for violence and crime; the 'law of retaliation establishes the principle that the offender is to suffer the same injury as the victim'.[47] The aim of this type of retributive justice is to ensure that there is balance in justice. This also has a limiting quality: only an eye for an eye, not two eyes for an eye, separating the proper measure of justice from the unbridled desire for revenge. God's just actions can also involve retribution: 'God takes up the cause of the one who has suffered, and rebalances the moral universe'.[48]

The Greek word used in the New Testament for justice is *dikaios*, commonly translated 'righteousness'. An unfortunate hermeneutical misunderstanding can arise from translating this word as 'righteousness'. The impression can be given that the New Testament emphasizes *individual* righteousness at the expense of social righteousness, or social justice.[49] Glen Stassen argues that righteousness is often understood as 'something like self-righteousness. [But] Jesus and Paul often criticized self-righteousness'.[50] Yet, Stassen says, communal justice and righteousness are part of the same fabric and must be exemplified in concrete, living ways.

While Jesus' ministry cannot be characterized solely in social justice terms, he was concerned for the weak and marginalized in society. He consorted with 'publicans and sinners' while criticizing the religious authorities for their misplaced concern for ceremonial minutiae rather than attending to matters of justice, righteousness and mercy (Luke 11.42). Jesus seems fully aware of the injustices of the reigning powers and freely disregards many of the social taboos of the time, healing and casting out demons on the Sabbath and associating with women, fishermen, Samaritans, tax collectors and prostitutes; forgiving their sins and restoring them to rightful living in society. In so doing, Jesus exposes the injustices of the dominant social orders and defends sinners, releasing them from the burden of sin and bidding them to carry out Jesus' liberating mission in the world.

Ultimately, viewed through the lens of justice, Christ's passion and death on the cross are both God's judgement upon sin – exposing sin and death for what they are, for their vicious grip on the social orders of the world – and the means by which God rescues, justifies and vindicates sinners, bringing them into restored relationships with himself and others. As the fullest picture of God's righteousness and justice, the cross simultaneously represents God's judgement, mercy, forgiveness and grace. In the unredeemed mind, the *justice* of the cross stands as a grave *injustice*: the innocent sufferer who dies on behalf of the sinful many. But paradoxically, it is the fullest expression of God's righteous justice towards his beloved creation. As Miroslav Volf puts it, there 'is a profound "injustice" about the God of the biblical tradition. It is called *grace*.'[51]

Palestinian Christians and justice
The Palestinian Christian approach to justice is one that attempts not only to address the inequity on the ground, but also to explore the ideological origins of these injustices. Palestinian Christian intellectuals maintain that Western and Israeli views of the Arab people, particularly the Palestinians, have continually led to policy and theology that is at best unaware and at worst unjust.

General influences
One prominent Palestinian intellectual who has influenced the Palestinian Christian approach to the conflict and justice is Edward W. Said. He changed the face of Middle Eastern studies with his 1978 book, *Orientalism*. This work challenged what then were the current methods of examining the Middle East (traditionally called the Orient by Western scholars), which he believed to be more 'a sign of European-Atlantic power over the Orient than it is a verdict discourse about the Orient'.[52] According to Said, Middle Eastern studies have been laced with an elusive Eurocentric predisposition

that views the Arab people, especially the Muslim majority, in a negative light. This understanding of the world – the Occidental superior and the Oriental inferior – has greatly but subtly influenced European and American societies, both in decision-making concerning political and military matters and in the theology embraced by religious institutions. Included in this scope of dogma is an ambivalent attitude towards Arab national aspiration, namely that of the Palestinian people. Alongside being an advocate for this cause, Said's work has shed light on why there has been doubt and inconsistency from the West towards Palestinian nationalism and desire for justice. Injustices are not just byproducts of strategic military and economic desires involving the Middle East, but are part of an all-encompassing, interwoven mindset in which the Arab peoples are viewed negatively.

While Said broadly focuses on how the West's generally negative perception of the Arab people creates injustice, contemporary Palestinian theologian Mitri Raheb specifically addresses how theology comes into play in matters affecting the Palestinian people. His assessment is that religious ideology concerning the land is so influential that it has not only entered into politics but has tainted our understanding of history. Raheb attests that traditionally, historians, archeologists and even Zionist leaders were persuaded that the local population of Palestine was a continual and integral part of the land. He cites that Marxist Zionist leader Ber Borochov, who strongly advocated for a Jewish state in *Eretz Israel* and even Israel's first prime minister, Ben Gurion, believed that the native population had not been drastically demographically affected by the various wars that had plagued the area down through the ages.[53] This inclusive idea did not survive in the development of Zionism, nor did it find its way into Christian perception of the events taking place in the land through the Zionist movement. Instead, both Zionism and certain Christian circles saw these events as fulfilment of prophecy, 'equating God's beloved people of the Bible with a contemporary group . . . as if there were no thirty centuries of history between'.[54] Many Palestinians believe that this perception of the Jews as a group, racially consistent with those who left Judea in the first century, is a myth. Raheb reinforces this idea by quoting Israeli historian Shlomo Sand's statement that, through nationalist aspirations, Judaism ceased to be 'a rich and diverse religious civilization [and] became an ancient people or race that was uprooted from its homeland'.[55]

The belief system in which the Jews are the only inheritors of the land can leave the fate of its non-Jewish residents as an inconsequential detail. As this ideology influences the policy of governments and the direction of the funds of Christian groups, the Palestinian people have been subject to persecution and neglect connected to the denial of their identity and their continual presence in the land. In 2009, Palestinian Christians from various denominations were inspired to challenge the concept that privilege based on race is an idea belonging to the Christian faith.

Prominent Palestinian theologians across denominational lines formulated the Palestine Kairos Document, which has become a defining document for Palestinian Christians. This document has drawn engagement, study and discussion across denominational lines as well as served as a basis for dialogue within the international Christian community, and even within some Jewish-Christian dialogue groups. As part of the Kairos Document, Palestinian Christian leaders encouraged the world's believers to no longer 'attach a biblical and theological legitimacy to the infringement of [Palestinian] rights' and to instead 'see the Word of God as a source of life for all peoples'.[56]

The subtle, negative attitude towards Arab Muslims became intertwined with Western political and military interests. This, together with the development of Zionism as a response to Jewish suffering in Europe and its resulting Christian Zionist theology, has created a religious-political background that has resulted in continual rejection of Palestinian national aspirations. This mindset has made it easier to delegitimize, or at least overlook, the consequences that any action would have for the Palestinian people. Their displacement and suffering can be disregarded because it is seen in light of a higher aim of bringing the 'original' people back to their land. To Palestinian Christians, addressing elements of oppression and inequality only addresses the surface issue. Achieving justice will therefore not truly be achieved if we only address the injustices themselves; instead we must embark on an extensive process of transforming the mentalities that lead to these very injustices.

Justice is the most important issue for all Palestinians in the Israeli–Palestinian conflict. Palestinians live with the pervasive sense that justice has eluded them for decades. As we discussed in the early chapters of this book, the Palestinian sense of injustice goes back to the Ottoman Empire, the Balfour Declaration, the British mandate, the UN Partition Plan, the Nakba and their betrayal by the surrounding Arab countries. It continues to this day with Israeli occupation and ongoing Western ambivalence towards the Palestinian plight.

Honest Palestinians acknowledge that throughout history Jews as a people have suffered enormous, organized injustices, especially during the horrific nadir of Nazi Germany. The Zionist movement was grounded in 'the right of every nation to self-determination, on the Jews' historical connection to the land of Israel and, as the tipping point, the persecution of the Jews in the 19th and 20th centuries.'[57] The historic, unjust suffering of the Jewish people is a key aspect of the Zionist claim to the land. The problem is that this expression of Israeli national self-determination, Palestinians argue, came at the expense of the Palestinian people, inflicting *them* with unjust suffering. As Chaim Gans suggests, the United Nations Partition Plan did not allow for the price to be paid by those who actually committed the atrocities against the Jews.[58] Consequently, Palestinians feel they have been forced to pay a debt they themselves never incurred. Moreover, Palestinians argue that there are systemic, structural injustices within the Israeli political system, both in the state as well as in the administration of the occupied territories. Many Palestinians would say that the state of Israel was conceived in injustice and continues to operate unjustly.

Palestinian liberation theology

Palestinian Christians ground their arguments about justice from the Bible, and analyze their current situation through a distinctly biblical lens. Recalling the centrality of justice for Palestinian Christians, Palestinian liberation theology most strongly articulates the Palestinian Christian position on justice. Like other liberation theologies, it arose as a reaction to a situation of conflict and injustice in order to address a growing need within the Christian community. It also developed as a way to counter arguments made by Christian Zionists that utilize a particular fundamentalist reading of the biblical texts to justify some of the current actions by the state of Israel. As previously discussed in the chapter on Palestinian hermeneutics, in *Justice, and Only Justice,*[59] Naim Ateek sets his exegesis within a christological and progressive hermeneutic that understands earlier sections of Scripture to be a cruder and more nationalistic form of revelation. Ateek considers later passages to be a more accurate expression of God's will since they exhibit a more universal form of revelation.

According to Ateek, the God represented in the book of Joshua represents a regression to a primal and nationalist conception of God that has been superseded by what we now know of God's nature through Christ. This hermeneutic renders certain passages in Joshua obsolete; these and similar passages are useful only insofar as they give a window into the historical progression of how people have conceived of God. However, it is a universalistic notion of God, such as is found in the prophets and the narrative of Christ's life and death for all humanity, that more accurately reflects God's nature. The same interpretation is true with respect to the land: '[I]f God loves this land and this people, that is a sign – a sacrament – that God loves each and every land and its peoples.'[60]

Having set out his hermeneutical key, Ateek examines the question of justice both as an overarching biblical theme and in light of the Israel–Palestine conflict. He asserts that biblical justice is both a virtue to possess and a relationship to maintain. God carries out acts of justice and is himself just. God's people are to apply themselves to a similar end as part of their worshipful response to God's own nature and activities. Injustice and inattention to matters of justice, in fact, negate the worship of a people (Isa. 1.11–17; Jer. 6.20). For social and political life, right worship will also be found alongside right behaviour, with a special emphasis on serving those on the margins of society. According to the prophets, God's heart is attuned to the needs of widows, orphans and strangers.

The liberation of these people becomes the centre of the church's social agenda, around which one is to formulate and influence social policies. Liberation theologies have a direct political expression, and political advocacy is a practical expression of this kind of life in God. For Ateek, peace is the fruit of justice; justice must precede peace. The cross shows not only the costliness of such peace but also God's judgement on sin and injustice in the world.

The proper responses to the costly work of the cross are to love one's neighbour and pursue justice for the poor and the oppressed.

As we began, we return to what many Palestinians, not just Palestinian Christians, would say is the serious lack of justice in their lives and homeland. Palestinians want justice and vindication in the face of the suffering they feel they have experienced at the hands of Israelis. And Israelis, while less inclined to talk about justice, are loath to admit to injustices they may have perpetrated if all they hear is a Palestinian desire for vengeance, for 'hurling the Jews into the sea'. True justice is desperately needed within the Israeli–Palestinian conflict; and while we will not admit to moral equivalencies, nevertheless, each side still has distinct claims for justice on their behalf from which they are not likely to part. Israelis and Palestinians, along with Israeli Messianic Jews and Palestinian Christians, need justice – a flexible, morally decisive, retributive and restorative, even merciful and loving justice – to flourish.

Messianic Jewish responses to the question of justice

While there is substantial output from Palestinian Christians on the subject of justice, it has been much neglected in Messianic Jewish writings. The issue of justice is a daily reality for the Palestinian community, whereas it is not a part of daily life and is therefore simply less directly relevant to the Israeli Messianic Jewish community. In our context of intractable conflict, justice is perceived as the primary concern for Palestinians whereas security is perceived as the primary concern for Israelis. This fundamental difference in perception seriously complicates theological dialogue and reflection. When working towards reconciliation, justice must become a more germane question for this community. Messianic Jewish theological reflection has focused on issues of Torah, eschatology and prophecy, as well as on social questions like abortion and humanitarian aid. Yet, given the theological attention afforded prophecy, eschatology and the purported theological underpinnings of the modern state of Israel, the Messianic Jewish community can and must do more to attend to the questions of justice posed within those very same veins of biblical thought. That is, prophetic moves of God have also always been expressions of his righteous justice. Even if the case is made that

Palestinians come under the category of 'strangers' in the land – a label that Palestinian Christians categorically reject – the God of Israel has much to say about how they are to be treated. How much more then are the residents of the land to be well treated.

Despite the meager contributions of Messianic Jewish thought to date on the question of justice, there are some exceptions. Daniel Juster, an Israeli-American Messianic Jew who resides in Israel, explores the promises given to the Jewish people regarding the land of Israel. His view is that biblical justice is not divorced from God's election of Israel; it is also not the *source* of present-day injustice. Rather, Israel's election in God is the foundation upon which Israel must pursue justice for the poor and neglected, for the outcast and the refugee. Israel's election, which includes the land promises, is of one piece with its vocation to be a light to the nations. The people of Israel have repeatedly failed in this vocational charge; but, from an eschatological perspective, the notion of Israel's election and vocation for justice are unchanged and must continue to be implemented.

Juster notes that influences of secular humanism have obfuscated a proper understanding of justice as a 'leveling equality'. He clarifies for the reader the difference between biblical justice and its modern secular counterpart. Biblical justice, Juster notes, is not reducible to equality.[61] The biblical ethos does provide equality for all as equally created in God's image before 'courts for crime, punishment, and restitution'. This equality, however, does not transfer to all aspects of individuals' 'gifts, talents, and callings.'[62] Juster then offers his definition of justice, as 'that order of righteousness whereby individuals and peoples can fulfill their God intended destinies'.[63] Juster makes the logical transition from individual destinies to corporate ones. Biblical justice is then defined, in the context of his discussion on corporate destinies, as *God's declared will for Israel and the nations*.[64] In the online book, 'The Law of Messiah Compiled as Mitzvot', Juster expresses his general view of justice:

> The Gospel is God's means of establishing justice. Micah summarized it well in his great verse that answers the question, '. . . *what does the* LORD *require of you but to do justice, and to love kindness, and to walk humbly with your God?'* (Micah 6:8 RSV) God has not changed. All

of the instruction of God is to be understood as the details of how to live out love for God and our fellows. In the Bible, love and justice are not opposed, but could be seen as a hyphenated word, 'love-justice'. When the law is broken, justice is satisfied by blood sacrifice or by paying the penalty. Love requires restitution to the one wronged; if the offender is truly repentant, this is his desire. God's love-justice provides the sacrifice of Yeshua so He can be both just and the justifier of those who are in Yeshua.[65]

In the instance of Israel, Juster notes that God's will is grounded in his covenant and sovereign election of Abraham.[66] In his discussion of the Israeli–Palestinian conflict, Juster argues that an unbiblical and humanistic version of justice limits its assessment of the conflict to its national and sympathetic components:

> It begins with the issue of empathy for the displaced Palestinian Arabs, who, in some cases, have had roots in the land for generations. It also begins with empathy for the Jews, who understandably need a homeland after so much suffering and persecution. How do we balance the claims of the Palestinian population and the refugees against the claim of the Jews, who have ancient roots in this land but have only returned in significant numbers over the last hundred-plus years – in some cases after being forced from Arab lands without any compensation for their loss?[67]

Juster appeals to the faith community to shun the type of reasoning embodied in the above citation, which he sees as characteristic of the unredeemed institutions of the nations. More specifically, Juster states that a humanistic and unbiblical assessment is expressed by a disproportionate emphasis on the suffering of both Palestinians and Jews, and the relative merits of their pleas for justice on the basis of their suffering. While not diminishing the importance of engaging biblical ethics related to human suffering, its root causes and relationships, Juster insists that one's analysis must include the idea that 'consequences result from failure to submit to the revealed will of God'.[68]

Juster applies this principle to both the Jewish and the Palestinian peoples. If the Jewish people fail to submit to the law of God, and replace it with human laws that contradict God's law, they will encounter God's resistance and consequently will experience suffering. In like manner, if Palestinians 'refuse to recognize what God says about the Jewish people and their connection to the land of Israel, then suffering will result'.[69]

Juster argues that the faulty reasoning concerning justice as equality or merely civil rights is a sad shadow of what true justice is meant to be. The conflict over the land is not simply about balancing the claims of Jews and their suffering against the claims of Palestinians and their suffering. Rather, for Juster, justice will reign when all are living in accordance with God's will, all fulfilling their particular callings. His interpretation of Scripture leads him to believe that the current state of Israel is in continuity with the Israelites of the Bible, and that the land of Palestine is consequently the legitimate property of contemporary Jewish people. He suggests that if the Palestinians do not acknowledge God's election of ethnic Israel and their rightful land claims, then they are questioning the foundation upon which their own possibility for national blessing rests:

> Justice in regard to the Land requires that there be a submission to what God has declared about this Land. The attainment of the Jewish people to their destiny in this Land opens the way for all nations to attain their inheritance. This is connected to Israel's priesthood. So if the Palestinians do not acknowledge God's promise, they are foundationally unjust and are themselves resisted by God and lose their rights in this Land. This resistance spreads to the other nations of the world, particularly those who are involved in resisting God's purposes for the Land, resulting in judgment for all the nations and a general blockage for all to obtain their inheritance.[70]

Juster would say that the nations will be judged according to their attitude towards Israel – the state and the people – and that Israel will be judged according to its attitude to God and his covenant. He does go on to say that everyone – Jews and non-Jews – are accountable for their actions and that Israelis are accountable for the way they treat foreigners, i.e. Palestinians, in their midst.

Juster is not the only voice representing Israeli Messianic Jewish reflections on social justice. Baruch Maoz, an Israeli Messianic Jewish pastor and a self-identified Zionist, has sought to integrate

Israel's election with the moral demands of the covenant. Maoz expresses his views of justice according to an eschatological understanding of the modern state of Israel and its covenantal expectations:

> Any theory of eschatology that weakens Israel's sense of moral responsibility towards others is faulty. Nor can it serve Israel's true interests: the Jewish people have twice been sent out of the land because their society had become cruel, unjust and ungodly. Any view of the present or future that assures Israel of possession of the land in spite of its sin misses the true burden of biblical prophecy. The prophets were concerned, as we should be, that the land should be filled with justice.[71]

Maoz, as does Ateek, affirms that only God can bring about absolute justice, the kind of justice that provides eschatological hope and which should motivate Israeli and Palestinian believers *now* and govern their choices *today*. Following Jesus humbly in service to others – believers and non-believers – is God's calling for his people.

Maoz notes that justice in the Bible was not a juridic abstraction, but rather was expressed in concrete circumstances in the form of case-law. He then stresses the moral requirement that God expected of Israel in order to be able to live in the land, and that this obligation was also true for the nations of the world wherever God had apportioned them their inheritance.

Lastly, Messianic Jewish theologian Richard Harvey has written an important contribution in a chapter entitled, 'Toward a Messianic Jewish Theology of Reconciliation in the Light of the Arab-Israeli Conflict'.[72] In this article, Harvey proposes discussion between the Messianic Jewish and Arab-Christian community in the context of the Middle East conflict. Harvey does not shy away from affirming that the difficult questions, including the issue of justice, need to be discussed between both communities. He also stresses the need for Messianic Jews to pursue justice, peace and reconciliation.[73]

Each 'side' – both Palestinian and Israeli – struggles to determine if and how one engages the other side's perceived grievances. Palestinian Christians have traditionally sought to articulate a theology of justice to make sense of their suffering. They see their place in the narrative as the unjustly vanquished and work to understand what the biblical narrative holds for them beyond biblically ordained ethnic defeat. Messianic Jews have tradition-ally articulated their theologies from the starting point of escha-tology, particularly Israel's eschatological triumph over its foes, buttressed by a lengthy narrative of national suffering. Clearly, these hermeneutical approaches conflict. They accentuate the pressing need for some kind of theological dialogue between these communities that might pave the way for reconciliation. Ideally, this theology would also address the concerns of both communi-ties as a part of that reconciling process.

Other Theological Frameworks that Affect Our Communities

We have briefly identified a few of the major theological conten-tions between the Messianic Jewish and Palestinian Christian communities. In addition, at times our discussions have touched on dispensationalism and liberation theology. Two other theol-ogies that affect our communities are supersessionism, and dual-covenant theology.

Supersessionism

Supersessionism (replacement theology), the idea that the church has replaced Israel as God's people, is rejected by the Messianic (and the wider) Jewish community. Within the Palestinian Chris-tian community, attitudes towards supersessionism vary greatly. While some Palestinian Christians openly embrace superses-sionism, others reject it entirely or certain aspects of it.[74] Superses-sionism has been the predominant view in Western church history since it was first adopted by the church fathers, most of whom polemicized against 'Judaism'. Throughout the history of the church, some extreme forms of supersessionism have contributed to anti-Semitism and violent actions against the Jews, including the myth of blood libel, the accusation that Jews engage in human sacrifice as part of their ritual practices.

'Softer' versions of supersessionism try to articulate the uniqueness of the Christian faith and the church's understanding of
radical discontinuity of the Old Testament promises to the people
of Israel, in light of the cross within salvation history. In order
to refrain from labelling all supersessionist theologians as necessarily (or even determinatively) anti-Semitic, it is important that
we define what is meant by supersessionism. Many Christians
who embrace softer versions of supersessionism love and pray for
the Jewish people in the hope that they will experience a national
spiritual regeneration resulting in their acceptance of Yeshua as
their Messiah. They also seek to formulate their theology in a
manner that does justice to the incarnation and the implications
of that event for their understanding of the identity of the people
of God.

Kendall Soulen identifies three types of supersessionism operative within Christian theology: punitive, economic and structural.[75] Punitive supercessionism, espoused by Origen, and
Martin Luther, among others, argues that Jews who reject Jesus
as the Messiah are thereby condemned by God and so forfeit their
place in the covenant and, consequently, the covenantal promises. In 'On the Jews and Their Lies', Luther employs vituperative
language to blame the Jews for the death of Christ, going so far as
to legitimize and provide theological justification for anti-Semitic
attitudes and policies:

> There is no other explanation for this than the one cited earlier from
> Moses, namely, that God has struck them with 'madness and blind-
> ness and confusion of mind.' So we are even at fault in not avenging
> all this innocent blood of our Lord and of the Christians which they
> shed for three hundred years after the destruction of Jerusalem, and
> the blood of the children they have shed since then (which still shines
> forth from their eyes and their skin). We are at fault in not slaying
> them. Rather we allow them to live freely in our midst despite their
> murdering, cursing, blaspheming, lying, and defaming.[76]

The second type of supersessionism is economic supersessionism,
which sees the Jewish people as the now-defunct vehicle of salvation for the nations, a function that has now been assumed by
the church. In contrast to punitive supersessionism, economic

supersessionism accounts for their replacement, not by virtue of their unique sinfulness in rejecting Christ as Messiah, but rather because the Jews have completed their role in God's salvific plan. The church is now the main protagonist in the narrative of salvation. Soulen writes, 'According to economic supersessionism, Israel is transient not because it happens to be sinful but because Israel's essential role in the economy of redemption is to prepare for salvation in its spiritual and universal form'.[77] Economic supersessionism says that Israel's role has served its purpose.

Finally, structural supersessionism refers to the standard narrative logic in which the Hebrew Scriptures become marginalized for shaping Christian theology. This form of supersessionism structures the biblical narrative in a way that portrays Israel's history 'as nothing more than the *economy of redemption in prefigurative form*'.[78] As Soulen points out, if one follows the logic of structural supersessionism to its natural end, the whole of the biblical canon as it stands is 'largely indecisive' for Christian faith. Because of the irrelevance of Israel's interactions with God, the canonical story of Israel and its relationship with the God of Israel has little or nothing to say about how that same God continues to interact within human history in general. Structural supersessionism is not only a politically incorrect posture to adopt in post-Holocaust chastened Christianity; it also posits a troubling theological incoherence in the biblical foundation for Christian faith.

Throughout church history, theologians and leaders have made use of one or more supersessionist approaches, often resulting in detrimental effects not only for the Jewish people but also for God's intention for the body of Messiah, constituted of Jews and Gentiles. From the time of the Roman Empire, which fused political imperialism with the Christian faith, Jews have suffered at the hands of the Christian West. What was established was not so much a city of God as an intolerant religio-political regime that placed the Jews in negative theological space, as a condemned and rejected people. This anti-Semitism has sadly characterized Western Christianity. In contrast, Eastern Christians cultivated a different historical dynamic with the Jewish people, one that is arguably more positive, though not without its share of misunderstandings and conflict. The problematic racist theological teaching concerning Jews characteristic of the West was not necessarily embraced by the Christians of the Middle East, nor did it become integral to their understanding.

Nevertheless, the events of the *Shoah* (Holocaust)[79] signified a marked change in global Christian thinking about the Jewish people. Daniel Rossing, founder of the Jerusalem Center for Jewish-Christian Relations, commented on Jewish-Christian relations in Israel today:

> Although in the modern era of 'enlightenment', reason and increasing secularization of Western society Christianity lost much of the direct political power and influence it had enjoyed for a millennia and a half, its centuries-old anti-Judaism remained largely unchallenged and eventually combined with modern 'scientific' racial theories to lay the foundations for the Holocaust. The Shoah in the heart of a continent that had been Christian-dominated for nearly two millennia was physically devastating for the Jewish people and left many Christians with a deep and painful sense of their own spiritual and moral bankruptcy.[80]

Most of European Christianity demonstrated moral and theological silence and complacency during the horrors of the Nazi era. Consequently, this called the legitimacy of their theology into question. Yet the prevailing sense of guilt among Western theologians following the Shoah also provided fresh ground for new theological understandings of the Jewish people.

Dual-covenant theology

Another response to the historical interaction between the church and the Jewish people is the development of 'dual-covenant theology'; namely, that there are two distinct and separate covenants for Jews and Gentiles. Although the twelfth-century Jewish theologian Maimonides admitted that 'Jesus the Christian' had a kind of legitimate, divinely appointed role among Gentiles (and so, arguably, may have held something akin to this view), it was advanced chiefly by Franz Rosenzweig, a twentieth-century Jewish theologian. Rosenzweig developed the notion that affirmed Jesus' salvific significance for the non-Jew but not for the Jews, who already enjoyed covenant relationship with God. He writes, 'We are wholly agreed as to what Christ and his church mean to the world: no one can reach the Father save through him. No one can reach the Father! But the situation is quite different for the one who does not have to reach the Father because he is already with him. And this is true of the people of Israel'.[81] Jews are saved, argued Rosenzweig, by virtue of their existing covenant with God. This arrangement was attractive to Jews and Christians alike. It framed the Jewish–Christian relationship in a neutral way. And, in light of the history of Christian anti-Semitism, especially the palpable guilt of the Holocaust, some Christians have embraced dual-covenant theology as a kind of psychological 'overcompensation' intended to restore their relationship with the Jewish people.[82]

While there is little doubt that certain forms of supersessionism contributed to the Shoah, dual-covenant theology is certainly not an adequate response to rid Christianity of these problematic theological formulations. Nowhere in the Bible is Jesus' redemptive activity depicted as exclusively for non-Jews. Paul himself, in fact, speaks of his anguish and sorrow concerning his fellow Jews' non-acceptance of Jesus' Messiahship (Rom. 9.1–3). Moreover, while the earliest Jewish Yeshua-believers in the nascent apostolic community struggled to make sense of how to integrate Gentiles within the predominantly Jewish faith community, there was never a question that the unity of the message of Jesus was intended for Jews as well as for Gentiles. Salvation is *from* the Jews (John 4.22), through the Jewish Messiah, the God of Israel. If he is God at all, he is also, of necessity, the God of the nations. Dual-covenant theology, while trying to find a way past the acrimony between Judaism and Christianity, does not fairly represent either faith, or what each faith claims about itself.

Dispensationalism

A dispensationalist reading of Scripture sees a series of chronological 'dispensations' or eras in history within the biblical narrative. In these dispensations, God involves himself in human affairs in different ways and under different covenants. The classical separation subdivides biblical history into seven main sections, the time of innocence from creation to the fall (Gen. 1 – 3), the time of conscience from the fall to the flood (Gen. 3 – 8), the time of human government from the flood to the call of Abraham (Gen. 9 – 11), the time of promise from the calling of Abraham to the giving of the law at Sinai under Moses (Gen. 11 – Exod. 19), the time of the law from Sinai to Calvary (Ex. 20 – Acts 1), the time of grace from Calvary to the kingdom (Acts 2 – Rev. 20), and the time of the kingdom and the thousand-year Messianic reign (Rev. 20 – 22).[83]

By viewing Scripture as unveiling a series of events, dispensationalists also tend to understand Scripture as revealing salvation *history*, from creation to the end times. Consequently, the Hebrew Scriptures are seen as key to interpreting the rest of Scripture. (The Palestinian Christian community, by contrast, tends to 'read back', using the New Testament and the person and work of Jesus as paradigmatic and typological for interpreting the Hebrew Scriptures; whereas the Messianic Jewish community bases their reading of Scripture on the fact that the early church, not having the New Testament, primarily understood their faith through the lens of the Tenach, seeing Torah as paradigmatic.) Consequently, as this 'read forward' hermeneutic is combined with dividing Scripture into separate periods, a strict distinction between the church and the Jewish people emerges based on covenants, specifically, the covenants given exclusively to the Jewish people, including the promise of the land of Israel as an eternal inheritance, and the covenant given to the Gentiles in Jesus.

Dispensationalist eschatology not only tends to focus on a literal interpretation of the events of Revelation but also places significant emphasis on the role of a restored land of Israel to the Jewish people. Echoes of this prophesied future for Israel are also anticipated in the book of Ezekiel. The biblical passage from Ezekiel 37.1–14 describes the prophet's vision of dry bones that God restores to life. A promise of national revival and territorial recovery follows as God promises the house of Israel:

> I am going to open your graves, and bring you up from your graves, O my people; and I will bring you back to the land of Israel. And you shall know that I am the LORD, when I open your graves, and bring you up from your graves, O my people. I will put my spirit within you, and you shall live, and I will place you on your own soil (Ezek. 37.12c–14a).

From within this particular framework of interpretation, the biblical 'land of Israel' becomes contiguous with a future hope for the restoration of a national entity. Many dispensationalists read prophecy as a sort of a futuristic *fait accompli*. This invites the temptation to ignore the moral responsibilities of individuals and groups. This dynamic is at play in the way the Messianic Jewish and Palestinian Christian congregations relate to one another. If the future is a foregone conclusion, there is little motivation to move towards reconciliation in the present, as present actions have no meaningful bearing on the future. This view also tends to neglect the conditional nature of prophecy.

The direct relationship which is drawn by many Messianic Jews between the Jewish people of the Bible and themselves as modern Jewish people also means that romanticized variations of biblical history become the overarching framework for interpreting contemporary history. As Lawrence Davidson, a Middle East scholar, puts it, this has meant that the mythical and romantic Palestine of the Bible holds more meaning than the political reality in Israel today.[84] The reality of the suffering of the Palestinian people as well as the secular nature of Israel is overlooked by this type of theology that views Israel in historical/mythical terms. It results in a situation where Palestinians can only be seen as the enemy and as those who are resisting the manifest will of God as it is translated in national terms.

In the Middle East, and particularly within the Messianic Jewish community, dispensationalism is the most prominent paradigm for interpreting apocalyptic literature. In dispensationalism, the apocalyptic genre in Scripture is given a much wider scope and is understood to include the prophetic literature, as well as the more traditional eschatological books of Daniel and Revelation. A literalist, futurist hermeneutic is then applied to these texts, which means that prophecy becomes pre-written history. Many believe that the fulfilment of this pre-written history is taking place now or will take place in the near future. Everything from 'wars and rumours of wars' to the apocalyptic beast is placed within this framework and projected as literal events and characters that will play a role in the end times which are yet to be fulfilled. The book of Revelation becomes a roadmap to expected events at the climax of history, before the fully established reign of God begins.

Those who hold to a dispensationalist view of Scripture saw the events of 1948 and 1967 as confirming evidence of dispensationalism's interpretive strength. They further viewed both historical moments as freighted with eschatological significance. That is, the restoration of Israel is not only a single, self-contained event but also a forerunner of a global restoration in which Jesus' millennial reign will extend throughout the earth. For many, Israel's eschatological manifest destiny is reason enough to warrant its economic, political and religious support from the wider Christian world.

The book of Revelation is also interpreted as a *climax* within history, the crowning point of prophetic fulfilment. Current events are seen as God involving himself in human history by exercising his power in order to bring the world under his dominion. This view of eschatology calls us to reframe our engagement with history and expects believers to be aware of what God is doing around us, namely, he established the state of Israel, is drawing the Jewish people to the land, and is preparing them for a spiritual revival before the end-time events of the apocalypse.

The theological implications of this kind of dispensationalist perspective – where God intervenes and acts directly in history – are controversial, but not without real merit. God *is* at work in the world; he is establishing his kingdom. The intuition, as is often colloquially put, to read the Bible in one hand and the newspaper in the other, with eschatological expectancy, is widespread. As reformed theologian Richard J. Mouw explains, this instinct is also one of dispensationalists' best attributes. Even though he writes that 'the dispensationalist perspective undercuts Christian social concerns', Mouw admits, 'Long before I had ever heard of Mother Theresa, I saw dispensationalists lovingly embrace the homeless in rescue missions. Whatever the defects of the older dispensationalism as a theological perspective, it embodied a spirituality that produced some of the most Christlike human beings I have ever known'.[85]

Eschatology also touches on the question of war and the use of violence, especially for believers. This is a particularly relevant question for Israeli and Palestinian believers as they live in the midst of a ferocious conflict and are regularly confronted with the issue of violence. Generally speaking, Israeli Messianic Jews subscribe – consciously or unconsciously – to 'just war' theory, and Palestinian Christians adhere to a pacifist or non-violent view.

For both believing communities, this is the result of a combination of the political realities of Israeli and Palestinian society, and the theological influences on both of these communities. For Messianic Jews, a sense of national duty and Israel's existential vulnerability in the context of Islamic anti-Zionist aggression is the primary context for their commitment to serve in the military.[86] In addition to the national context, theological influences also play a limited role, including the influence of dispensationalist thinking and its attendant eschatological scenarios. Messianic Jews often see the conflict as having a spiritual dimension with demonic forces active in the conflict to prevent Israel from achieving its destiny. For Palestinian Christians who, unlike their Israeli counterparts, are not required to do military service, the pacifist/non-violent tradition has been very influential in shaping attitudes towards war.

In any conflict, including the Israeli–Palestinian one, it is tempting to simply withdraw from the ethical dilemmas that surround injustice, violence and even conditions of war. But the implications of our faith in Jesus call us deeply into the complexities of the world, especially in the face of injustice. Mere withdrawal is never an adequate response to injustice. Pacifists and non-pacifists alike can agree on this point, even as they disagree on what shape engaging that injustice will take. While a thorough exploration of these traditional positions is beyond the scope of this book, it is enough to say that the well-established debate between Christian just war subscribers and Christian pacifists is not new, and the arguments between them can be intractable.

Charity about theological positions

Sadly, within the current debate, the terms 'supersessionism' or 'replacement theology' as well as dual-covenant theology and 'dispensationalism' are invoked as labels – often, inaccurately – to dismiss and malign real points of theological disagreement. Certainly, there are forms of supersessionism that should not form any part of 'Christian' theology, including anything that rejects the Jewish heritage of the Christian faith, seeks to purge all biblical Jewish influence from Christianity, or refuses to ascribe ongoing covenantal significance to, at least, Jewish believers in Jesus.

In the New Testament, Paul fought for the inclusion of non-Jews in the new community of faith, arguing against his Jewish opponents who did not allow Gentiles to meet God as non-Jews. These Pauline opponents advocated for circumcision and full Torah observance from these Gentiles as a prerequisite to their inclusion in Israel's covenant community. The reverse should be true now, where Messianic Jews should be free to meet with God without abandoning their identities and cultural context as Jews who believe in Jesus, despite the dominance of a non-Jewish culture in the church.

Messianic believers must also recognize that the logic of supersessionism does not necessarily entail the logic of anti-Semitism or traditional Christian hatred of Jews and Judaism, any more than the logic of dispensationalism necessitates a hatred of Palestinians over and against the Jews. The contemporary Middle East context is unique and needs to be related to on its own terms. Palestinian Christians do not have the same historical and theological 'baggage' towards historical Judaism as their European counterparts. It behoves Palestinian Christians to affirm their Jewish brothers and sisters in their identity and to encourage them to embrace their heritage, just as they desire to be affirmed in their own Palestinian identity. The instinctive fear that each side has concerning the other is understandable. Theological labels can facilely function as code to help sort out who might be an intellectual friend or foe. However, they are also easily misapplied, precluding genuine engagement with the other, fostering preconceived perceptions, and masking the fears each side has of the other.

Caricaturing any interlocutor according to one's own fears must be resolutely resisted. Each side must avoid the trend within both communities to label, and thereby dismiss, other views. Labelling a theologian who does not agree with a dispensationalist view of Israel as an anti-Semitic replacement theologian; or, likewise, labelling a theologian who maintains that there is a particular relationship between God and the state or the people of Israel as a politically right-wing Zionist, are examples of the kind of behaviour to avoid. Above all, a commitment to intellectual charity and a posture of hermeneutical humility should characterize our theological discussions.

9.

Towards a Theology of Reconciliation

One of our hopes in writing this book is to offer insights that might help Israeli Messianic Jews and Palestinian Christians to live as reconciled and reconciling members of Christ's body and be witnesses of his grace to their respective communities. We also pray that our readers who live outside the region will embrace and support the vision of reconciliation we articulate. Our desire is to be joined in heart and action in the service of reconciliation.

Our fallen human natures incline us to grow *incurvatus in se* ('curved in upon ourselves'). This is true both individually and communally. As a result, we become indifferent to one another, even as we meet to worship the same God in our separate congregations.[1] Our lives are complicated by our context. For Messianic Jews life includes military service, regional military instability, economic, family and congregational pressures, and the challenge of being a minority whose faith is seen by many as a betrayal of our people. For Palestinian Christians, all of the above apply, minus military service, but with the addition of living as Arabs in a Jewish state, Gaza, or the West Bank, in a combination of partial self-rule and Israeli military rule. For the Israeli Messianic Jewish community, fundamentalist Islam and its regional spread is seen as the main hindrance to achieving Middle East peace; whereas for Palestinian Christians, Israeli policies of continued occupation, checkpoints and expanding settlements are seen as the main roadblocks to peace. All of these factors tempt even the most optimistic among us to grow weary, become cynical and lose hope for a political solution.

As we noted in the introduction of this book, biblical reconciliation has two main aspects, the vertical and the horizontal. The vertical aspect of reconciliation between God and humanity comes about through God's saving gift of his Son. As a result of the cross, the horizontal dimension of reconciliation, the outworking of the restored relationship between God and humanity is manifest in healed and restored relationships between people. It was God's initiative to reconcile the world to himself through the sacrificial death of Jesus. At the cross, the relationship that had been broken by human rebellion and sin was healed. Reconciliation is the theological concept that describes the setting right and restoration of broken relationships (divine-to-human and human-to-human). In this process God's grace is revealed, sin is judged as sin, its debt is paid and sinners are forgiven. They are released to live free of guilt and to joyfully accept their responsibility to now live in righteous relational order towards God, people and creation. The vertical and horizontal aspects of reconciliation are interdependent and mutually reinforcing, and bear witness to one another. True 'horizontal reconciliation' is dependent on prior 'vertical reconciliation'. Without total embrace of the vertical aspect of reconciliation, there can be no true or complete horizontal reconciliation. God's reconciliation is not confined to relationships between God and humanity, and person to person. God has reconciled *all things* to himself.[2] Thus, reconciliation has an all-encompassing cosmic dimension. As we primarily focus the following discussion in the realm of divine–human relationships, we would do well to remember that reconciliation is more about God than about human beings. It is because of this inclusivity that humanity has reason for hope. In God's purposes, even intractable conflicts can be resolved.

As part of his covenant with Israel, God established covenantal law as a way of ordering social relationships among people and between the Israelites and God. Diligently following the Torah would lead to the creation of a just and blessed community. This community would then become the witness of God's agent of salvation, Israel, before all the nations of the earth.[3] Abraham, the great father and model of faith, was called a righteous man, not by virtue of any inherent moral superiority but because of his faith in God. This faith was expressed through his relationship with God and, consequently, with others.

The vertical–horizontal dynamic continues into the New Testament. The writer of 1 John puts the matter starkly: 'If anyone says,

"I love God," and hates his brother, he is a liar; for he who does not love his brother whom he has seen cannot love God whom he has not seen' (1 John 4.20 ESV). Fulfilling this 'horizontal' dimension of our obedience often presents a unique challenge in our Middle Eastern setting. However, our interpersonal animosities are a smaller dimension of a much larger problem that God has already solved. The once 'inevitable' enmity between Jew and Gentile is broken down by the cross of the risen Christ. The enmity that was fuelled by idolatrous egocentricity and ethnocentricity is judged at his cross. In Christ, all ethnicities are freed to uniquely become what God intends them to be. This is an objective that cannot be achieved through slavish attention to self and nation, but only through obedient reverence to Christ, lived out in service of others.

Though not an unqualified parallel, the situation of the early church bears a striking resemblance to the current conflict between Israelis and Palestinians within the community of faith. Like the conflicting parties within the Ephesian church, Israeli Messianic Jews and Palestinian Christians are two *believing* communities in a conflict that bears seriously on their identity in the Messiah. As in Ephesus, the conflict in the Holy Land today expresses itself through ethnic divisions, national enmities and a lack of (or refusal to) fellowship with one another. This stance is inexcusably justified through theologies that fail to faithfully account for what God in Christ has done for *both* Palestinian and Jewish believers. Furthermore, whether intentionally or not, this conflict is at times supported and sometimes financed by members of the global church who fail to recognize the serious implications this conflict has for the entire body of Christ in the world. Just as the solution to the problem of partisan and doctrinal division in the early church was christological,[4] so too is it the solution for the divided church in the Holy Land. *Jesus* alone is our peace. Our identities, narratives and national aspirations will only find their true and lasting meaning in him.

Aspects of a Theology of Reconciliation

We believe reconciliation to be the heart of the gospel. It is God's good news that he has reached out in love to fallen, rebellious humanity. God himself has entered into his creation to redeem and rescue it from the results of sin. Reconciliation is holistic, and is definitively set in the context of relationship with God, self, others and the creation. In the biblical sense, true reconciliation is a process of discipleship in Christ through the power of the Holy Spirit and is primarily expressed in relationships within the church. Reconciliation is costly and usually demands far more than we would comfortably give. To fully embrace God's mission of reconciliation requires deep understanding of God's heart and mission in the world, a commitment to obedience, and ardent trust in God's provision.

We have already related to practical steps of reconciliation; now we examine the *theo*-logic of those steps. To the extent that this theology serves our communities by giving them more 'light' and less 'heat', it will have served its purpose. We are not proposing our model in order to create a 'new community of reconcilers'. That would cast judgement on or become arrogant towards those who refuse to live in reconciliation – the 'irreconciling'. Rather, our motivation is one of freely extending the grace, and hopefully some of the wisdom, we have gained on the journey.

As a biblical–theological approach to the Israeli–Palestinian conflict, and to all conflicts in which believers are pitted against one another, a theology of reconciliation announces, first, that *reconciliation is a complete, sufficient work that God both freely initiated and achieved for his people*. While this reconciliation has already been achieved through the death and resurrection of Messiah, there are aspects of reconciliation that need to be lived out in the here and now. The Holy Spirit continually empowers his body to live as reconciled people, being agents of reconciliation through the life, death and resurrection of Jesus. Believers are the beneficiaries and partakers of Christ's completed work of reconciliation. It is not something we achieve or appropriate outside of his completed victory. The *via dolorosa* that Jesus walked on our behalf once and for all, to reconcile us to God, is a road we cannot and will never have to walk.[5] This way was his alone. Our only adequate response should be worshipful awe and loving obedience that seeks to know him more deeply.

Second, by appropriating our reconciliation with God and others, reconciliation in our lives is both *a present theological reality as well as an eschatological task.* This task must shape our lives until his kingdom comes in fullness. As his kingdom is already in our midst but is not yet fully realized, so too is reconciliation both already here and not yet. Regardless of our unique circumstances, in Christ we are reconciled to God and are commissioned to be ministers of reconciliation to each other and to the world. As members of his body, believers *are* the reconciled and the reconciling. Jesus Christ becomes the source of our identity. Our wounds, including the wounds of our communities' narratives, find healing in his wounds. Each member of Christ's body is now free to embrace their God-given ethnic identity while at the same time eschewing the capacity of the state to demand absolute allegiance or obedience when those demands are in conflict with the ethics of the kingdom. Israeli followers of Yeshua are free to fellowship with their Palestinian Christian brothers and sisters as are Palestinians also free to fellowship with their Israeli brothers and sisters in Jesus. As those reconciled to God, we celebrate our redemption and derive the foundation of our identity in nothing other than Christ. Our identity in Messiah takes precedence over our ethnic identity, but does not replace it or remove it.

As the reconciling, for his sake, we seek to serve each other and the world. We trust him for assuring the fullness of our communities' identities and destinies.

Third, *our ethnic, political or theological differences do not give us liberty to let go of or withdraw, physically, emotionally or intellectually from our fellow members of Christ's body.* In light of what God has done for us in Christ, to do so would be akin to refusing each other table fellowship, the heart of our ongoing mutual witness. In fact, as Palestinian and Israeli members of Christ's body, we were *never* permitted to let go of one another in word (theological reflection) or deed (table fellowship). The results of having done so are plainly evident in the schism between our communities today.[6] Israeli Messianic Jews, as members of Christ's body, are incomplete in and of themselves without Palestinian Christians; the reverse is equally true. The members of Christ's body witness to one another in their worship and love of him. This mutual witness includes respectfully listening to how each community reads and interprets the Bible, and celebrates how each has discerned Christ in their particular community. We allow our community's biblical hermeneutics to be informed by a reconciling hermeneutic, in which 'the other' is not only accounted for but also acknowledged as a necessary partner in our theological work. 'What persons from one culture bring from that culture to their reading of the text may illuminate dimensions or implications of the text itself that persons of another culture may not have seen so clearly.'[7]

Fourth, by virtue of our walking as reconcilers in the way of the cross, our relationships will be marked by *genuine vulnerability, repentance, a commitment to forgiveness, and an enduring hospitality* towards one another. We actively pursue relationships with each other, despite the psychological discomfort it brings. We repent when we've wounded one another, and we choose to forgive when we inevitably suffer because of these relationships. In this, we follow in the footsteps of our Lord who has freely forgiven us. The wounds we experience in our relationships need no longer fuel resentment and animosity, nor do they fatalistically determine our identities. Our identities are firmly rooted in the wounded, risen body of Christ.

Two important corollaries follow here when, because of that vulnerable humility, the pain of reconciling relationship seems too great to continue. First, we remember that *the cost of not reconciling far exceeds the suffering entailed as a result of pursuing reconciliation.* Again, it is not unlike the dynamic within a marriage. God has placed our communities in relationship by virtue of our mutual membership in the body of Christ. Relationship among Christ's members is not something we have the option to either embrace or avoid. It is a joyful truth and a divine mandate. However, on account of the theo-political conflict between us, we readily admit that this marriage-like relationship is a source of much pain, anger and bitterness for both parties. We have consistently betrayed one another in the midst of the conflict by ignoring each other's cries for help. The temptation to divorce – to walk away from one another; to refuse fellowship; to disparage the other; to seek allies near and far in our defence against the other; to gossip, slander, and malign – is enticing. These dissociating actions can seem to alleviate our anger, disappointment and pain. Nevertheless, insulating our communities from this relational pain will not cause the broken relationship, or its agony, to disappear. To withdraw from our participation in the body of Christ will rather lead to our own spiritual malaise.

The second corollary is even more serious: *The failure of one side to move towards its apparent enemy*[8] *in reconciliation gives the other side no excuse to relax in its commitment to reconcile.* Neither side is given a theological escape clause. It is inevitable that each side will be tempted to withdraw because of the failures of the other. This is a temptation that will likely grow *stronger* in the process of reconciliation, even as the real work of reconciliation is becoming well established. Yet the only way forward is towards God and one another, even if the other side does not reciprocate in ways we would have hoped for or if the relationship appears to 'give' us nothing.

Fifth, in the process of reconciliation, forgiveness is not a one-time event. It is a long-term process in which *we commit ourselves to continue to forgive and pursue relationship.* We do this prayerfully, confident in Jesus' power to communicate and to correct us and our inadequate and at times errant theologies. In the same manner, we also trust him to correct our errant brothers and sisters. We trust him that he has and will continue to communicate and correct us through the gentle admonitions of the Holy Spirit. Ultimately, we are all called to trust *Jesus* for his righteous judgement as each person confesses their sins of thought, word and deed against their forgiven enemy. Each community must resist the temptation to establish its identity in anything other than Christ. And jointly, we pray for all our brothers and sisters in the body of Messiah to root their identity firmly in Jesus the Messiah. We extend forgiveness when they do not. We ask God to forgive us when we do not.

Sixth, another aspect of reconciliation is justice. We acknowledge that the issues of justice and reconciliation are inextricably interwoven. Justice is not a quality we can attain on its own; neither is reconciliation a goal we can reach without addressing justice. The concept of justice in the Bible is complex and multifaceted. Many discussions of justice in the public sphere focus on either retributive or restorative justice. While it is beyond the scope of this book to address this in depth, we acknowledge and affirm the importance of an holistic approach to reconciliation that must take a position on justice in our context. In Psalm 85.10 we read that mercy and truth meet, justice and peace kiss. Mercy, compassion, truth-telling and relationship are all components of true justice. As Miroslav Volf writes, 'To agree on justice in conflict situations you must want more than justice; you must want embrace. There can be *no justice without the will to embrace*. It is however, equally true that there can be no genuine and lasting embrace without justice.'[9] Our work in this book has begun to address some of the foundational issues involved in justice, such as listening to one another and acknowledging the other's grievances.

In the history chapter and in the presentation of the various theological positions, we have tried to make space for the other to articulate their position, to recognize where the backgrounds of each side affect their positions, and to highlight areas of disagreement and grievance with love and respect. We believe this is the beginning of addressing the issues involved in reconciliation. We are aware that our work is partial and recognize the necessity of further theological work that is beyond the scope of this book. The perfect model of loving relationship among the persons of the Trinity is often invoked as a theological metaphor for relationships within the church. However, this model is nearly impossible to emulate and it often discourages more than inspires! The more apt theological metaphor for our relational conflict is the wounded, broken and pierced body of Christ on the cross, the iconic centrepiece of a theology of reconciliation. The scars he endured for our sake are evidence of the high cost of love, and of the reconciliation he achieved on our behalf. We recall the words of Jürgen Moltmann:

> The cross is not and cannot be loved. Yet only the crucified Christ can bring the freedom which changes the world because it is no longer afraid of death. In his time the crucified Christ was regarded as a scandal and foolishness. Today, too, it is considered old fashioned to put him in the center of the Christian faith and of theology. Yet only when men are reminded of him, however untimely this may be, can they be set free from the power of the facts of the present time, and from the laws and compulsions of history, and be offered a future which will never grow dark again.[10]

Beyond the cross is the resurrection of Jesus. He remains alive and walks with us daily in our quest to live out his life in the world.

His kingdom is not of this world, but it has come. It has broken through in the redeemed, reconciled lives of his followers who live simultaneously in two realities. It is through the power of his resurrection that we are enabled today to embody reconciliation in our relationships. However important we may feel them to be, our contexts of conflict are ultimately of marginal significance. This is because he has already walked the context of the most intractable conflict, through death and into resurrected life. In that he has given himself fully to us, we have received the same power.

A Hermeneutic of Reconciliation

How does a theology of reconciliation shape the way we might approach and interpret Scripture? As we have discussed already, Palestinian Christians and Israeli Messianic Jews navigate various political and theological differences related to and impacted by the larger conflict. In addition, both communities seek to rein-force their own communal identities, which are challenged by the conflict. The nature of their respective hermeneutics, reflecting their theological self-understandings and the shared perceptions of threat to their identities, has meant that there has been little fruitful dialogue between the two sides. Because the biblical hermeneutics of each community provide an essential foundation for its sense of identity, legitimacy and self-worth, each community's hermeneutics also tend to be hermetically sealed from the other. Each tends towards defensiveness, self-protection and insularity.

In a hermeneutic of reconciliation, we approach Scripture together, inviting and stimulating an interpretive process that produces theological and biblical insights. This process can yield new understandings that may be quite distinct from the under-standings gained by approaching Scripture separately. Coming to the Scriptures together is a sign of our fellowship in Christ and our love for each other. We may not agree on specific points of interpretation (and even less on historical narratives), but by reading together and truly listening to the other, we allow the Holy Spirit to firmly and transparently ground our collective iden-tities in the living God. It is God alone who merits our love and adoring worship. We invite the Holy Spirit to quiet our reflexive hermeneutical postures – our intellectual tendencies of defensive aggression – so that we may learn to hear what God is saying to us through the other community.

It follows that in a hermeneutic of reconciliation, not only do we read Scripture *together*, but we also read Scripture *for each other* in light of the redemptive work of Christ's life, death and resurrection. The distinctions between Messianic Jews and Palestinian Christians remain, including their unique hermeneutical perspectives. However, the cross does away with the notion that these differences in interpretation are legitimate grounds for estrangement, discrimination, hostility and self-justification. When reading Scripture together, as citizens of the kingdom of heaven and in the shadow of the cross, we read not simply for ourselves, but also for our community, our neighbour and even our 'enemy'. These are the people and relationships to which the texts, and the Lord of the texts himself, point us.

As is true in a theology of reconciliation, the hermeneutic derived from this theology also expects, even wisely *anticipates*, vulnerability to being wounded. Even as we joyfully affirm that Christ has put to death the hostility that once separated us, we remember that reconciliation involves exposure to pain and a willingness to continue to love even as we inevitably and sometimes unconsciously wound each other. The exercise of theology is not immune to being offensive. Given the history of world wars, theology is not only not immune, but is capable of causing enormous damage on a cold war basis and in real military engagement.

As limited, frail, and redeemed-yet-fallen beings, our intellectual pursuits, our approaches to Scripture and our often irreconcilable theologies reflect humanity's God-given capacity both for fantastic creativity as well as the disorientation of sin. Our theologies can offend and wound our neighbour.

Moving towards a theology of reconciliation requires a willingness to become vulnerable before one another. As co-authors of this book, we have met in our respective homes and in a modest office in Jerusalem to discuss how this book should be framed, what we should discuss, and how each of our respective communities will respond to the ideas we present together. The process has necessitated considerable flexibility and intentionality. At times, we have disagreed forcefully about the ideas shared here and agonized over a sense of mutual misunderstanding and hermeneutical approaches that threaten our most sacred cows: our sense of community identity and calling before God based upon our community's reading of Scripture. We have doubted the commitments of the other to our own good. We have wondered at times if our partner is pressuring us to compromise our deep convictions, resulting in a betrayal of our community or even of our own identity for the sake of the other. We have hoped that the other would recognize the truth of our position and abandon the falseness of theirs.

There has been real suffering, even mundane kinds of 'deaths', involved in our work of reconciliation. We have experienced the exhaustion, confusion and frustration that are inevitable aspects of any human relationship. (Our relationship extends beyond the efforts of this book; we, along with our families, have been friends – intentionally reconciling friends – for many years.) So, we honestly challenge each other: 'The way you approach this verse is divergent from the way we do', or, 'This notion that is precious to you is *offensive* to me and my community, even as I can acknowledge that your understanding of it is precious to you and your community. I believe your exegesis and hermeneutical approach is sorely wrong on this point!' Nevertheless, we are given no liberties to be released from this relationship; to do so would impoverish and compromise our shared life in Christ. Indeed, even writing this book together, as an act of reconciliation, is not without real risk and has involved suffering and testing for each of us.

Seeking release from our reconciling relationship would also jeopardize our shared vocation in witnessing to the reconciling reality of God in Christ to the world. The Israeli–Palestinian conflict is not beyond God's sovereign authority! We believe that this kind of shared kingdom life is possible for our respective communities in our broken part of the world. We share in his life, and therefore, we share a secure identity in him. Reconciliation will not necessarily look like perfectly attuned harmony between us, but it will be evident in our continued commitment to sharing life in the Messiah together for his sake.

The Limits of Theology

As the apostle Paul says, 'we see through a glass, darkly' (1 Cor. 13.12 AV), even as we pray that Christ would shine out ever more clearly in the life of our communities of faith. Our cultural, linguistic and even ethnic lenses can illumine as well as distort the truth of the Bible. Our understandings of history, our 'sacred' communal narratives, our biblical hermeneutics and even our most beloved theologies nourish us. At the same time, they have the potential to become god-like idols, enslaving and deceiving us as to the source of our life and salvation, and sealing us off from loving relationship with one another and from the God who calls us out of ourselves into fuller, deeper relationship with him and others through the Messiah. As we mentioned earlier, a posture of epistemic humility is both an essential gift from God as well as a virtue we must cultivate, especially because we are regularly tempted to believe ourselves the possessors of the truth, rather than among the once-hopelessly-lost whom the Truth has rescued.

In this book we have sought to nuance often-made simplistic arguments about our conflict. We have attempted to honour the real differences that divide us, endeavouring to position the conversation in a biblically oriented direction towards reconciliation. We recognize that we cannot offer a complete picture or a full accounting of the suffering and hopes each community carries. As limited contributions to the conversation, our insights and exhortations are humbly offered to people of goodwill in each of our respective communities and beyond. A theology of reconciliation can help to reshape our theo-political imaginations. This is important, but it is not *the way*. Jesus is the Way. He is the Truth. He is Life.

The theology of reconciliation we offer here is more a description of a way of life and a direction to walk in rather than 'principles to apply in a conflict'. It is an invitation to love our sister or brother whose ethnicity represents the 'enemy' in our political conflict. It is the way Jesus walked for all humanity, especially for those who believe. He walked this path on our behalf and *on behalf of all who are forgiven in him*, including those with whom we are in conflict. We cannot claim the comfort and reconciliation of the cross while rejecting the way of Jesus. He calls us out of worshipful obsession with our own communities towards relationship with our 'enemy' in a radically new community marked by its relationship to God in Christ. We live out a theology of reconciliation by embracing the identity we each have received at Christ's cross. He shows us that this kind of life involves suffering for the sake of love. He calls us to love God and our neighbour, without fear of the inevitable suffering, promising not to abandon us in it and inviting us deeper into his life. He has positioned us in his kingdom, which is already in our midst. Just as he provided Israel with the Torah to structure a just society that would bear witness to him, so he continues to give us the means whereby we can live together as a reconciled community, bearing witness of his love and healing power to the world.

Perhaps the most immediate 'suffering' for many of us who are involved in reconciliation is primarily psychological. Besides being looked at suspiciously from many within our own communities for meeting with the 'other', our greatest hindrance to embracing God's provision of reconciliation is the one that lies within us. Making the decision to meet together with 'the other side' is the first step; however, what happens once we get there presents a whole new menu of psychological challenges. It will be helpful to briefly explain how this has played out in our context and offer some wisdom we have gained over the years about the reconciliation process. We noted a disclaimer above; we are not offering a surefire method of 'principles to apply in a conflict', but rather we are seeking to be imitators of God. However, if, by the power of the Holy Spirit, we will do the latter, then the wisdom of applying tested principles will certainly not hinder our efforts for reconciliation.

Our New Identity in the Messiah

In previous sections, we discussed challenges faced by Israeli Messianic Jews and Palestinian Christians. We also need to address the dynamics present when these two peoples in conflict meet, and the consequent effect on their identities. As those who were dead and are now alive in Messiah, we cannot continue our lives as though God had not visited this world. The divine in-breaking of God begins most decisively at the incarnation, expressing God's loving commitment to his creation in its brokenness. He is a God who chooses to involve himself with his fallen creation, drawing people to himself in covenant partnership, and loving them even to the point of a cruel and ignominious death. As Oliver O'Donovan puts it, 'The sacrificial death of God's Messiah is the event to interpret all events, which alone can offer human existence the cosmic meaning which it demands.'[11] Jesus' life, death and resurrection make the historical narrative coherent and meaningful. He is the fixed point in history. Any theology that does not anchor its centre in the resurrection of Jesus is bound to miss the radical implications of that event for our lives in the here and now. If his incarnation represents the definitive point of God's in-breaking within our material world, his resurrection means that we are empowered with his life to be his catalysts of transformational change in our present world.

Identities in conflict

Having a healthy sense of individual and collective identity is one of the most basic human psychological needs.[12] As we have already explored, as believers in Jesus, our identity is intimately connected to our theological narratives, which provide a sense of legitimacy and coherency to life. Identity is an integral and legitimate aspect of being human, made in God's image. Our identities, like our theologies, can easily become distorted by sin and result in bondage to a narcissistic ethnocentricity when held or pursued as an ultimate priority.

The Israeli–Palestinian conflict presents considerable challenges to Israeli Messianic Jewish and Palestinian Christian identity. For many Israelis and Palestinians, meeting with someone from the other side is considered a betrayal of their own group. Unfortunately, this is also true for some believers. Both communities have theological reasons for adopting this position, but there are also sociological and psychological factors at work. As an example, some Palestinian Christians refuse to meet with Israelis because, in their view, to do so would represent a form of 'normalization', or cooperation with the occupation, thereby giving legitimacy to the injustices Israel has imposed upon the Palestinian people. By refusing to meet, they symbolically communicate that justice is a precondition to reconciliation. Similarly, some Israeli Messianic Jews refuse to meet with Palestinian Christians for theological or political reasons, for example that Palestinian Christians are supersessionist, or anti-Israel, and that to engage in dialogue with them would be to compromise on theological truth. They make agreement on theological and political points a precondition to dialogue. There is strong social pressure within each group to refuse to meet with the other. Clearly, when any kind of meeting is already considered doomed to failure, neither posture is conducive to reconciliation

As believers, we are often affected by the wider context of our ethnic communities. Israelis and Palestinians often mirror one another in how they view themselves and their group, and these views bear directly on prospects for peace. Daniel Bar-Tal writes about how Israelis and Palestinians tend to identify as the victims in the conflict; each sees themselves and their in-group surrounded by a hostile and unsympathetic world.[13] To achieve some measure of security for one's threatened identity, each tends to fixate on the weaknesses of the other group while too highly elevating its own group's innocence. Every nation or people group has a sense of its cherished uniqueness and national calling, but when identity is established in opposition to or by denigrating others, it can become a spiritual obstacle to fellowship with one's brother or sister from the wider 'enemy' group.

Modern social identity theory recognizes the significance of categorization and the way in which being categorized as a member of a larger group provides an important concept of the self for individuals. Henri Tajfel proposed the idea that self-esteem and pride are often derived from membership in a particular group. As a result of this relationship between self-esteem and group membership, we are able to increase our individual self-esteem through enhancing the status of the group to which we belong. Exploring the legacy of Tajfel's work on social identity theory, Michael Hogg writes, '[E]valuatively positive social identity became the main motivation behind social identification, and it in turn was explicated in terms of the operative of an individual motive to maintain or enhance self-esteem . . . It was this formulation that inspired most social identity research that dealt with intergroup relations, intergroup conflict, ethno-linguistic identity, and so forth.'[14] This is particularly relevant for our purposes. To use examples from our context; for an Israeli to claim that Israel is the best country in the world (or, as is often stated, 'the only democracy in the Middle East'), the self-esteem of the particular individual identifying himself as a member of that group (Israel) will be enhanced because the status of the category is considered superior to other categories. So to be a member of 'Israel' is better than being a member of any other country. The same is also the case for a Palestinian claiming that Palestine is the best country in the world.

Similarly, negative claims about others also help to reinforce our sense of identity and superiority. We build up our own sense of ourselves at the expense of others, especially when we are in conflict with them. If a Palestinian makes a claim that Israel is the worst country in the world (or 'the worst abuser of human rights'), the self-esteem of that particular Palestinian will be enhanced through inferring that the other group is inferior. Again, the same will also be the case for an Israeli inferring that Palestine is the worst country in the world. Using this method of social categorization, the whole world becomes divided into 'us' and 'them', fostering exclusion and hostility against those who belong to another social category.

When we elevate ourselves in opposition to others, to our enemies, we are on a dangerous path that often leads to dehumanization. History is littered with examples of nationalist movements that began with a sense of national calling and a desire to achieve liberation and ended in tragedy, chauvinism, xenophobia and genocide. All nations or people groups have a sense of uniqueness and national calling. However, if this is predicated on opposition to other groups, it may become a form of idolatry. This mentality challenges the truth that all people are sinners in need of God's grace and mercy. After sin entered the world, the first murder occurred against the background of Cain's comparison with his brother Abel. Appreciation of our own particularity has its place, but when it stands in the way of fellowship, it is at odds with the universal message of Christ. Undue emphasis on our uniqueness results in building walls between 'us and them' when our focus should be (as we shall see) on living in the reality that the wall of partition has been broken down.

An obstacle to reconciliation is present when one group sees itself as superior to or as replacing another group. This is not new; believers have faced this issue before. Indeed, the New Testament has much to say about divisions within the body of the Messiah caused by ethnic identity and enmity. The New Testament deals with the new reality we face since the coming of the Messiah, and its implications for our personal, communal and intergroup identity. In his epistles, Paul deals with these and other thorny intergroup relations as they affect the community of faith.

God redefining our identity

Much of Paul's work deals with who God is and who the people of God are. These concepts anchor his theology. When God chose Israel, he intended Israel to be a light to the nations, a commission they failed to achieve. Jesus, the embodiment of Israel, fulfilled Israel's intended purpose, doing what Israel alone 'was called to do but could not, namely . . . on behalf of the whole world' (referencing Phil. 2 and Rom. 1 – 8).[15] In his letters, Paul reaffirms Israel's election while redefining it. Paul argues that those who believe in Jesus as the Messiah and in his faithfulness to Israel's calling are God's people.[16] Arguing that God's love was behind his election of Israel (Deuteronomy), so too Messiah's love motivates his desire for all people (Jews and non-Jews alike) to become God's renewed people. From Abraham, God intended to create for himself one family comprised of those who believed in him and were faithful to him. In Jesus, this family is made up of those who believe in the gospel, contrasted with all who do not, whether Jews or non-Jews. N.T. Wright writes, 'The doctrine of justification by faith was born into the world as the key doctrine underlying the *unity* of God's renewed people'.[17] In effect, God redefines the boundaries of identity around Messiah followers (see also Romans 9 – 11), according to faith in God rather than by Israel's covenant faithfulness. This identity is now available to Jew and Gentile alike.[18] This enlarges and reinterprets the family of God, following God's original intention to expand the eschatological kingdom of Israel to include the nations. Just as we do not choose our physical siblings, so too we do not choose our spiritual siblings, with whom we share fellowship and have mutual responsibility. This applies to both Israelis and Palestinians.

Jesus as the anchor of our identity

In Philippians 3:1–11 Paul writes to counter those who would put their confidence in 'the flesh', or in their personal identity credentials, over their identity in the Messiah. He writes, 'If someone else thinks they have reasons to put confidence in the flesh, I have more: circumcised on the eighth day, of the people of Israel, of the tribe of Benjamin, a Hebrew of Hebrews; in regard to the law, a Pharisee; as for zeal, persecuting the church; as for righteousness based on the law, faultless' (Phil. 3.4–6 NIV). Yet all these identity markers – birth, belonging or personal achievement[19] Paul counts as rubbish (or 'garbage') in comparison to his identity in the Messiah, 'But whatever were gains to me I now consider loss for the sake of Christ. What is more, I consider everything a loss because of the surpassing worth of knowing Christ Jesus my Lord, for whose sake I have lost all things. I consider them garbage, that I may gain Christ' (3.7–8 NIV). Paul is not dismissing these elements of his identity as irrelevant or inconsequential. Similar to his argument in Galatians 3.28 that 'there is neither Jew nor Gentile, neither slave nor free, nor is there male and female, for you are all one in Christ Jesus.' Paul is saying that these identities are still present, but they are irrelevant to our relationship with God and hence to our identity in the Messiah, since our relationship to the Father is grounded in our being 'in him'.

In our context, the identity credentials for Messianic Jews include being ethnically Jewish, living in the land of Israel, and being the remnant who have accepted the revelation of Jesus as the Messiah. For Palestinian Christians, this could be that they were born and live in the land where Jesus was born, lived, taught, was crucified and rose again; and that they are a faithful testimony living out their Christian identity on this same land from the time of the early church.

Another dynamic is at work in the conflict of identities between Israelis and Palestinians. Power is an issue as the groups identify themselves as those who are weaker and those who are more powerful. The weaker party can act to define itself in such a way as to appease the stronger party and ensure a positive social status. We can see this with Israeli Palestinians in the state of Israel and Palestinian Christians in the West Bank and Gaza who sometimes downplay important aspects of their identity for social acceptance and success. Yet, as believers, we are not limited to these identities. Jesus' act on the cross transforms our fleshly identities and frees us from the roles of victim and oppressor. We are affirmed in our identity as believers. This gives us security to reach out to others without falling into the divisive mentality of 'us' versus 'them'.[20]

In Philippians 3, Paul sees his overarching identity as being one who is anchored in Jesus, uniting him with all those who are also anchored in Jesus. Identity credentials that previously distinguished and separated him as a Jew from others are now considered as secondary to his primary identity as a believer and follower of Jesus the Messiah. His previously significant identity as circumcised, a Hebrew, a Jewish Benjaminite, a Pharisee, a persecutor of the church and a faultless follower of the Torah, are demoted to the category of fleshly identity. His *primary and principal* identity as a follower of Jesus unites him with other followers of Jesus, regardless of their ethnicity, culture, class, or any other identity category.

In Philippians 2, Paul describes Jesus as stepping down from his exalted, glorified position with the Father to put on flesh and submit to death on the cross. In so doing, Jesus identified with us and abolished boundaries between humanity and God. Following the example Jesus set for us, we too must be willing to cross boundaries and put aside those parts of our identity that exclude others, anchoring our identity in the Messiah. Paul argues, 'In your relationships with one another, have the same mindset as Christ Jesus' (Phil. 2.5) who emptied himself to identify with us, thus bringing us into himself and rescuing us from the bondage of sin. The process of finding our ultimate identity in the Messiah and imitating his example enables us to embrace others and influences our attitude and approach towards them. There is no hope or future in our fleshly identity. As compared to our eternal identity in the Messiah, our fleshly identity is temporal.

It is important to note that choosing the Messiah will entail following in his footsteps and taking our vocation seriously. This can cause our own community to 'exile' us, and send us 'outside the camp' (Hebrews 13). In our context of conflict this dimension is present when we meet with believers from the other side (often perceived as the enemy in the eyes of our own people) and we are then ostracized. Choosing the Messiah as the anchor of our identity will motivate us to prioritize fellowship with other believers as higher than other aspects of our identity, even if it is costly.

Our attitude towards others

When God chose the Jewish people, he set them apart from (not above) other nations. With Jesus' coming, non-Jews were invited into the people of God. In Romans 9 – 11 Paul addresses believers' attitudes towards Jewish believers and Jews who do not believe in the Messiah. Paul honours the heritage of the Jewish people and addresses the faithful remnant who are ethnically Jewish and believe in Jesus. This remnant, of which Paul is a part, is proof of God's continuing faithfulness to the Jewish people.

These Jewish believers struggled with what the Messiah meant for non-Jews, whom they called Gentiles (godless and hopeless pagans). Many Gentiles, called 'God-fearers', were disillusioned and unfulfilled by the Greco-Roman pantheon, which was replete with idolatry and temple prostitution, and were drawn to worship with Jews. Apart from the contact of Jews with such God-fearing Gentiles, there was indeed a deep-seated mistrust of Gentiles by Jews, not least of all because they were a source of ritual contamination and reviled as idolaters. For pious Jews, even selling material to a Gentile that would be used in their idolatrous cults, or purchasing food in the market that had previously been offered up to a pagan deity, was warned against by the Jewish community leaders (and apparently even a problem for Christians in the Pauline communities, cf. 1 Cor. 8). Such *Halachic* (based on the rulings of Jewish law) discussions make up a considerable part of the later codified Jewish law in the Mishnah.[21] A balanced picture of first-century Jewish attitudes towards Gentiles is represented in the following citation from S. McKnight:

> Judaism of the Second Temple period is known for (1) its emphasis on monotheistic universalism (that God is truly one and God of all; cf. Sir. 13:15; 18:13; Philo *Decal.* 64); (2) its friendliness to Gentiles (Philo *Flacc.* 94); (3) its apparent permission to Gentiles to participate at various levels (e.g., synagogue attendance) in Judaism (Josephus *J.W.* 2.412–16); (4) its participation in Hellenistic education (Philo *Vit. Mos.*

1.23–24; Josephus *Ant.* 15.373; *J.W.* 1.602); and (5) its continual intermarriage (Josephus *Ant.* 2:91–92). At times this assimilation resulted in overt apostasy (Philo *Spec. Leg.* 1:56-7; *Vit. Mos.* 2.193–208; Josephus *Ag. Ap.* 1:180).[22]

Having emphasized the positive dimensions of Jewish relations with Gentiles, McKnight then fills in the negative side of this relationship. This was seen in Jewish resistance to Gentiles and paganism because of Gentile 'sinfulness', which prevented eating meals together, the prohibition of Gentile (full) participation in Temple worship, the exhortation to avoid intermarriage (in spite of the intermarriage noted above, cf. Ezra!),[23] the tendency to revolt against religious reforms (cf. 1 Macc.), and finally that the Gentiles would one day be judged and punished by God.[24] McKnight notes, however, the positive Jewish attitude towards the proselyte who had truly abandoned his or her idolatry.[25]

When these Gentiles responded to Jesus and became part of the community of Jesus followers, did they first have to become *Jewish*? In Acts 15 we see that the apostles affirmed that one's relationship with Jesus, not one's ethnicity, determines who is a part of the people of God. Belief in the Messiah (regardless of ethnicity) does not place us 'above' others. Just as God has shown us mercy by including us in the people of God, he seeks to extend this same mercy to others. In our context of conflict, regardless of the conflicting and divided communities that separate Messianic Jews and Palestinian Christians, we must humbly acknowledge one another's different but equally important roles in the body of the Messiah.

As non-Jews began to respond to the gospel message, they soon outnumbered Jewish believers and gained prominent positions in church leadership. Tensions between the Jewish and non-Jewish believing communities heightened regarding issues of Torah observance and church practice, and, while encouraging uniqueness within the body of Messiah, Paul also emphasized fellowship as a higher goal.

The idea of celebrating our diversity is more than an idealistic nod to the principle of pluralism. It has important consequences for our two communities in the Holy Land. In Romans 14, Paul deals with issues of community and urges his readers to avoid judging one another. He writes, 'Let us therefore no longer pass judgement on one another, but resolve instead never to put a stumbling-block or hindrance in the way of another' (Rom. 14.13). Paul was specifically addressing the issues of what food was permitted, and which days were to be considered holy. The clear message is that we should not be critical of the other's choices, but are to be sensitive to each other and the influence of our choices on them. He is definite when he writes, 'If your brother or sister is being injured by what you eat, you are no longer walking in love. Do not let what you eat cause the ruin of one for whom Christ died. So do not let your good be spoken of as evil. For the kingdom of God is not food and drink but righteousness and peace and joy in the Holy Spirit' (Rom. 14.15–17).

Finally, our attitude towards non-believers (Jewish or otherwise) should be one of humility. We are all created in the image of God, fallen and undeserving recipients of God's gracious forgiveness and redemption. His gift of salvation is equally available to all humanity.

Unity within our new identity

Particularly in Romans 9 – 11, Paul dealt with the attitudes of non-Jews towards Jews. This is significant as it has implications for Israeli and Palestinian believers to be careful concerning their attitudes towards Jews. By implication, this applies to our attitudes towards Muslims and those from other religious backgrounds. In Romans 10.15 Paul writes, 'How beautiful are the feet of those who bring good news!' We have opportunity to be a blessing to the non-believing community in whose midst we live. Returning to Jewish attitudes toward Gentiles, Paul addresses this in Ephesians 2. Unity in the body of Messiah and our attitudes towards one another have implications for our community as a dwelling place of the Holy Spirit. Our unity is also a declaration to evil powers. In part, the challenge of reconciliation emerges from this, 'for our struggle is not against flesh and blood, but against the rulers, against the authorities, against the powers of this dark world and against the spiritual forces of evil in the heavenly realms' (Eph. 6.12 NIV).

It is important to remember that during the Second Temple period, Israel was living under occupation by a foreign power.

Rome was not an easy taskmaster for the Jews. Culturally and religiously the two communities found themselves in constant conflict. Rome was the oppressor and the Jewish people were victims. Jews at that time were very concerned for ritual purity. The presence of an occupying military power, together with Hellenistic influences, caused the Jewish population to strongly emphasize their God-given particularity in terms of the extreme differences between the two cultures and religious expressions.

In Ephesians 2 we encounter the most decisive chapter on ethnic rivalry and animosity in the Scriptures. The chapter includes Paul's attempt[26] to counter the attitudes of the 'us' versus 'them' mentality. When Paul wrote Ephesians, he was dealing with the mutual enmity between Jews and Gentiles. The ethno-religious makeup of Judaism automatically excluded Gentiles from full participation in the commonwealth of Israel.[27] In Ephesians 2.11–12 (RSV), Paul writes, 'Therefore remember that at one time you Gentiles in the flesh, called the uncircumcision by what is called the circumcision, which is made in the flesh by hands – remember that you were at that time separated from Christ, alienated from the commonwealth of Israel, and strangers to the covenants of promise, having no hope and without God in the world.' In this passage, Paul outlines the issues of ethnic animosity, presenting the Jewish perception to his largely non-Jewish audience. This indicates that there was no separation between Jewish ethnic and religious identity. Jewish thinking during this time[28] was largely determined by what Yee calls their 'covenantal ethnocentrism' which 'prompted their exclusive attitude toward the Gentiles'.[29] Their attitude emphasized the 'otherness' of Gentiles, as detailed in the previous verses – they were uncircumcised, outsiders from Israel and the covenants, hopeless (as they lacked knowledge of the one true God) and without God.[30] All these elements later became clear boundary lines between Jews and Gentiles.[31] The ethno-religious overtone of verses 11–12 is juxtaposed with the following verses:[32]

But now in Christ Jesus you who once were far away have been brought near by the blood of Christ. For he himself is our peace, who has made the two groups one and has destroyed the barrier, the dividing wall of hostility, by setting aside in his flesh the law with its commands and regulations. His purpose was to create in himself one new humanity out of the two, thus making peace, and in one body to reconcile both of them to God through the cross, by which he put to death their hostility. He came and preached peace to you who were far away and peace to those who were near. For through him we both have access to the Father by one Spirit' (Eph. 2.13–18 NIV).

Jesus dealt with ethnic rivalry and animosity on the cross, and his actions allowed for these two groups to become one.[33] Jesus came to reconcile both parties to God, and to preach both to those who were far away (Gentiles) and to those who were near (Jews). These verses critique the previous Jewish attitude towards Gentiles, and their turning of 'Israel's privileges into ethnic and national assets' which became 'a boundary marker . . . separating and distinguishing Jews from the rest of humanity' resulting in an exclusive ethnic religion. It is the hostility (the ethnic rivalry and animosity) that has been dealt with, not the differences themselves. Jews and non-Jews retain their distinctiveness. These verses contend that Israel's previous election did not automatically result in reconciliation with God, or inclusion into the expanded people of God. Peace with God is now a result of reconciliation between Jews and Gentiles. This is the goal of ethnic reconciliation presented here.[34] Furthermore, this passage emphasizes that Jesus established a new unified, but not homogenized, community. This is a theological statement concerning who God is and what Jesus did on the cross. Paul continues:

> Consequently, you are no longer foreigners and strangers, but fellow citizens with God's people and also members of his household, built on the foundation of the apostles and prophets, with Christ Jesus himself as the chief cornerstone. In him the whole building is joined together and rises to become a holy temple in the Lord. And in him you too are being built together to become a dwelling in which God lives by his Spirit (Eph. 2.19–22 NIV).

Gentiles who have come to faith in Messiah Jesus are then no longer foreigners and strangers, but part of God's people. Jews and Gentiles together are a holy temple to the Lord, and a vessel for the indwelling of God's Spirit. God's creation of a people that would be a blessing to the nations (as circumcision, Torah and the commonwealth of Israel were supposed to be) was never intended to be an ethnocentric exclusive identity. Through Jesus, God has established a multi-ethnic religion and multi-ethnic covenant, large enough to encompass all who believe, regardless of background.

The cross is the means by which God has, 'in his flesh', removed the barrier so that true peace between Jew and non-Jew (and Palestinian and Israeli) can be realized. This union can be thought of as a marriage, in which a man and a woman come together as one body, but retain their distinctive male and female identities. God's covenant with the Israelites required that they take on external, socially constructed symbols such as circumcision and dietary restrictions to mark themselves as separate and distinct. In the New Testament, we see these external markers of identity as something to be celebrated.

At Pentecost, the Holy Spirit came upon the disciples. They began to speak in the languages of the tribes and nations present in the city, 'Parthians, Medes, Elamites, and residents of Mesopotamia, Judea and Cappadocia, Pontus and Asia, Phrygia and Pamphylia, Egypt and the parts of Libya belonging to Cyrene, and visitors from Rome, both Jews and proselytes, Cretans and Arabs – in our own languages we hear them speaking about God's deeds of power' (Acts 2.9–11). Although the context of this text[35] is Jews and religious proselytes from these nations, we can extrapolate to say that tribes, tongues, language, race, religious laws, and other such external symbols of identity were all included and embraced.

It is clearly not God's intention that we suppress what makes us unique and particular, whether it is our ethnicity, our nationality, or something less fundamental to who we are. God does not want us to deny our Jewish or Palestinian identity, nor our wider identification with our communities. Rather, God's intention is that 'all the nations' he has made 'shall come and bow down before [him] . . . and shall glorify [his] name' (Psalm 86.9). Similarly, Revelation 15.4b states that 'all nations will come and worship before you.' Markus Barth writes:

> The 'one new man' is apparently not an international, intercultural, sexless or historical superman . . . Similarly, neither Jews nor Gentiles

become colorless and meaningless internationals: both of them approach God together; circumcision and uncircumcision are now but a 'so-called' barrier between God and men, and among men. Now Jews and Gentiles are joined and built together –instead of boasting at the expense of one another.[36]

Particularity and diversity are thereby maintained, though we are changed by the cross. Our particularity is not to be a source of enmity but of celebration.

There are very practical problems that arise when people from different social groups come together in community. Paul was addressing the problems on a practical level. In many ways, some of these same issues face the Israeli and Palestinian believing communities today. We see this in the political and theological realm, and also (for they are connected) in our lifestyle choices. We should keep these principles in mind as we seek to engage each other in fellowship. Our identities matter, but they are not an excuse for insensitive egocentricity. Our choices affect others and we are required to consider their impact.

Although the Lord's Supper is not the context of Paul's exposition here (though he does mention that our reconciliation is 'by the blood of Christ' which evokes the imagery of the Lord's Supper in Eph. 2.23), it is nonetheless the ritual expression of these truths. This is beautifully expressed by Gordon Smith:

> On the one hand, our fellowship is derivative of our communion with Christ, and on the other, we know this communion with Christ only when we are in fellowship with one another. Our experience of Christ is mediated to us through the community of faith . . . The Lord's Supper is a rite of reconciliation: Our peace is with Christ and with one another. When we meet we discern both the presence of the risen Christ, who hosts the meal, and also the body, the community of faith of which we are a part . . . Indeed, as Thomas Aquinas put it, the Eucharist is 'the sacramental sign of church unity'. It is the declaration – by ritual sign – that we are at peace with one another . . . Each time we gather to do so on the assumption that all Christians are, as a matter of principle, welcome at this table, this observance. We 'discern the body' (1 Cor. 11:29) each time we gather and celebrate the church catholic – women and men from every nation and tribe and language.

In this event we are in fellowship with the Lord of glory. And in this event we are accepted by Christ as we welcome others even as Christ welcomed us (Rom. 15:7).[37]

In his reflections above, Smith notes that 'to exclude someone from the table because he or she is not of our denomination or church tradition is to fail to discern the body of Christ.' Are we guilty of excluding each other? Here we have a ready indication of how close, or far, we are from the spiritual reality of God's creation of 'one new man out of the two'. It is here, at the place of our ritual communion in the body and blood of Christ, that we see the importance of developing and living out a theology that positions us together at the table of the Lord, and not one that prevents us from this act of communion. As we noted, the context of the text is not that of the Lord's Supper, but surely this is the ritual expression of the truths Paul is discussing. The focus of his words is the radical transformation of the status of both non-Jews and Jews in Christ who are now God's joint dwelling place:

> So then you are no longer strangers and aliens, but you are citizens with the saints and also members of the household of God, built upon the foundation of the apostles and prophets, with Christ Jesus himself as the cornerstone. In him the whole structure is joined together and grows into a holy temple in the Lord; in whom you also are built together spiritually into a dwelling-place for God (Eph. 2.19–22).

The application of this passage is germane to our discussion of Messianic Jews and Palestinian Christians today. We cannot draw a direct parallel between our ethnic conflict and the situation of Jews and Gentiles addressed in Ephesians. Jews and Judaism have changed significantly in the past two thousand years, and Palestinian Christians hardly constitute godless pagans as the context indicated at the time. Yet, even within our communities of faith, we find a strong ethnic–religious divide, in effect comprising a new 'us' versus 'them' attitude. What we can do is derive principles from this passage as the ethnic animosity of that time is mirrored in our ethnic and religious differences today. What we see emphasized most strongly in Ephesians 2 is to be careful that our fleshly identity, our ethnic identity and religious vocation, will not be obstacles to reconciliation, and that the people of God, this 'one new humanity', will not be exclusive.

Paul continues his discussion of unity in Ephesians 3. He discusses God's intention *from the beginning* that there be fellowship between Jews and non-Jews; an intention that was kept hidden but accomplished in Jesus our Messiah. Paul writes:

> Surely you have heard about the administration of God's grace that was given to me for you, that is, the mystery made known to me by revelation, as I have already written briefly. In reading this, then, you will be able to understand my insight into the mystery of Christ, which was not made known to people in other generations as it has now been revealed by the Spirit to God's holy apostles and prophets. This mystery is that through the gospel the Gentiles are heirs together with Israel, members together of one body, and sharers together in the promise in Christ Jesus . . . this grace was given me . . . to make plain to everyone the administration of this mystery, which for ages past was kept hidden in God, who created all things. His intent was that now, through the church, the manifold wisdom of God should be made known to the rulers and authorities in the heavenly realms, according to his eternal purpose that he accomplished in Christ Jesus our Lord (Eph. 3.2–6,8b,9–11 NIV).

Once again we see the cosmic context of reconciliation. In this is revealed the ultimate victory of Jesus on the cross and his ongoing purpose for humanity. The intent was, through the body of Christ, to exhibit God's wisdom and glory to the cosmic powers that opposed God's grace. The process of reconciliation is often a spiritual battleground. God's purposes of love and grace stand everlastingly opposed to the destructive, divisive plans of the powers that rule the fallen creation. God's kingdom has come; it has broken through in Christ and his followers who faithfully live according to the principles of the kingdom of God.

Conclusion

The well-known parable of the Good Samaritan epitomizes unconditional love of one's neighbour, but what shocked those who heard Jesus' story was that the one whom Jesus chose to illustrate true love belonged to the community of the 'other'.[38] He was considered a second-class citizen and an outsider, looked upon with scorn by the religious Jews of that time.[39] To situate this kind of person as the exemplary protagonist was scandalous. The story was Jesus' brilliant answer to the expert in religious Jewish law who asked him, 'Teacher . . . what must I do to inherit eternal life?' (Luke 10.25 NIV) In response, Jesus asked the man, 'What is written in the [Torah]? How do you read it?' The man answered, 'Love the Lord your God with all your heart and with all your soul and with all your strength and with all your mind' and 'Love your neighbour as yourself,' quoting two important verses from the Torah. Jesus replied, 'You have answered correctly' and 'Do this and you will live.'

The man was not satisfied with the answer, and asked for clarification: 'Who is my neighbour?' This was essentially a question of *Halacha* (Jewish law). He was asking towards whom did he have neighbourly obligations. Jesus probes the man's interpretation of Torah through the telling of this great parable:

'A man was going down from Jerusalem to Jericho, when he was attacked by robbers. They stripped him of his clothes, beat him and went away, leaving him half-dead. A priest happened to be going down the same road, and when he saw the man, he passed by on the other side. So too, a Levite, when he came to the place and saw him, passed by on the other side. But a Samaritan, as he travelled, came where the man was; and when he saw him, he took pity on him. He went to him and bandaged his wounds, pouring on oil and wine. Then he put the man on his own donkey, brought him to an inn and took care of him. The next day he took out two denarii and gave them to the innkeeper. "Look after him," he said, "and when I return, I will reimburse you for any extra expense you may have." Which of these three do you think was a neighbour to the man who fell into the hands of robbers?' The expert in the law replied, 'The one who had mercy on him.' Jesus told him, 'Go and do likewise' (Luke 10.30–37 NIV).

This story would have been unsettling to its hearers, just as it would no doubt have been to the expert in the law. When Jesus asked which of the three constituted 'a neighbour', the expert could not even bring himself to say the word 'Samaritan' but only *'the one* who had mercy on him.'[40] The Samaritans and Jews had a long history of racial, religious and political enmity that dated back as far as 722 BCE. There are different views as to the origins of the Samaritans. According to 2 Chronicles 30.1 – 31.6 the claims that the northern tribes of Israel were all exiled by the Assyrians and therefore those who occupied the land (Samaritans) were from non-Israelite origins is rejected by the Hebrew Bible. This passage states that not all of the people from the northern kingdom were exiled by the Assyrians. Some remained even after the Assyrian conquest of the land in the eighth century BCE. In addition, when Israel was conquered by Assyria, many people were exiled from the land, and foreigners were 'transplanted' in their place. The Samaritans were thus a mixed group. They perceived themselves as the guardians and the true keepers of the Mosaic covenant. Judeans, however, perceived them as practising a deviant, syncretistic version of Yahweh worship.[41]

When the exiled Israelites returned to the land and rebuilt their temple, conflict ensued between them. The Samaritans had erected a rival temple in their religious centre. Scholarly opinion is divided on the issue of the placement of the Samaritan temple, although many believe it was built on Mt Gerizim, opposite Shechem. In 128 BCE the Hasmonean leader, John Hyrcanus, initiated an attack on Samaria and destroyed the Samaritan temple. During Jesus' childhood, a number of Samaritans desecrated the temple in Jerusalem by scattering dead people's bones around this central holy site.[42] The Gospel of John records some Judeans who opposed Jesus, and disparagingly referred to him as a 'Samaritan' (John 8.48). A clear example of the ethnic and religious hostilities is demonstrated when Jesus was refused Samaritan hospitality as he and his disciples passed by Samaria on their way to Jerusalem. He was then asked by his enraged disciples, 'Lord, do you want us to call fire down from heaven to destroy them?' (Luke 9.54).[43]

Jesus carefully composes his story, from the setting on the road to the particular characters. The winding road descends from the mountainous heights of Jerusalem down to the small town of Jericho on the desert plain hundreds of metres below sea level. Jesus' hearers knew the road was dangerous. The victim is beaten by thieves, stripped of his clothing and possessions, and left unconscious by the wayside. Jesus purposefully leaves out details regarding this person's identity. The easiest way to determine which group someone belonged to was by their clothing or their accent. Lacking either of these socially descriptive elements, it was impossible to know to which group this victim belonged. In the Second Temple period, Jericho was a priestly city where priests would live and make preparations during the times of the year when they were not working in the temple.[44] Thus, it was common for priests and Levites to use this road. When the first man, a priest, saw the wounded man, he deliberately passed by him on the other side, avoiding the ritual contamination that would have resulted (and rendered him temporarily unfit for temple service) had he come into contact with a dead body. Jesus' story, however, seems to indicate that the priest was travelling from Jerusalem to Jericho, perhaps returning home after his temple service. The second traveller, a Levite, also passed by the wounded man. Ironically, it is a Samaritan, a member of a competing ethno-religious group, far from his religious centre and a stranger on this road, who stops and cares for the victim. It's not a usual road for a Samaritan to travel; his presence on the road is more striking than that of the priest or the Levite. It is interesting to note that the Mishnah (the earliest layer of the rabbinic corpus)[45] makes reference to Samaritans in the context of prohibited contact that had the potential to render a Jew unclean.[46] By bringing a Samaritan into the discussion, Jesus redirects the legal parsing about neighbourly obligations and instead focuses on an indiscriminate expression of love that mirrors God's own love towards humanity. Any human being, created in his image, is a 'neighbour'.

Our communities know the road upon which Jesus set his parable. The members of our communities can identify which town is Israeli and which is Palestinian. Sometimes just by looking at a person, or hearing their accent, we can make quick judgements about a person – 'One of us?' or 'One of them?' Through the example of the Samaritan, Jesus upends our instinctive categories and invites us to see the world with new eyes.

In an Israeli context, the Samaritan might take the form of a religious, bearded Muslim from a national-religious party dressed in traditional attire as he passes through West Jerusalem. For Palestinians, the Samaritan might take the form of a young Jewish settler with a knitted *kipah* and uncurled side-locks from a West Bank settlement, passing by Beit Jala. For a Messianic Jew, the Samaritan could be a Palestinian liberation theologian; for a Palestinian Christian, a Christian Zionist theologian.

Like the Samaritan, we must be willing to extend neighbourliness to the 'other', even to our perceived enemy. It is *our* responsibility to go out of our way to love and engage one another, even if that means we do so at *our own expense,* just as the Samaritan cared for the wounded man; giving of his time, energy and finances without thought of reimbursement. To be a neighbour means we are called to *actively show mercy* towards each other. What does mercy look like when we encounter one another? Perhaps it means listening to one another with love and openness, refusing to insist on first defending our own position. When we do this, our conversational partner from the 'enemy camp' may be given a real hearing, and *real dialogue can then take place.* What does mercy look like in terms of land? Perhaps it means letting go of some of our ideas of entitlement. What does mercy look like in terms of justice? Perhaps it means showing more compassion than judgement. What does mercy look like in terms of eschatology? Perhaps it means rethinking some of our theological ideas that fail to seek the other's good. What does mercy look like in terms of identity? Perhaps it means making meaningful room for one another within our group. We the co-authors, and the members of our communities, are responsible for grappling with these difficult questions.

We invite all our brothers and sisters in the body of Christ, especially our fellow community members, to join us and embrace the theological promise and challenge we have presented in this book. May God empower us by his Spirit, that we may live our lives sacrificially *for his sake.*[47]

APPENDIX:

Stages of Reconciliation

Because reconciliation is neither a single event nor a linear process, it is best described in stages.[1] People progress at their own pace, and it is impossible to generalize what 'works' since everyone has a different path towards reconciliation. However, Musalaha has identified stages that people experience on their journey towards reconciliation. These surprisingly reliable signposts provide some orientation to participants when the process seems uncomfortably chaotic or futile.

The essential elements of reconciliation are found in these four principles developed by John Dawson:

1. *Confession*: Stating the truth; acknowledging the unjustness of hurtful action by oneself or one's group towards other individuals or groups.
2. *Repentance*: Turning from unloving to loving actions.
3. *Reconciliation*: Giving and receiving forgiveness, and pursuing intimate fellowship with previous enemies.
4. *Restitution*: Attempting to restore what has been damaged or destroyed, and seeking justice wherever one has power to act or to influence.[2]

These principles find their application in the stages of reconciliation developed by Musalaha (outlined here). As newly established relationships deepen, one finds places where confession and repentance are both necessary and valuable for the health of the relationship (Stages 1 and 2). At this pivotal point, one or both of the individuals in the relationship might decide to part ways. The perceived costs of reconciling and making restitution can seem overwhelming, risky and even imprudent (Stage 3). But when one or both parties can reclaim self-identity and grow in it (Stage 4), they find the movements through reconciliation and restitution far less psychically threatening than they once believed and are now willing to work together in a more honest, open way (Stages 5 and 6).

Stage 1: Establishing Relationships

It is no accident that the idea of Musalaha was initially developed in the early 1990s, a time characterized by hope and optimism. With the beginning of the Oslo peace process, many Israelis and Palestinians thought that peace was finally imminent. This hope was also reflected within the two believing communities, and the first Israeli and Palestinian believers who came to Musalaha meetings were full of excitement, confident that the road to reconciliation was readily achievable. After all, they thought, would not a shared faith in Jesus the Messiah make the differences that hinder reconciliation easily fade away? That was the confident expectation.

Theoretically, there are many approaches to reconciliation. Some methods advocate an interpersonal approach, focusing on individuals and building personal relationships between them, which can then be applied to larger groups. Others argue for an intergroup approach, where the focus is on group dynamics, claiming that conflict is never merely about individuals but instead about two identities or nations.[3]

Musalaha attempts to combine these two methods, finding it important to address both interpersonal and intergroup elements. In the first stage, however, the interpersonal approach is more important to establish friendships and build a measure of trust. When launching immediately into an intergroup discussion about divisive issues – as happened at that first meeting at the Baptist Village – the participants will quickly meet with discouragement. By first working to establish friendships and cultivating a sense of care for the other, there is greater mutual flexibility to discuss contentious issues.

The problem is that once participants have begun to establish a relationship and a sense of appreciation for each other, they hesitate to raise the divisive issues. Because they do not want to jeopardize the fragile new relationships, it is easy for participants on both sides of the divide to get stuck in what Musalaha's staff refers to as the 'Hallelujah!' stage. Participants are happy and excited to come together for worship and fellowship but refuse to move beyond that and discuss harder questions. They say, 'We are already reconciled! We all love Jesus and that is enough. We don't need to talk about things that we do not agree on.' Participants often need gentle prodding towards these painful realities.

Additionally, this 'Hallelujah!' attitude often functions as a form of self-protection against deeper, more conflicted emotions that each side experiences in their initial encounter with the other. For instance, in every conflict one side is more powerful than the other. In the first flush of acquaintance, the more powerful party often feels that reconciliation has been achieved by merely establishing relationships with the less powerful. To delve further would risk compromising that 'feeling of reconciliation'. Simultaneously, although they also enjoy the blossoming relationships, the less powerful party becomes aware of a growing frustration at this stage. They realize that if this moment constitutes reconciliation, then it is inadequate. While they may not yet feel free to voice their frustration, they do not fully share that sense of 'reconciliation'. They desire to release their pent-up emotions and to change the imbalance of power.

Stage 2: Opening Up

Research has shown that bringing Israelis and Palestinians together for a meaningful encounter reduces social distance and lack of acceptance of the other.[4] However, it has also shown that a one-time encounter and its limited positive effects cannot be sustained without continued face-to-face meetings and encouragement to maintain relationships. Therefore, the second stage involves developing and deepening these new friendships through more follow-up meetings. By increasing their sense of vulnerability and the real possibility of being hurt, participants demonstrate a growing dedication to reconciliation and can begin to discuss issues related to the conflict.

Now intergroup dynamics begin to emerge. Where participants once saw each other merely as individuals, participants now see the other as members of a larger group – as *Israelis* or as *Palestinians*.

As these aspects come into view in the deeper discussions, people start unloading their grievances on each other. Often participants make accusations that shock their new friends. In Musalaha meetings, the Palestinian participants often initiate this process by telling the Israelis about their lives and the suffering they endure because of the occupation. They have a felt need to be heard and known. They cannot complain to the Israeli government, and they cannot argue with the soldiers in the Israeli army. They do not have any other avenues for expressing their frustrations with their daily humiliations and trials. So, when they meet Israelis, especially those who have stepped forward for the purpose of reconciliation, the Palestinians feel as though they finally have a chance to talk about their experiences with a representative of the oppressing group. And they sincerely believe that if these Israelis truly hear about their lives and the difficulties they face, then they will try to help and advocate for them within the political system.

Naturally enough, the Israeli participants feel uncomfortable when the Palestinians share their frustrations. Put on the defensive, they feel as though they are being personally attacked for national grievances. Often, they meet the Palestinians' anger with their own anger. The Israelis feel as though they have come to meet with Palestinians out of a genuine desire to make friends, to learn and to fellowship. Instead, they now find themselves being ambushed, blamed for the occupation, and made to feel responsible for the suffering of their Palestinian brothers and sisters. Sometimes they respond with their own grievances and counter the Palestinian accusations with accusations of their own. Others answer the Palestinians with theological justifications of Israeli actions and appeal to an interpretation of the Bible that confidently claims that God promised the land to the Jewish people, thereby discounting any Palestinian objections. Who would argue with God?

Many times, at this stage in the process, participants are hurt by the discussions. Their pain is evident. The honeymoon of friendship is over. Whatever suspicions they may have quietly harboured about the other side are now forcefully confirmed. This stage has played out similarly in history: In the late 1990s, the peace process was undone as extremists on both sides of the conflict perpetrated violent attacks. Israelis and Palestinians began to mistrust each other again, and people on both sides would say, 'They never wanted peace with us. It was all a part of their strategy, to lull us to sleep and then strike us when we least expected it.' In the same way, at this stage, Musalaha participants often feel betrayed by the individual friends who now appear to be belligerent group members: 'I didn't sign up for this. Why should I come here and listen to *them* complain about *us*?' Even the language used reveals the subtle shift from interpersonal to intergroup dynamics.

Additionally, they think that the other side does not properly understand the validity of their theological beliefs: 'If they really knew what I believe, they would understand me and we would get along.' Both Israeli and Palestinian believers believe this to be the case. As a result, they often feel they need to explain their theology when they first meet. To some extent, it is true that Israeli Messianic Jews and Palestinian Christians do not know much about one another. But when the issues that divide them are brought into sharper focus, they realize that they fundamentally disagree about how to understand the Bible. Indeed, they disagree about the most fundamental aspects of life and faith. And what the other side is saying about the Bible is not just wrong, in which case it could be dispassionately corrected. It is offensive and communally threatening, and therefore must be rejected and fought.

Stage 3: Withdrawal

Because of the difficult discussions, many simply withdraw from the process.[5] This is a normal, even healthy response, and an expected part of the reconciliation process. Disruption and withdrawal followed the collapse of Oslo as well. In 2000 the second *intifada* erupted, and the relationship between Israelis and Palestinians reached near total disconnection. Among believers, this was a difficult period as well, as both Israeli and Palestinian believers felt pressure to join in the larger conflict. To a greater or lesser extent, both believing communities experienced emotional struggles balancing their sense of national identification with their identification with their fellow brothers and sisters from the other 'camp'.[6]

After Musalaha participants' initial excitement fades and their sense of betrayal and injury ferment, many find that engaging with the other side is simply too painful, too disappointing, too hopeless, and they withdraw. Theological truths that are foundational to their sense of identity cannot be cavalierly compromised just to appease the other party. Some try to negotiate or dictate the terms of their engagement, offering fellowship on the condition of theological agreement. Since they believe they do not and seemingly *cannot* agree, the possibility for fellowship ends. Because they perceive themselves as taking a theologically principled stand, these participants also feel little compunction about ending the relationships.

An often unseen but powerful layer complicates these fledgling relationships. There are Christians throughout the world, who are neither Israeli nor Palestinian, who do not live with the daily fears and humiliations, but who still have a *theological* stake in the conflict. On one side there are evangelicals, dispensationalists and Christian Zionists, who believe that any territorial concession of Israel's land to Palestinians or other Arab states violates God's will. On the other side are mostly liberal Protestant Christians who elevate the principles of social justice and non-violence and see the Palestinian Christian struggle as an ideal venue to demonstrate the truth of their doctrine.

Both these outside forces are tempted to view Israeli and Palestinian believers as proxies in a larger theological battle. Their influence has been increasingly felt in the conflict, especially in the last decade since the second intifada. With the support and financial backing of foreign institutions, both sides hold conferences and seminars and produce books and documentaries, most of which present an overly simplified version of the conflict, championing one side and vilifying the other. In all of these forums, Israeli and Palestinian believers are encouraged to cultivate their sense of identity as victims and to withdraw from conciliatory action.

As enablers of the conflict, these outside influences have harmed the process of reconciliation, and the effects of their efforts reverberate throughout both Israeli Messianic Jewish and Palestinian Christian theology. Many leaders on both sides are becoming increasingly aware of the problem and are seeking to develop a more locally relevant, indigenous theology. However, equally evident on both sides, leaders often financially and politically depend on the outside supporters and, as one would expect, risk much by reconsidering their hard-line position. Withdrawing from relationships with the other seems like the better bet; to move towards one another in reconciliation presents too many risks.

Stage 4: Reclaiming Identity

In most conflict situations, a group's sense of identity is fundamentally challenged. Conflicts tend to force each side to view itself as the pure victim and the other as the pure aggressor.[7] This dynamic is the same for both Israelis and Palestinians, who each see their group as the primary victim of the conflict. But, in forums of reconciliation, when the 'victims' meet their 'aggressors', this sense of identity as blameless victim is called into question. They realize they cannot continue to see themselves or the others so simplistically. This is a trying period as each side must challenge strongly held perceptions of 'who we are'. This moment, the fourth stage, is also an opportunity for the participants to reclaim their own identity – no longer as 'pure victim', but with a more accurate and, in many ways, more secure understanding of one's self and group.

For reconciliation to occur, each side's identity must be affirmed. The goal of meeting with one's perceived enemy is not to do away with distinguishing characteristics, but rather to be enriched, challenged and humbled by the differences of the people whom God has called to his kingdom. The distinctiveness of Israeli Messianic Jewish and Palestinian Christian identity must be affirmed at every stage, but it cannot be done *at the expense of the other*. The emphasis now is each participant's unshakeable identity as children of God, heirs of the kingdom, and members of the body of Christ. The participants are freed to abandon the idolatry of their self-protective sense of victimhood and to ground themselves in the identity of the Victim-Who-Is-Victor, Jesus the Messiah. Indeed, the securest form of identity is one that is forged at the foot of the cross.

With their identities affirmed as Israelis and Palestinians, and as equally valued members in the body of Christ, the participants now have a sympathetic awareness of the 'other side'. Each side is freed to affirm the other's identity because they themselves have also been affirmed. In appraising and valuing the identity of the other, each is freed to deal with one's own identity. As John Paul Lederach writes, 'The journey through conflict toward reconciliation always involves turning to face oneself. Jacob has to face his fear. To turn toward his brother, his enemy, he first has to deal with himself, his own fears, and his past actions.'[8]

Decision Point

Having moved through several of the initial stages, the participants now face a decision. Do they continue in the path of reconciliation, now knowing that it is a path of genuine suffering? Or do they stop here? Participants reach this decision point at various stages, but it usually happens after the initial glow of friendship has been challenged, and even after a period of withdrawal. But despite these difficulties, many participants choose the high road of love and empowered vulnerability; that is, they decide to commit to dialogue and relationship with those who were once their enemies. Alongside the sting of realizing that life's entrenched problems are far more complex than they once thought, they have experienced the joy of coming to know people on the other side. Accepting that reconciliation is often a painful process requiring vulnerability and trust, many still continue to walk in its path.

Once participants have made this decision, they usually remain involved and engaged. Although they may revisit the decision from time to time, they know that the cost of total withdrawal is catastrophic and full of despair. Not unlike the pain of childbirth endured for the sake of a baby, participants realize that the pain of reconciliation is worth the rewards.

Stage 5: Committing and Returning

Now committed to reconciling work, participants deepen their relationships and take greater risks for reconciliation. Securely grounded in their identity in Jesus, the participants have developed the capacity to listen to the other side's grievances without feeling fundamentally threatened. They enjoy a confidence in the reciprocity of their relationship with the other, knowing that their grievances will also receive a respectful hearing. The two may still robustly disagree; in fact, it is likely that they will. But the participants enjoy a new freedom to truly hear and accept others and their differences for what they are.

This freedom is accompanied by a deeper appreciation of one's moral responsibility for the perpetuation of the conflict, as well as for the failings of one's own group. Far from self-hatred, the participant has developed a capacity for healthy self-criticism, made possible because of the restoration of trust within the relationship. (This self-critical stance is crucial to the process, but it must also be balanced. If only one side adopts it, resentment will grow.) When both sides are secure enough to be self-critical, relational progress can be made. This does not imply that both sides must agree that both are *equally* guilty, or that guilt and blame must be apportioned symmetrically. This expectation does not reflect the dynamics of conflict in real life. It is important enough that the participants forego instinctive self-justification and acquire a willingness to seek after the truth, even if it does not portray their communities in the best possible light.

Now the question of justice is raised. Crucial to genuine reconciliation, asking questions related to justice naturally emerge within honest, self-critical assessment of each side's actions in the conflict: 'How have I [or my community] contributed to injustice?' and 'How can I help bring about justice?' Each participant must face the conflict, in all of its ugliness, and ask themselves, 'How am I involved in this? What is my moral responsibility?' There can be no true reconciliation without justice, just as there can be no true justice without reconciliation.

It is also here that participants take more risks for the cause of reconciliation. For some, just continuing to meet with the other side is a risk, especially if they have been hurt in the process of reconciliation. (For instance, many Musalaha participants face judgement, being viewed as traitors or heretics by their own community.) By continuing to be involved, they indicate their willingness to risk being hurt and misunderstood again. For others, it may mean getting involved outside the framework of Musalaha, advocating for reconciliation as well as sharing the message of reconciliation within their spheres of influence. This avenue shares the same risks of being accused of treachery or heresy. Yet others may decide to commit to the friends they have made during Musalaha meetings. For Israelis and Palestinians to maintain friendships where the political, cultural and social norms dictate separation involves true risk.

Stage 6: Taking Steps

Finally, the participants plan and take practical, tangible steps towards reconciliation. Often participants engage in confession and forgiveness, especially those who have played an active role in the conflict. While this may occur earlier in the process, it is often in the sixth stage that participants are able to ask for forgiveness and to forgive without feelings of bitterness, anger and guilt.

The participants often acquire a shared vision for joint actions and advocacy. They have honestly assessed their complicity within the conflict, or their roles in perpetuating injustice, and aim towards actually achieving justice. Self-criticism alone is not enough; the question of how one might be contributing to injustice is truly answered through actions for the sake of justice. Musalaha participants who have reached this stage are clearly committed to the process of reconciliation and are able to inspire and invite others to join the cause. Motivating others happens best through example. People may be curious and want to know about efforts at reconciliation. Even if one's friends disagree with Musalaha's reconciliation encounters, the act of speaking openly about one's reconciling friendships with those who were once enemies is a powerful witness. In recent years Musalaha has seen a small core-group of dedicated Israelis and Palestinians committed to reaching out, taking risks, and working for transformation of their societies through reconciliation.

Musalaha is a small organization and has little influence in the political sphere. However, this applied process of reconciliation has and continues to have a significant impact on many individuals' lives. The individuals who persevere tend to be quite effective at motivating others and bringing about real change within their communities. The courageous commitments of the few can inspire and influence the many, and can help to shape the prevailing culture.[9] As we have consistently emphasized, the ground, possibility and success of appropriating the reconciliation God has provided for us in Christ is based on the reality of that provision and its implications for our new identity in him.

Bibliography

'A Moment of Truth (Kairos Palestine): A Word of Faith, Hope, and Love from the Heart of Palestinian Suffering' (Bethlehem, 2009).

Abdel Jawad, Saleh. 'The Arab and Palestinian Narratives of the 1948 War.' Pages 72–114 in *Israeli and Palestinian Narratives of Conflict, History's Double Helix* (ed. Robert I. Rotberg; Bloomington: Indiana University Press, 2006).

Abu El-Assal, Riah. 'The Birth and Experience of the Christian Church: The Protestant/Anglican Perspective, Anglican Identity in the Middle East.' Pages 131–40 in *Christians in the Holy Land* (ed. Michael Prior and William Taylor; London: World of Islam Festival Trust, 1994).

—. *Caught in Between: The Story of an Arab Palestinian Christian Israeli* (London: SPCK, 1999).

Adiv, Ehud. 'Politics and Identity: A Critical Analysis of Israeli Historiography and Political Thought.' Pages 19–44 in *Across the Wall: Narratives of Israeli–Palestinian History* (ed. Ilan Pappé and Jamil Hilal; London, New York: I.B. Tauris, 2010).

Aghazarian, Albert. 'The Significance of Jerusalem to Christians.' Pages 99–106 in *Christians in the Holy Land* (ed. Michael Prior and William Taylor; London: World of Islam Festival Trust, 1994).

Al-Dabbagh, Moustafa M. *Biladuna Filastin* (Our Country Palestine) (Kofr Qar: Israel, 2nd edn, 1991).

Ali, Michael Nazir. 'Christians in the Holy Land.' Pages 161–8 in *Christians in the Holy Land* (ed. Michael Prior and William Taylor; London: World of Islam Festival Trust, 1994).

Ateek, Naim. *Justice, and Only Justice* (Maryknoll, NY: Orbis Books, 1989).

—. *Palestinian Cry for Justice* (Maryknoll, NY: Orbis Books, 2008).

—. 'Putting Christ at the Centre: The Land from a Palestinian Christian Perspective', in *The Bible and the Land: An Encounter* (ed. Lisa Loden, Peter Walker and Michael Wood; Jerusalem: Musalaha, 2000).

Augsburger, David W. *Conflict Mediation across Cultures, Pathways and Patterns* (Louisville, KY: Westminster John Knox Press, 1992).

Awad, Alex. *Palestinian Memories: The Story of a Palestinian Mother and Her People* (Bethlehem: Bethlehem Bible College, 2008).

Bailey, Kenneth. *Jesus through Middle Eastern Eyes: Cultural Studies in the Gospels* (Downers Grove, IL: InterVarsity Press, 2008).

Barak, Oren. 'The Failure of the Israeli-Palestinian Peace Process, 1993–2000'. *Journal of Peace Research* 42:6 (November 2005): pp. 719–36.

Baramki, Gabriel. 'The Spiritual Significance and Experience of the Churches: The Orthodox Perspective.' Pages 141–2 in *Christians in the Holy Land* (ed. Michael Prior and William Taylor; London: World of Islam Festival Trust, 1994).

Bar-On, Dan and Sami Adwan. 'The Psychology of Better Dialogue between Two Separate but Interdependent Narratives.' Pages 205–24 in *Israeli and Palestinian Narratives of Conflict: History's Double Helix* (ed. Robert I. Rotberg; Bloomington: Indiana University Press, 2006).

Bar-On, Mordechai. 'Conflicting Narratives or Narratives of a Conflict: Can the Zionist and Palestinian Narratives of the 1948 War Be Bridged?' Pages 142–73 in *Israeli and Palestinian Narratives of Conflict: History's Double Helix* (ed. Robert I. Rotberg; Bloomington: Indiana University Press, 2006).

Bar-Tal, Daniel and Gavriel Salomon. 'Israeli–Jewish Narratives of the Israeli–Palestinian Conflict, Evolution, Contents, Functions and Consequences.' Pages 19–46 in *Israeli and Palestinian Narratives of Conflict: History's Double Helix* (ed. Robert I. Rotberg; Bloomington: Indiana University Press, 2006).

—. *Living with the Conflict: Socio-Psychological Analysis of the Jewish Society in Israel* ([Hebrew] Jerusalem: Carmel, 2007).

Barth, Markus. 'Conversion and Conversation: Israel and the Church in Paul's Epistle to the Ephesians'. *Interpretation* 17 (1963), pp. 3–24.

Becker, Adam H. and Annette Yoshiko Reed, eds. *The Ways that Never Parted: Jews and Christians in Late Antiquity and the Early Middle Ages* (Minneapolis: Fortress, 2007).

Ben-Shmuel, Philip D. 'Hagshama: A Theology for an Alternate Messianic Jewish Zionism', in *The Land Cries Out: Theology of the Land in the Israeli-Palestinian Context* (ed. Salim J. Munayer and Lisa Loden; Eugene, OR: Wipf & Stock, 2012).

Ben-Gurion, David. 'David Ben-Gurion, Broadcast to the Nation, May 15, 1948'. http://www.jewishvirtuallibrary.org/jsource/History/bgbroad.html (accessed 24 October 2012).

Benvenisti, Meron. *Sacred Landscape: The Buried History of the Holy Land since 1948* (Berkeley: University of California Press, 2000).

Berkowitz, Ariel and Devorah. *Torah Rediscovered: Challenging Centuries of Misinterpretation and Neglect* (Lakewood, CO: First Fruits of Zion, 1996).

Blau, Joshua. *A Grammar of Christian Arabic, Based Mainly on South-Palestinian Texts from the First Millennium, Corpus Scriptorum Christianorum Orientalium*, vols 267, 276, 279, Subsidia Tom. 27–9 (Louvain: Secretariat du Corpus SCO, 1966–7).

Brock, Brian. *Singing the Ethos of God: On the Place of Christian Ethics in Scripture* (Grand Rapids, MI: Eerdmans, 2007).

Buber, Martin. 'Politics and Morality.' Pages 169–73 in *A Land of Two Peoples: Martin Buber on Jews and Arabs* (ed. Paul R. Mendes-Flohr; New York: Oxford University Press, 1983).

Bulliett, Richard W. 'Empires of the Sand: The Struggle for Mastery in the Middle East, 1789–1923 (Review)'. *The Middle East Journal* 54:4 (2000), p. 667.

Butler, Judith. *Parting Ways: Jewishness and the Critique of Zionism, New Directions in Critical Theory* (New York: Columbia University Press, 2012).

Calder, Mark. '"Enclosures of Hymns for the Lambs of Your Flock": Syriac Orthodox Scripture, Tradition and Modernity in the Competition for Souls'. *The Competition for Souls: The Contemporary Christian Communities in the Holy Land* (Jerusalem: Van Leer Institute, 14 June 2011).

Cannon, Mae Elise. *Social Justice Handbook: Small Steps for a Better World* (Downers Grove, IL: InterVarsity Press, 2009).

Carr, David. *Time, Narrative, and History* (Bloomington and Indianapolis: Indiana University Press, 1986).

Chartier, Roger. 'Reading Matter and "Popular" Reading: From the Renaissance to the Seventeenth Century.' Pages 269–81 in *A History of Reading in the West* (ed. Cavallo Guglielmo and Roger Chartier; Amherst, MA: University of Massachusetts Press, 1999).

Coggins, R.J. 'The Samaritans in Josephus.' Pages 257–73 in *Josephus, Judaism and Christianity* (eds. L. H. Feldman and G. Hata; Detroit: E.J. Brill, 1987).

Cohen, Boaz. 'Introduction.' *Everyman's Talmud* (ed. A. Cohen; New York: Schocken Books, 1975).

Cohen, Gili. 'Study: IDF Officers Identify More as Israeli than Jewish' http://www./news/diplomacy-defense/study-idf-officers-identify-more-as-israeli-than-j haaretz.comewish.premium-1.469791 (accessed 14 October 2012).

Cohen, Shaye J.D. *The Beginnings of Jewishness: Boundaries, Varieties, Uncertainties* (London: University of California Press, 1999).

—. *From the Maccabees to the Mishnah* (Philadelphia: Westminster, 1987).

Cohn-Sherbok, Dan and Dawoud El-Alami. *The Palestine–Israeli Conflict: A Beginner's Guide* (Oxford: Oneworld, rev. edn, 2003).

Cox, Brian. *Faith-Based Reconciliation: A Moral Vision that Transforms People and Societies* (USA: Xlibris Press, 2007).

Crombie, Kelvin. 'Michael Solomon Alexander and the Controversial Jerusalem Bishopric'. *Mishkan* 15 (1991): pp. 1–12.

Currie, Mark. *Postmodern Narrative Theory* (Houndmills: Palgrave, 1998).

Davidson, Lawrence. 'Christian Zionism as a Representation of American Manifest Destiny'. *Critique: Critical Middle Eastern Studies* 14 (2005): pp. 157–69.

Davis, Alan T. *Anti-Semitism and the Christian Mind* (New York: Herder and Herder, 1969).

Dawson, John. 'Hatred's End: A Christian Proposal to Peacemaking in a New Century.' Page 236 in *Forgiveness and Reconciliation: Religion, Public Policy, and Conflict Transformation* (ed. Raymond G. Helmick, S.J., and Rodney L. Peterson; Radnor: Templeton Foundation Press, 2001).

Del Sarto, Raffaella A. 'Israel's Contested Identity and the Mediterranean' (2002) 7 http://ies.berkeley.edu/research/DelSartoIsraelMed.pdf (accessed 14 October 2012).

Doumani, Beshara. *Rediscovering Palestine: Merchants and Peasants in Jabal Nablus, 1700–1900* (Berkeley: University of California Press, 1995).

Dumper, Michael. 'Faith and Statecraft: Church-State Relations in Jerusalem after 1948.' Pages 56–181 in *Palestinian Christians, Religion, Politics and Society in the Holy Land* (ed. Anthony O'Mahony; London: Melisende, 1999).

Elwell, Walter A. *Evangelical Dictionary of Theology* (Grand Rapids, MI: Baker Academic, 2nd edn, 2007).

Epp-Tiessen, Esther. 'Conquering the Land.' Pages 52–74 in *Under Vine and Fig Tree* (ed. Alain E. Weaver; Telford, PA: Cascadia, 2007).

Eusebius, *Ecclesiastical History* 4.5.1–4, in J.A. Stevenson, *A New Eusebius: Documents Illustrating the History of the Church to AD 337*, new edition revised by W.H.C. Frend (London: SPCK, 1985).

Fattah, Kamal Abdul and Wolf-Dieter Hutteroth. *Historical Geography of Palestine, Transjordan and Southern Syria in the Late Sixteenth Century* (Erlangen; Fränkische Geographische Ges., 1977).

Fearon, James D. 'What Is Identity (as We Now Use the Word)?' (Stanford University Department of Political Science, 1999) http://www.stanford.edu/~jfearon/papers/iden1v2.pdf (accessed 17 September 2012).

Finkelstein, Norman. *Image and Reality of the Israel–Palestine Conflict* (London: Verso, 1995).

Flannery, Edward H. *The Anguish of the Jews: Twenty-Three Centuries of Antisemitism* (New Jersey: Paulist Press, 2nd edn, 2004).

Flusser, David. 'Paganism in Palestine.' Pages 1065–1100 in *The Jewish People in the First Century*, vol. 2 (ed. S. Safrai and M. Stern; Amsterdam: Van Gorcum, 1976).

Foster, Zachary J. 'Arab Historiography in Mandatory Palestine, 1920–1948.' Master's thesis (Georgetown University, 2011).

Fruchtenbaum, Arnold. *Israelogy: The Missing Link in Systematic Theology* (Tustin, CA: Ariel Ministries, 1992).

Gans, Chaim. 'Palestinians Were Made to Pay an Unfair Price.' Ha'aretz (27 June 2009) http://www.haaretz.com/hasen/spages/1094908.html (accessed 15 August 2011).

Gelber, Yoav. *Palestine 1948: War, Escape and the Emergence of the Palestinian Refugee Problem* (Brighton/Portland: Sussex Academic Press, 2nd edn, 2006).

Gera, Gideon. 'Israel and the June 1967 War: 25 Years Later'. *Middle East Journal* 46:2 (Spring 1992): pp. 229–43.

Geraisy, Sami F. 'Socio-Demographic Characteristics: Reality, Problems and Aspirations within Israel.' Pages 45–55 in *Christians in the Holy Land* (ed. Michael Prior and William Taylor; London: World of Islam Festival Trust, 1994).

Glatzer, Nahum N. *Franz Rosenzweig: His Life and Thought* (New York: Schocken Books, 1961).

Goble, Phillip E. and Salim Munayer. *New Creation Book for Muslims* (Pasadena, CA: Mandate Press, 1989).

Goetz, R. 'Joshua, Calvin, and Genocide'. *Theology Today* 32 (1975): pp. 263–74.

Gordon, Robert P. *Holy Land, Holy City: Sacred Geography and the Interpretation of the Bible* (Carlisle: Paternoster Press, 2004), pp. 104–6.

Gruenler, R.G. *Meaning and Understanding* (Grand Rapids, MI: Zondervan, 1991).

Hainthaler, Theresia. *Christliche Araber vor dem Islam* (Leuven: Peeters, 2007).

Hajjar, Lisa. 'Human Rights in Israel/Palestine: The History and Politics of a Movement'. *Journal of Palestine Studies* 30:4 (Summer 2001), pp. 21–38.

Halabi, Rabah and Nava Sonnenschein. 'School for Peace: Between Hard Reality and the Jewish–Palestinian Encounters.' Pages 278–9 in *Beyond Bullets and Bombs* (ed. Judy Kuriansky; Westport, CN: Praeger, 2007).

Halkin, Hillel. 'Was Zionism Unjust?' *Commentary* (November 1999) http://www.commentarymagazine.com/article/was-zionism-unjust/ (accessed 27 August 2012).

Hammer, Joshua. *A Season in Bethlehem: Unholy War in a Sacred Place* (New York: Free Press, 2003).

Hanafi, Sari. 'Dancing Tango during Peacebuilding: Palestinian-Israeli People-to-People Programs for Conflict Resolution.' Pages 139–56 in *Beyond Bullets and Bombs* (ed. Judy Kuriansky; Westport, CT: Praeger, 2007).

Hanania, Agnes D. 'Churches of the Holy Land Obligations and Expectations: A View from the Holy Land.' Pages 203–16 in *Christians in the Holy Land* (ed. Michael Prior and William Taylor; London: World of Islam Festival Trust, 1994).

Harrill, J. Albert. 'The Use of the New Testament in the American Slave Controversy: A Case History in the Hermeneutical Tension between Biblical Criticism and Christian Moral Debate'. *Religion and American Culture* 10:2 (2000), pp. 149–86.

Hartman, David. *Israelis and the Jewish Tradition: An Ancient People Debating Its Future* (New Haven: Yale University Press, 2000).

Harvey, Richard. *Mapping Messianic Jewish Theology: A Constructive Approach* (Milton Keynes: Paternoster Press, 2009).

—. 'Toward a Messianic Jewish Theology of Reconciliation in the Light of the Arab-Israeli Conflict: Neither Dispensationalist nor Supersessionist?' Pages 82–103 in *The Land Cries Out: Theology of the Land in the Israeli-Palestinian Context* (ed. Salim J. Munayer and Lisa Loden; Eugene, OR: Wipf & Stock, 2012).

—. 'A Typology of Messianic Jewish Theology'. *Mishkan* 57 (2008): pp. 13–23.

Hayes, Richard. *The Moral Vision of the New Testament* (New York: HarperCollins, 1996).

The Helsinki Consultation theological group. http://www.helsinkiconsultation2012.org/index.php/en/statement-en (accessed 20 January 2013).

Heschel, Abraham Joshua. *God in Search of Man: A Philosophy of Judaism* (New York: Farrar, Strauss and Giroux, 1976).

Hilal, Jamil. 'Reflections on Contemporary Palestinian History.' Pages 177–215 in *Across the Wall: Narratives of Israeli–Palestinian History* (ed. Ilan Pappé and Jamil Hilal; London, New York: I.B. Tauris, 2010).

Hitti, Philip. *History of the Arabs* (New York: Palgrave Macmillan, 2002 [1937]).

Hogg, Michael. 'Intragroup Processes, Group Structure and Social Identity.' Pages 65–94 in *Social Group and Identities: Developing the Legacy of Henri Tajfel* (Oxford: Butterworth-Heinemann, 1996).

Holwerda, David E. *Jesus and Israel: One Covenant or Two?* (Grand Rapids, MI: Eerdmans, 1995).

Horsley, Richard, 'Jesus Confronting Empire'. Pages 56–86 in *Challenging Empire: God, Faithfulness and Resistance* (ed. Naim Ateek, Cedar Duaybis and Maurine Tobin; Jerusalem: Sabeel, 2012).

Hudson, Michael C. 'Developments and Setbacks in the Palestinian Resistance Movement'. *Journal of Palestine Studies* 1:3 (Spring 1972): pp. 64–84.

Hyvärinen, Matti. 'Towards a Conceptual History of Narrative'. Collegium (2006) http://www.helsinki.fi/collegium/e-series/volumes/volume_1/index.htm (accessed 25 January 2010).

Isaac, Munther. *A Biblical Theology of the Land: With a Special Emphasis on the Palestinian Church* (Oxford Centre for Mission Studies), forthcoming in 2014.

—. 'Reading the Old Testament in the Palestinian Church Today: Joshua 6 – A Case Study.' Pages 217–33 in *The Land Cries Out: Theology of the Land in the Israeli-Palestinian Context* (ed. Salim J. Munayer and Lisa Loden; Eugene, OR: Wipf & Stock, 2012).

Israel Ministry of Foreign Affairs http://www.mfa.gov.il/MFA/Peace+Process/Guide+to+the+Peace+Process/Declaration+of+Establishment+of+State+of+Israel.htm (accessed 19 October 2012).

Isseroff, Ami. 'Zionism: The History of Zionism and the Creation of Israel' http://www.mideastweb.org/zionism.htm (accessed 29 July 2012).

Itzhaki, Yedidya. 'What Is Jewish Secularism?' http://www.posenfoundation.com/literaryprojects/haaretz-supplement.html (accessed 14 October 2012).

Jenkins, Phillip. *The Lost History of Christianity: The Thousand-Year Golden Age of the Church in the Middle East, Africa and Asia – and How It Died* (New York: HarperOne, 2008).

Jenson, Matt. *Gravity of Sin: Augustine, Luther and Barth on 'homo incurvatus in se'* (London: T&T Clark, 2006).

Juster, Daniel. 'Covenant and Dispensation'. *Mishkan* 1:2 (1985):, pp. 34–5.

—. *Growing to Maturity: A Messianic Jewish Guide* (Denver: Union of Messianic Jewish Congregations, 1987).

—. 'A Messianic Jew Looks at the Land Promises.' Pages 63–81 in *The Land Cries Out: Theology of the Land in the Israeli–Palestinian Context* (ed. Salim J. Munayer and Lisa Loden; Eugene, OR: Wipf & Stock, 2012).

—. http://www.tikkunamerica.org/halachah/intro-dj.php (accessed 1 June 2013).

Karsh, Efraim. *Fabricating Israeli History: The 'New Historians'* (Portland, OR: Frank Cass, rev. edn, 2000).

—. *Palestine Betrayed* (New Haven, CT: Yale University Press, 2010).

—. 'Rewriting Israel's History'. *Middle East Quarterly* (June 1996): pp. 19–29. Also available online: http://www.meforum.org/302/rewriting-israels-history (accessed 10 September 2012).

Kassis, Riad. *Why Don't We Read the Book that Jesus Read?* (Beirut: Clarion Publishing House, 2008).

Katanacho, Yohanna. 'Christ Is the Owner of Haaretz'. *Christian Scholar's Review* 34 (2005): pp. 425–41.

—. 'Introduction to the Church of the Arabs' (unpublished as of August 2012), pp. 5–6.

—. 'Palestinian Protestant Theological Responses to a World Marked by Violence'. *Missiology* 36:3 (July 2008): pp. 289–305.

—. 'A Palestinian Reading of Psalm 87: Jerusalem Is the City of God.' Pages 181–99 in *The Land Cries Out: Theology of the Land in the Israeli-Palestinian Context* (ed. Salim J. Munayer and Lisa Loden; Eugene, OR: Wipf & Stock, 2012).

Kaufman, Debra. 'Is There Such a Thing as "Jewish Identity"?' http://www.secularjewishculture.org/jewish_identity_.html (accessed 14 October 2012).

Khalaf, Issa. 'The Effect of Socioeconomic Change on Arab Societal Collapse in Mandate Palestine'. *International Journal of Middle East Studies* 29:1 (Feb. 1997): pp. 93–112.

—. *Politicism in Palestine: Arab Factionalism and Social Disintegration 1939–1948* (New York: State University of New York Press, 1991).

Khalidi, Rashid. 'Arab Nationalism: Historical Problems in the Literature'. *American Historical Review* 96:5 (1991): pp. 1363–73.

—. *The Iron Cage: The Story of the Palestinian Struggle for Statehood* (Boston: Beacon Press, 2007).

—. *Palestinian Identity: The Construction of Modern National Consciousness* (New York: Columbia University Press, 1997).

Khalidi, Tarif. 'Palestinian Historiography: 1900–1948'. *Journal of Palestine Studies* 9:2 (Aug. 1980): pp. 59–76.

Khalidi, Walid. *All that Remains: The Palestinian Villages Occupied and Depopulated by Israel in 1948* (Washington, DC: Institute for Palestine Studies, 2006).

—. 'Plan Dalet Revisited'. *Journal of Palestine Studies* 18 (1988): pp. 3–70.

Khoury, Geries. *Arab Christians: Rootedness, Presence, Openness* (Jerusalem: Al-Liqa', 2006).

Kimmerling, Baruch and Joel S. Migdal. *The Palestinian People: A History* (Cambridge: Harvard University Press, 2003).

Kinbar, Carl. 'Israel, Torah and the Knowledge of God'. *Kesher* 24 (2010): pp. 18–37.

Kinzer, Mark S. *The Nature of Messianic Judaism* (Hartford, CT: Hashivenu Archives, undated).

—. *Post Missionary Messianic Judaism: Redefining Christian Engagement with the Jewish People* (Grand Rapids, MI: Brazos, 2005).

—. 'Scripture and Tradition.' Pages 29–38 in *Voices of Messianic Judaism* (ed. Dan Cohn-Sherbok; Baltimore: Lederer, 2001).

Kjaer-Hansen, Kai, and Bodil F.Skjøtt, eds. 'Facts and Myths about the Messianic Congregations in Israel'. *Mishkan* 30–1 (1999).

—. *Joseph Rabinowitz and the Messianic Movement: The Herzl of Jewish Christianity* (trans. David Stoner, additions by Birger Petterson; Grand Rapids, MI: Eerdmans, 1995 [1988]).

Kraybill, Ron. 'The Cycle of Reconciliation.' Pages 73–8 in *Seeking and Pursuing Peace: The Process, the Pain, and the Product* (ed. Salim J. Munayer; Jerusalem: Musalaha, 1998).

Kupermintz, Haggai and Gavriel Saloman. 'Lessons to Be Learned from Research on Peace Education in the Context of Intractable Conflict'. *Theory into Practice* 44:4 (2005), p. 295.

Laqueur, Walter. *A History of Zionism* (New York: Schocken Books, 1976).

League of Arab States, Khartoum Resolution, 1 September 1967 http://www.cfr.org/international-peace-and-security/khartoum-resolution/p14841 (accessed 29 November 2011).

Lederach, John Paul. *The Journey toward Reconciliation* (Scottdale, PA: Herald Press, 1999).

Levine, Lee L. *The Ancient Synagogue: The First Thousand Years* (New Haven, CT: Yale University Press, 2005).

Lizorkin-Eyzenberg, Eli. http://jewishstudies.eteacherbiblical.com/2012/08/the-jewish-sabbath-what-took-place-in-between-the-testaments/#_ftn65 (accessed 19 May 2013).

Loden, Lisa. 'Messianic Jewish Views on Israel's Rebirth and Survival in Light of Scripture.' Page 46 in *Christian Perspectives on the Israeli–Palestinian Conflict* (ed. W. Brown and P. Penner; Pasadena, CA: William Carey University Press, 2008).

Lustick, Ian S. *For the Land and the Lord: Jewish Fundamentalism in Israel* (USA: Council on Foreign Relations, 1988).

—. 'Israeli History: Who Is Fabricating What?' *Survival: Global Politics and Strategy* 39:3 (1997), pp. 156–66.

Luther, Martin. 'On the Jews and Their Lies.' Pages 137–306 in *Luther's Works*, vol. 47, American Edition (55 vols; ed. Jaroslav Pelikan and Helmut T. Lehmann; Philadelphia: Muehlenberg and Fortress, and St Louis: Concordia, 1955–86).

Maalouf, Tony. *Arabs in the Shadow of Israel: The Unfolding of God's Prophetic Plan for Ishmael's Line* (Grand Rapids, MI: Kregel, 2003).

MacIntyre, Alasdair. *After Virtue: A Study in Moral Theory* (Notre Dame: University of Notre Dame Press, 1984).

—. *Whose Justice? Which Rationality?* (Notre Dame: University of Notre Dame Press, 1988).

MacKinnon, Catherine. *Women's Lives, Men's Laws* (Cambridge: Harvard University Press, 2005).

Madanat, Suheil. *The Life of Roy Whitman* (Beirut: Baptist Publishing, 1995).

Maoz, Baruch. 'Jerusalem and Justice: A Messianic Jewish Perspective'. Pages 150–73 in *Jerusalem Past and Present in the Purposes of God* (ed. P.W.L. Walker; Cambridge: Tyndale House, 1992).

—. *Judaism Is Not Jewish: A Friendly Critique of the Messianic Movement* (Ross-shire: Christian Focus Publications, 2003).

Masalha, Nur. *The Bible and Zionism: Invented Traditions, Archaeology, and Post-Colonialism* (London: Zed Books, 2007).

—. *Expulsion of the Palestinians: The Concept of Transfer in Zionist Political Thought, 1882–1948* (Beirut: Institute for Palestine Studies, 1992).

—. *The Palestine Nakba: Decolonising History, Narrating the Subaltern, Reclaiming Memory* (London: Zed Books, 2012).

Massad, Hanna. 'The Theological Foundation for Reconciliation between the Palestinian Christians and the Messianic Jews.' Unpublished PhD dissertation (Fuller Theological Seminary, 2000).

McDermott, Gerald.
http://www.yale.edu/faith/jewishchristianconference/documents/Gerald_McDermott.pdf (accessed 1 June 2013).

McKnight, Scot. 'Gentiles.' Pages 259–65 in *Dictionary of Jesus and the Gospels* (ed. Joel B. Green, Scot McKnight and I. Howard Marshall; Downers Grove, IL: InterVarsity Press, 1992).

McRay, Jonathan. *You Have Heard It Said: Events of Reconciliation* (Eugene, OR: Wipf & Stock, 2010).

Mendes-Flohr, Paul. 'Preface.' *A Land of Two Peoples: Martin Buber on Jews and Arabs* (ed. Paul R. Mendes-Flohr; New York: Oxford University Press, 1983).

Meron, Ya'akov. 'Why Jews Fled the Arab Countries'. *The Middle East Quarterly* 2:3 (September 1995), pp. 47–55.

Mink, Louis O. 'History and Fiction as Modes of Comprehension.' Pages 59–60 in *Historical Understanding* (ed. Brian Fay, Eugene O. Golob and Richard T. Vann; Ithaca, NY: Cornell University Press, 1987).

Mishnah, tractate *Shevi'it* [Seventh Year] 8:10 (trans. Jacob Neusner; New Haven, CT: Yale University Press, 1988).

Mitchell, Timothy. *Colonising Egypt* (London: University of California Press, 1991).

Moltmann, Jürgen. *The Crucified God* (London: SCM Press, 2001).

Morris, Benny. *The Birth of the Palestinian Refugee Problem Revisited* (Cambridge: Cambridge University Press, rev. edn, 2004).

—. 'Derisionist History'. *New Republic* (28 November 2009) http://www.tnr.com/article/books-and-arts/derisionist-history?page=0,2 (accessed 27 August 2012).

—. 'The New Historiography: Israel Confronts Its Past'. *Tikkun* (Nov.–Dec. 1988): pp. 19–23, 99–102.

—. 'Refabricating 1948'. *Journal of Palestine Studies* 27:2 (Winter 1998): pp. 81–95.

—. *Righteous Victims: A History of the Zionist-Arab Conflict, 1881–2001* (New York: Vintage Books, 2001).

Mouw, Richard J. 'What the Old Dispensationalists Taught Me'. *Christianity Today* 39:3 (6 March 1995), p. 34.

Munayer, Salim J. 'Beyond Bells and Smells: The Gap between Eastern and Western Christianity' http://www.musalaha.org/articleview.asp?ID=46 (accessed 27 February 2013).

—. 'The Cross and Reconciliation.' Pages 69–81 in *Journey through the Storm: Musalaha and the Reconciliation Process* (ed. Salim J. Munayer; Beit Jala: Nour Print and Design Company, 2011).

—. 'Discernment and Reconciliation amidst the Fog of War.' Pages 82–95 in *Journey through the Storm: Musalaha and the Reconciliation Process* (ed. Salim J. Munayer; Beit Jala: Nour Print and Design Company, 2011).

—. 'The Ethnic Identity of Palestinian Arab Christian Adolescents in Israel.' Unpublished PhD dissertation (University of Wales, Cardiff: Oxford Centre for Mission Studies, June 2000).

—. *Hosea*, Asia Bible Commentary Series (ed. Bruce J. Nicholls and Sang-Bok David Kim; Manila, Philippines: Asia Theological Association, 2010), pp. 8–19, 313–19.

—. 'The Theological Challenge the State of Israel Poses to Palestinian Christians'. *St Francis Magazine* (2008) http://www.stfrancismagazine.info/ja/ (accessed 15 August 2011).

—. 'The Theology of the Land.' *The Land Cries Out: Theology of the Land in the Israeli–Palestinian Context* (ed. Salim J. Munayer and Lisa Loden; Eugene, OR: Wipf & Stock, 2012).

Murre-van den Berg, Heleen. *Syriac Christianity* (Oxford: Blackwell, 2007).

Muslih, Muhammad Y. *The Origins of Palestinian Nationalism* (New York: Columbia University Press, 1988).

Nazzal, Nafez. *The Palestinian Exodus from Galilee, 1948* (Beirut: Institute for Palestine Studies, 1978).

Nerel, Gershon. 'Attempts to Establish a Messianic Jewish Church in Eretz-Israel'. *Mishkan* 28 (1998), pp. 35–44.

—. 'From Death to Life: The Restoration of Jewish Yeshua-Believers in the Land of Israel.' Pages 168–88 in *Israel: His People, His Land, His Story* (ed. Fred Wright; Eastbourne: Thankful Books, 2005).

—. 'Life from the Dead: Modern Jewish Yeshua-Believers and the Historic Churches' (Yad Hashmonah: unpublished paper, 2004).

—. 'Messianic Jews'. *Mishkan* 27 (1997), p. 19.

—. 'Messianic Jews and the Modern Zionist Movement.' Pages 75–84 in *Israel and Yeshua* (ed. Torlief Elgvin; Jerusalem: Caspari Center, 1993).

—. '"Post Mission" and "Messianic Judaism" – Semantics and Reality: A Response to Mark Kinzer, "Post Missionary Messianic Judaism Three Years Later: Reflections on a Conversation Just Begun"' (Jerusalem: Robert Lindsey Lectures, 2008).

—. 'Torah and Halakhah among Modern Assemblies of Jewish Yeshua-Believers: An Israeli Response to Arnold Fruchtenbaum.' Pages 152–65 in *How Jewish Is Christianity? 2 Views of the Messianic Movement* (ed. Louis Goldberg; Grand Rapids, MI: Zondervan, 2003), pp. 152–65.

Nielsen, Jørgen S. 'Preface.' Pages vii–xii in *Christian Arabic Apologetics during the Abbasid Period (750–1258)* (ed. Samir Khalil Samir and Jørgen S. Nielsen; Leiden: Brill, 1994).

O'Donovan, Oliver. *The Desire of Nations: Rediscovering the Roots of Political Theology* (Cambridge; New York: Cambridge University Press, 1996).

—. 'The Political Thought of the Book of Revelation'. *Tyndale Bulletin* 37 (1986): pp. 61–94.

O'Mahony, Anthony. 'Palestinian Christians: Religion, Politics and Society, c.1800–1948.' Pages 9–55 in *Palestinian Christians: Religion, Politics and Society in the Holy Land* (ed. Anthony O'Mahony; London: Melisende, 1999).

'Palestinian Kairos Document.' World Council of Churches (2009)
http://www.oikoumene.org/fileadmin/files/wcc-main/2009 pdfs/Kairos%20Palestine_En.pdf (accessed 10 November 2010).

Pappé, Ilan. 'The Bridging Narrative Concept.' Pages 194–204 in *Israeli and Palestinian Narratives of Conflict: History's Double Helix* (ed. Robert I. Rotberg; Bloomington: Indiana University Press, 2006).

—. *The Ethnic Cleansing of Palestine* (Oxford: Oneworld, 2006).

—. 'Histories and Historians in Israel & Palestine'. *Transforming Cultures eJournal* 1:1 (March 2006), pp. 33–42.

—. *The History of Modern Palestine: One Land, Two Peoples* (Cambridge: Cambridge University Press, 2004).

Peters, Joan. *From Time Immemorial: The Origins of the Arab-Jewish Conflict over Palestine* (New York: Harper and Row, 1984).

Posen, Felix.
http://www.secularjewishculture.org/strands_of_jewishness.html (accessed 14 October 2012).

Prior, Michael. 'Pilgrimage to the Holy Land, Yesterday and Today.' Pages 169–99 in *Christians in the Holy Land* (ed. Michael Prior and Williams Taylor; London: World of Islam Festival Trust, 1994).

—. '"Power" and "the Other" in Joshua: The Brutal Birthing of a Group Identity'. *Mission Studies* 23 (2006), pp. 27–43.

—. '"You Will Be My Witnesses in Jerusalem, in All Judaea and Samaria, and to the Ends of the Earth": A Christian Perspective on Jerusalem.' Pages 96–140 in *Palestinian Christians: Religion, Politics and Society in the Holy Land* (ed. Anthony O'Mahony; London: Melisende, 1999).

Pritz, Ray. *Nazarene Jewish Christianity: From the End of the New Testament Period until Its Disappearance in the Fourth Century* (Jerusalem: Magnes Press, 1992).

Rae, Murray. *History and Hermeneutics* (London: T&T Clark, 2005).

Raheb, Mitri. 'Contextual Palestinian Theology as It Deals with Realities on the Ground'. Christ at the Checkpoint Conference (Bethlehem: Bethlehem Bible College, 17 March 2010). http://www.christatthecheckpoint.com/index.php/lectures (accessed 8 August 2011).

—. 'Displacement Theopolitics: A Century of Interplay between Theology and Politics in Palestine.' Pages 9–32 in *The Invention of History: A Century of Interplay between Theology and Politics in Palestine* (ed. Mitri Raheb; Bethlehem: Diyar Publisher, 2011).

—. *The Invention of History: A Century of Interplay between Theology and Politics in Palestine* (Jerusalem: Diyar Publisher, 2011).

—. 'Shaping Communities in Times of Crises' http://www.mitriraheb.org/index.php?option=com_content&view=article&id=363:shaping-communities-in-times-of-crises&catid=33:english&Itemid=20 (accessed 27 February 2013).

Ramon, Amnon. *Christians and Christianity in the Jewish State* (Jerusalem: Jerusalem Institute for Israel Studies, 2011), forthcoming.

Redekop, Vern Neufeld. *From Violence to Blessing: How an Understanding of Deep-Rooted Conflict Can Open Paths to Reconciliation* (Ottawa: Novalis, 2002).

Regehr, Keith Allen. 'Justice and Forgiveness: Restorative Justice Practice and the Recovery of Theological Memory.' Doctoral thesis (University of Waterloo: Ontario, 2007).

—. 'Justice and Forgiveness: Restorative Justice Practice and the Recovery of Theological Memory.' Unpublished MTh thesis (University of Waterloo: Ontario, 2007), p. 47 (referencing J. Scullion, 'Righteousness, Old Testament'. Pages 724–36 in *Anchor Bible Dictionary* [vol. 5; ed. David Freedman; Toronto: Doubleday, 1992]). Available online: http://uwspace.uwaterloo.ca/bitstream/10012/3489/1/ Keith%20Regehr%20Thesis.pdf (accessed 1 April 2013).

Reuther, Rosemary. *Faith and Fratricide: The Theological Roots of Anti-Semitism* (New York: Seabury Press, 1974).

—. *To Change the World* (New York: Crossroad, 1981).

Rimmon-Kenan, Shlomith. 'Concepts of Narrative.' *Collegium* (2006) http://www.helsinki.fi/collegium/e-series/volumes/ volume_1/index.htm (accessed 20 January 2010).

—. 'The Story of "I": Illness and Narrative Identity'. *Narrative* 10 (2002): pp. 9–27.

Roberson, Ronald G. *The Eastern Christian Churches: A Brief Survey* (Rome: Pont. Institutum Studiorum Orientalium, rev. edn, 1990).

Rossings, Daniel. 'Microcosm and Multiple Minorities: The Christian Communities in Israel.' Pages 28–42 in *Israel Yearbook and Almanac* (ed. N. Greenwood; Jerusalem: IBRT Translation/ Documentation, 1999).

—. 'The Twelve Points of Berlin Viewed through the Prism of Jewish-Christian Relations in Israel Today'. Paper presented at the Jerusalem Rainbow Club, Jerusalem (December 2009).

Rotberg, Robert I. 'Building Legitimacy through Narrative.' Pages 1–18 in *Israeli and Palestinian Narratives of Conflict: History's Double Helix* (ed. Robert I. Rotberg; Bloomington: Indiana University Press, 2006).

—. 'Preface.' Pages vii–viii in *Israeli and Palestinian Narratives of Conflict: History's Double Helix* (ed. Robert I. Rotberg; Bloomington: Indiana University Press, 2006).

Rouhana, Nadim M. 'Zionism's Encounter with the Palestinians: The Dynamics of Force, Fear and Extremism.' Pages 115–41 in *Israeli and Palestinian Narratives of Conflict* (ed. Robert I. Rotberg; Bloomington: Indiana University Press, 2006).

Rubin, Milka. 'Arabization versus Islamization in the Palestinian Melkite Community during the Early Muslim Period.' Pages

149–61 in *Sharing the Sacred: Religious Contacts and Conflicts in the Holy Land, First–Fifteenth Centuries CE* (ed. Arieh Kofsky and Guy G. Stroumsa; Jerusalem: Yad Izhak Ben Zvi, 1998).

Sabbah, Michel. 'Reading the Bible Today in the Land of the Bible.' *Latin Patriarchate of Jerusalem* (1993).
http://www.lpj.org/newsite2006/patriarch/pastoral-letters/1993/readingthebible_en.html (accessed 1 May 2011).

Sabella, Bernard. 'Palestinian Christians: Challenges and Hopes' http://www.al-bushra.org/holyland/sabella.htm (accessed 22 November 2011).

—. 'Socio-Economic Characteristics and Challenges to Palestinian Christians in the Holy Land.' Pages 82–95 in *Palestinian Christians: Religion, Politics and Society in the Holy Land* (ed. Anthony O'Mahony; London: Melisende, 1999).

Sadan, Zvi. 'Halakic Authority in the Life of the Messianic Community'. *Kesher* 24 (Summer 2010).
http://www.kesherjournal.com/pdf/Issue-24/Halakic-Authority-in-the-Life-of-the-Messianic-Community.pdf (accessed 2 February 2013).

Said, Edward. 'New History, Old Ideas'. *Al-Ahram Weekly On-line*, no. 378 (21–7 May 1998).
http://weekly.ahram.org.eg/1998/378/pal2.htm (accessed 27 August 2012).

—. *Orientalism* (New York: Vintage Books, 1978).

Sand, Shlomo. *The Invention of the Jewish People* (London: Verso), 2009.

Schiff, Ze'ev and Ehud Ya'ari. *Israel's Lebanon War* (trans. Ina Friedman; New York: Simon & Schuster, 1984).

Schwartz, Joshua. 'On Priests and Jericho in the Second Temple Period'. *The Jewish Quarterly Review* 79 (July 1988): pp. 23–48.

Schwartz, William E. 'Towards Understanding Churches in the Middle East: A Western Evangelical Perspective'. *MECC Perspectives* (1986), pp. 43–5.

Scofield, C.I. *Rightly Dividing the Word of Truth* (New Jersey: Loizeaux Brothers, n.d. [1896]).

Segev, Tom. 'The June 1967 War and the Palestinian Refugee Problem'. *Journal of Palestine Studies* 36:3 (Spring 2007), pp. 6–22.

Shahîd, Irfan. *Byzantium and the Arabs in the Fourth Century* (Washington, DC: Dumbarton Oaks, 1984).

Shapira, Anita. 'The Past Is Not a Foreign Country: The Failure of Israel's "New Historians" to Explain War and Peace'. *New Republic* (29 November 1999): pp. 26–36. Also available online: http://ontology.buffalo.edu/smith/courses01/rrtw/Shapira. htm (accessed 27 August 2012).

Shemesh, Moshe. 'The Palestinian Society in the Wake of the 1948 War: From Social Fragmentation to Consolidation'. *Israel Studies* 9 (2004): pp. 86–100.

Shenk, Calvin E. 'The Middle Eastern Jesus: Messianic Jewish and Palestinian Christian Understandings'. *Missiology* 29 (2001): pp. 403–16.

Shlaim, Avi. *The Iron Wall: Israel and the Arab World* (New York: W.W. Norton, 2000).

—. 'The War of the Israeli Historians'. *Annales* 59:1 (January–February 2004), pp. 161–7.

Shulam, Joseph. 'Doing Messianic Jewish Halacha' http://www.netivyah.org/articles/Doing_Messianic_Jewish_Halacha.pdf (accessed 3 February 2013).

—. *Hidden Treasures: The First Century Jewish Way of Understanding the Scriptures* (Jerusalem: Netivyah, 2008).

—. 'Rabbi Daniel Zion: Chief Rabbi of Bulgarian Jews during World War II'. *Mishkan* 15 (1991): pp. 53–7.

Skarsaune, Oskar. *In the Shadow of the Temple* (Downers Grove, IL: InterVarsity Press, 2002).

Skarsaune, Oskar and Reidar Hvalvik, eds. *Jewish Believers in Jesus: The Early Centuries* (Peabody, MA: Hendrickson, 2007).

Skjøtt, Bodil F. 'Messianic Believers and the Land of Israel: A Survey'. *Mishkan* 26 (1997), pp. 72–81.

Smith, Barbara Herrnstein. 'Narrative Versions, Narrative Theories.' Pages 213–36 in *On Narrative* (ed. W.J.T. Mitchell; Chicago: University of Chicago Press, 1981).

Smith, David I. *Learning from the Stranger: Christian Faith and Cultural Diversity* (Grand Rapids, MI: Eerdmans, 2009).

Smith, Gordon T. *A Holy Meal: The Lord's Supper in the Life of the Church* (Grand Rapids, MI: Baker, 2005).

Smooha, Sammy. Research on Palestinian-Israeli/Arab identity in Israel http://soc.haifa.ac.il/~s.smooha/page.php?pageId=162 (accessed 9 November 2011).

Solomon, Norman. 'Covenant' (Oxford, 2001) http://www.bc.edu/dam/files/research_sites/cjl/texts center/conferences/solomon.htm (accessed 30 April 2013).

Soulen, Kendall, *The God of Israel and Christian Theology* (Minneapolis: Fortress Press, 1996).

Stassen, Glen H. *Just Peacemaking: Transforming Initiatives for Justice and Peace* (Louisville, KY: Westminster John Knox Press, 1992).

Steinberg, Shoshana and Dan Bar-On. 'Dialogue in the Midst of an Ongoing Conflict: A Group Process of Israeli Jewish and Palestinian Students.' Page 148 in *Beyond Bullets and Bombs* (ed. Judy Kuriansky; Westport, CT: Praeger, 2007).

Stern, David. 'The Land from a Messianic Jewish Perspective.' Pages 37–54 in *The Bible and the Land: An Encounter* (ed. Lisa Loden, Peter Walker and Michael Wood; Jerusalem: Musalaha, 2000).

—. *Messianic Jewish Manifesto* (Clarksville, MD: Jewish New Testament Publications, 1991).

Stirk, Peter M.R. *The Politics of Military Occupation* (Edinburgh: Edinburgh University Press, 2009).

Stone, Lawson G. 'Ethical and Apologetic Tendencies in the Redaction of the Book of Joshua'. *Catholic Biblical Quarterly* 53 (1991): pp. 25–35.

Strengholt, Jos M. *Gospel in the Air: 50 years of Christian Witness through Radio in the Arab World* (Zoetermeer: Boekencentrum, 2008).

Tajfel, H. and J.C. Turner. 'The Social Identity Theory of Intergroup Behavior.' Pages 7–24 in *Psychology of Intergroup Relations* (ed. S. Worchel and W.G. Austin; Chicago: Nelson-Hall, 2nd edn, 1985).

Tal, David. 'The Forgotten War: Jewish–Palestinian Strife in Mandatory Palestine, December 1947–May 1948'. *Israel Affairs* 6:3–4 (2000): pp. 3–22.

Tarazi, Paul Nadim. 'Covenant, Land and City: Finding God's Will in Palestine'. *The Reformed Journal* 29 (1979): p. 11.

—. *Land and Covenant* (St Paul, MN: OCABS Press, 2009).

—. 'An Orthodox Christian Response to the Inclusive Language Lectionary'. *Word Magazine* (April 1984) http://www.orthodoxresearchinstitute.org/articles/bible/tarazi_inclusive_language_lectionary.htm (accessed 18 May 2011).

Thomas, Robert L. *Evangelical Hermeneutics: The New Versus the Old* (Grand Rapids, MI: Kregel, 2002).

Toews, John E. *Romans: Believers Church Bible Commentary* (Scottdale, PA and Kitchener, ON: Herald Press, 2004).

Toth, Anthony B. 'History as Ideology'. *Journal of Palestine Studies* 31:2 (Winter 2002): pp. 85–6.

UNDOC, Acquisition of Land in Palestine (1 January 1980) http://unispal.un.org/unispal.nsf/eed216406b50bf6485256ce-10072f637/7d094ff80ff004f085256dc200680a27?OpenDocment.

Van Rompay, Lucas. 'Opkomst en groei van onafhankelijke volkskerken in het Oosten tot aan de Arabisch-islamitische veroveringen (451–641).' Pages 17–34 in *Oosterse Christenen binnen de wereld van de Islam* (ed. H. Teule and A Wessels; Kampen: Kok, 1997).

Vanhoozer, Kevin. *Is There a Meaning in This Text?* (Grand Rapids, MI: Zondervan, 1988).

Volf, Miroslav. *Exclusion and Embrace: A Theological Exploration of Identity, Otherness, and Reconciliation* (Nashville: Abingdon Press, 1996).

Walker, Peter. *The Weekend that Changed the World: The Mystery of Jerusalem's Empty Tomb* (Louisville, KY: Westminster John Knox Press, 2000).

Warshawsky, Keri Zelson. 'Returning to Their Own Borders: A Social Anthropological Study of Contemporary Messianic Jewish Identity in Israel.' Unpublished PhD dissertation (The Hebrew University of Jerusalem, 2008).

Wright, Chris. *The Mission of God* (Downers Grove, IL: InterVarsity Press, 2006).

Wright, Christopher. 'A Christian Approach to Old Testament Prophecy Concerning Israel.' Pages 1–19 in *Jerusalem: Past and Present in the Purposes of God* (ed. Peter Walker; Cambridge: Tyndale House, 1992).

Wright, N.T. *Paul: In Fresh Perspective* (Minneapolis: Fortress Press, 1995).

—. *Way of the Lord* (Grand Rapids, MI: Eerdmans, 1999).

Wyshogrod, Michael. *The Body of Faith: Judaism's Corporeal Election* (New York: Seabury Press, 1983).

Yee, Tet-Lim N. *Jews, Gentiles and Ethnic Reconciliation: Paul's Jewish Identity and Ephesians*, Society for New Testament Studies Monograph Series 130 (Cambridge: Cambridge University Press, 2005).

Younan, Munib and Frederick M. Strickert. *Witnessing for Peace: In Jerusalem and the World* (Minneapolis: Fortress, 2003).

Zerubavel, Yael. 'A Secular Return to the Bible? Reflections on Israeli Society, National Memory, and the Politics of the Past.' Page 31 in *AJS Perspectives, Association for Jewish Studies: Center for Jewish History*, New York, NY (Spring 2011).

Zerwick, Francis. 'The Good Samaritan'. *The Furrow* 6 (1955), pp. 291–5.

Endnotes

Introduction

[1] For more on Palestinian-Israeli/Arab identity in Israel, see the research of Sammy Smooha, professor of sociology at the University of Haifa http://soc.haifa.ac.il/~s.smooha/page.php?pageId=162 (accessed 9 Nov. 2011).

[2] Another unique book related to our topic is that of Dan Cohn-Sherbok and Dawoud El-Alami, *The Palestine–Israeli Conflict: A Beginner's Guide* (Oxford: Oneworld, rev. edn, 2003) in which the authors (one a diasporic Jewish rabbi/scholar and one a Palestinian Islamic law scholar) discuss the conflict in separate chapters followed by a debate.

[3] We use the term 'Israel-Palestine' to refer to the traditional region of the Holy Land, which includes the present-day state of Israel and the Israeli-occupied territories of the West Bank – also known as Judea, Samaria and the Gaza Strip.

1. A Brief History of the Israeli–Palestinian Conflict

[1] https://docs.google.com/file/d/0B-5-JeCa2Z7hV2szWm1VYmV-lckE/edit (accessed 1 June 2013).

[2] Lee L. Levine, *The Ancient Synagogue: The First Thousand Years* (New Haven: Yale University Press, 2005), pp. 210–14.

[3] Ami Isseroff, *Zionism: The History of Zionism and the Creation of Israel* http://www.mideastweb.org/zionism.htm (accessed 29 July 2012).

[4] Isseroff, *Zionism*.

[5] Benny Morris, *Righteous Victims: A History of the Zionist-Arab Conflict, 1881–2001* (New York: Vintage, 2001), p. 5.

⁶ Ilan Pappé, *The Ethnic Cleansing of Palestine* (Oxford: Oneworld, 2006), pp. 10–11. See also Morris, Righteous Victims, p. 14.

⁷ 'Pogrom' is a Yiddish term derived from Russian, meaning 'to destroy', and is used to denote the organized massacre of Jews.

⁸ Morris, *Righteous Victims*, pp. 8–15. Identifying a number of massacres against Jews that took place in Arab countries, Morris writes, 'the underlying attitude, that Jews were infidels and opponents of Islam, and necessarily inferior in the eyes of God, prevailed throughout Muslim lands down the ages' (11). Under the Christian Russian Empire, he writes that the 'reality of Jewish life . . . was one of continuous discrimination and insecurity and occasional oppression and violence' (14).

⁹ Morris, *Righteous Victims*, pp. 15–19. *Hovevei Zion* (Lovers of Zion) groups sponsored this initial wave of immigration, the first aliyah ('ascension', or immigration). The immigrants of the first aliyah began arriving to Palestine in 1882, establishing settlements and purchasing land.

¹⁰ Morris, *Righteous Victims*, p. 20.

¹¹ Morris, *Righteous Victims*, pp. 20–21.

¹² Walter A. Elwell, *Evangelical Dictionary of Theology* (Grand Rapids, MI: Baker Academic, 2nd edn, 2007), p. 1307.

¹³ Walter Laqueur, *A History of Zionism* (New York: Schocken, 1976), p. 106.

¹⁴ Morris, *Righteous Victims*, p. 23.

¹⁵ Morris, *Righteous Victims*, p. 75.

¹⁶ 'Palestine' here refers to the territory comprising the three *sanjaks* (districts) of Acre, Nablus and Jerusalem, within the *vilayet* (province) of Ottoman Syria. See Morris, *Righteous Victims*, p. 7.

¹⁷ B. Kimmerling and J.S. Migdal, *The Palestinian People: A History* (Cambridge: Harvard University Press, 2003), p. 6.

¹⁸ Kimmerling and Migdal, *Palestinian People*, p. 6.

¹⁹ Kimmerling and Migdal, *Palestinian People*, pp. 7–8.

²⁰ Morris, *Righteous Victims*, pp. 6–7.

²¹ Kimmerling and Migdal, *Palestinian People*, p. 16; Morris, *Righteous Victims*, pp. 5–6. Also, Rashid Khalidi, *Palestinian Identity: The Construction of Modern National Consciousness* (New York: Columbia University Press, 1997), pp. 94–6.

²² Morris, Righteous Victims, p. 29; Kimmerling and Migdal, *Palestinian People*, p. 75. For more on the development of Palestinian identity and

the overlapping loyalties that came with being a part of the Ottoman Empire in its final days, see R. Khalidi, *Palestinian Identity*, pp. 63–88.

23 Morris, *Righteous Victims*, pp. 68–70; Kimmerling and Migdal, *Palestinian People*, p. 79. The territory McMahon refers to in his letters was not clearly defined. It was not clear if Palestine was to be included in the area marked for Arab independence. However, the Arabs certainly assumed that it was included.

24 Morris, *Righteous Victims*, p. 38. The goal of land purchase was for the eventual establishment of a state.

25 Morris, *Righteous Victims*, pp. 37, 42–5.

26 R. Khalidi, *Palestinian Identity*, p. 95.

27 R. Khalidi, *Palestinian Identity*, p. 99; Morris, *Righteous Victims*, p. 50; Pappé, *Ethnic Cleansing*, pp. 17–19.

28 R. Khalidi, *Palestinian Identity*, p. 100; Morris, *Righteous Victims*, pp. 24–5. The Kishinev pogrom of 1903 was particularly brutal: forty-nine people were slaughtered, hundreds wounded, and around fifteen hundred Jewish homes and shops were destroyed.

29 Morris, *Righteous Victims*, pp. 50–52. Jewish labour was central to the tenets of Socialist-Zionism, which attached a great deal of importance to the renewal of the Jewish body as well as the Jewish soul. Traditionally, Jews had been excluded from agriculture and manual labour in the Diaspora, and the proponents of Jewish labour saw the reversal of this trend as an important part of Zionist ideology.

30 R. Khalidi, *Palestinian Identity*, pp. 124–7. R. Khalidi's survey also covers other important newspapers, including *Al-Mufid, Al-Muqtabas, Al-Muqattam* and *Al-Ahram*. See also R. Khalidi, *Iron Cage: The Story of the Palestinian Struggle for Statehood* (Boston: Beacon, 2007), pp. 90–104; Morris, *Righteous Victims*, pp. 62–6.

31 R. Khalidi, *Palestinian Identity*, p. 114.

32 Morris, *Righteous Victims*, p. 54; R. Khalidi, *Palestinian Identity*, pp. 99–100.

33 Morris, *Righteous Victims*, p. 53.

34 R. Khalidi, *Palestinian Identity*, pp. 105–6.

35 Morris, *Righteous Victims*, p. 33. The Palestinians looked to the McMahon–Hussein correspondence as international support for their national aspirations, but they were ignored by the British.

36 Morris, *Righteous Victims*, pp. 92–102; Kimmerling and Migdal, *Palestinian People*, pp. 89–90.

37 Morris, *Righteous Victims*, pp. 112–13.

38 Morris, *Righteous Victims*, pp. 112–16; Kimmerling and Migdal, *Palestinian People*, pp. 91–2.

39 Morris, *Righteous Victims*, pp. 126–7; Kimmerling and Migdal, *Palestinian People*, p. 90.

40 Kimmerling and Migdal, *Palestinian People*, p. 111; Morris, *Righteous Victims*, p. 130.

41 Kimmerling and Migdal, *Palestinian People*, p. 119; Morris, *Righteous Victims*, pp. 132–3.

42 Pappé, *Ethnic Cleansing*, p. 14.

43 R. Khalidi, *Iron Cage*, pp. 107–8; Morris, *Righteous Victims*, p. 153.

44 R. Khalidi, *Iron Cage*, pp. 68–9; Morris, *Righteous Victims*, p. 145.

45 Morris, *Righteous Victims*, pp. 138–44.

46 Morris, *Righteous Victims*, p. 159.

47 Morris, *Righteous Victims*, p. 160; R. Khalidi, *Iron Cage*, p. 122.

48 Morris, *Righteous Victims*, p. 158.

49 Morris, *Righteous Victims*, pp. 161, 164, 166–7.

50 Morris, *Righteous Victims*, pp. 176, 179. Although loosely unified, the different factions often acted alone. The King David Hotel bombing, for example, was carried out by the Irgun Z'vai Leumi (IZL; a national military organization) without coordinating with the Haganah. See also Kimmerling and Migdal, *Palestinian People*, p. 146.

51 http://unispal.un.org/unispal.nsf/eed216406b50bf6485256ce-10072f637/7d094ff80ff004f085256dc200680a27?OpenDocument.

52 Morris, *Righteous Victims*, pp. 184–6.

53 Morris, *Righteous Victims*, pp. 180–4; Kimmerling and Migdal, *Palestinian People*, p. 147.

54 Morris, *Righteous Victims*, p. 186.

55 Morris, *Righteous Victims*, pp. 190–91.

56 Morris, *Righteous Victims*, pp. 198–201.

57 Morris, *Righteous Victims*, pp. 201–4. See also David Tal, 'The Forgotten War: Jewish–Palestinian Strife in Mandatory Palestine, December 1947–May 1948', *Israel Affairs* 6:3–4 (2000): pp. 12–15.

58 Morris, *Righteous Victims*, pp. 204–206; and Kimmerling and Migdal, *Palestinian People*, p. 158.

59 Walid Khalidi, 'Plan Dalet Revisited', *Journal of Palestine Studies* 18:1 (1988): pp. 3–37, which includes three appendices, including the text of Plan Gimmel [Plan C] and texts of Plan Dalet [Plan D]. The article is also available online: http://www.palestine-studies.org/enakba/Khalidi,%20Plan%20Dalet%20Revisited.pdf (accessed 17 Nov. 2011).

60 'The Zionist leadership openly declared – two months *before* the end of the Mandate [in March] – it would seek to take over the land and expel the indigenous population by force: Plan Dalet.' Pappé, *Ethnic Cleansing*, p. 41 (emphasis original). Y. Gelber argues, 'Although it provided for counter-attacks, Plan D was a defensive scheme . . . Plan D was not "ideological" as the Palestinians portray.' He adds that 'reading Plan D as it is, without deconstructing it to change its meaning, show that there is no correlation between the actual text and the significance, background, and outcomes that the Palestinian scholars and their Israeli colleagues assign it.' Yoav Gelber, *Palestine 1948: War, Escape and the Emergence of the Palestinian Refugee Problem* (Brighton/Portland: Sussex Academic Press, 2nd edn, 2006), pp. 304, 306. For the historiographical debate, see Saleh Abdel Jawad, 'The Arab and Palestinian Narratives of the 1948 War', in *Israeli and Palestinian Narratives of Conflict: History's Double Helix* (ed. Robert I. Rotberg; Bloomington: Indiana University Press, 2006), pp. 72–114. A persistent critic of Israel's so-called 'new historians', Efraim Karsh has also put forward the argument that Palestinians, but particularly the corrupt Arab states, rather than Israel, are the true source of Palestinians' acknowledged suffering. See also Efraim Karsh, *Palestine Betrayed* (New Haven: Yale University Press, 2010). For his arguments against the new historians see also Efraim Karsh, *Fabricating Israeli History: The 'New Historians'* (Portland, OR: Frank Cass, rev. edn, 2000).

61 Morris, *Righteous Victims*, pp. 207–9; R. Khalidi, *Iron Cage*, p. 133; Kimmerling and Migdal, Palestinian People, p. 161.

62 Meron Benvenisti, *Sacred Landscape: The Buried History of the Holy Land since 1948* (Berkeley: University of California Press, 2000), pp. 116–17.

63 Pappé, *Ethnic Cleansing*, p. 91; Morris, *Righteous Victims*, p. 207.

64 The first stage (Dec. 1947–Mar. 1948) of Palestinian flight involved approximately 75,000 people from the upper and middle classes due to rumours of war. The second stage (Apr.–June 1948) involved the flight of 200,000–300,000 Palestinians deprived of their leadership and prior to the arrival of Jewish forces. The third (July–Oct. 1948) was triggered when the IDF forcibly exiled over 100,000 Palestinians. IDF operations in the Galilee and Negev instigated the fourth stage, in which 100,000–150,000 Palestinians fled or were expelled from their homes. Issa Khalaf, 'The Effect of Socioeconomic Change on Arab Societal Collapse in Mandate Palestine', *International Journal of Middle East Studies* 29:1 (Feb. 1997): p. 93; Ilan Pappé, *The History of Modern*

Palestine: One Land, Two Peoples (Cambridge: CUP, 2004), p. 143; Ilan Pappé, 'The 1948 Ethnic Cleansing of Palestine', *Journal of Palestine Studies* 36:1 (2006): p. 7; Benny Morris, *The Birth of the Palestinian Refugee Problem Revisited* (Cambridge: CUP, rev. edn, 2004), pp. 52–57, 61–131, 197–216.

[65] Morris, *Righteous Victims*, p. 252; Kimmerling and Migdal, *Palestinian People*, p. 156.

[66] Morris, *Righteous Victims*, p. 257.

[67] Pappé, *History of Modern Palestine*, p. 146. This influx of Jewish refugees has often been cited as exculpatory evidence for Israel in its role in the creation of the Palestinian refugee problem. See Ya'akov Meron, 'Why Jews Fled the Arab Countries', *Middle East Quarterly* 2:3 (September 1995): pp. 47–55, and Tom Segev, 'The June 1967 War and the Palestinian Refugee Problem', *Journal of Palestine Studies* 36:3 (Spring 2007), pp. 6–22, esp. 7.

[68] R. Khalidi, *Iron Cage*, p. 133.

[69] R. Khalidi, *Iron Cage*, pp. 136–8.

[70] Pappé, *Ethnic Cleansing*, p. 220.

[71] Morris, *Righteous Victims*, p. 295.

[72] Pappé, *Ethnic Cleansing*, p. 236.

[73] Morris, *Righteous Victims*, pp. 270–71.

[74] Morris, *Righteous Victims*, pp. 271–4.

[75] Morris, *Righteous Victims*, p. 284.

[76] Morris, *Righteous Victims*, p. 289.

[77] Morris, *Righteous Victims*, pp. 299–301.

[78] Morris, *Righteous Victims*, p. 304–5. Their deployment was due to misinformation they received from the Soviet Union.

[79] Pappé, *History of Modern Palestine*, pp. 302–6; also Morris, *Righteous Victims*, pp. 302, 305–6.

[80] Morris, *Righteous Victims*, pp. 309–10.

[81] Morris, *Righteous Victims*, pp. 321, 324–5, 326.

[82] Pappé, *History of Modern Palestine*, pp. 311–31; also Morris, *Righteous Victims*, p. 329.

[83] Morris, *Righteous Victims*, pp. 331, 335–6.

[84] A copy of the Khartoum Resolution is available on the Council on Foreign Relations website http://www.cfr.org/international-peace-and-security/khartoum-resolution/p14841 (accessed 29 Nov. 2011).

[85] Morris, *Righteous Victims*, pp. 345–6; also Gideon Gera, 'Israel and the June 1967 War: 25 Years Later', *Middle East Journal* 46:2 (1992): p. 234.

[86] Peter M.R. Stirk, *The Politics of Military Occupation* (Edinburgh: Edinburgh University Press, 2009), p. 45.

[87] Morris, *Righteous Victims*, p. 341.

[88] R. Khalidi, *Iron Cage*, p. 138.

[89] Morris, *Righteous Victims*, p. 363; R. Khalidi, *Iron Cage*, p. 138; Gera, 'Israel and the June 1967 War', p. 236; also Moshe Shemesh, 'The Palestinian Society in the Wake of the 1948 War: From Social Fragmentation to Consolidation', *Israel Studies* 9:1 (2004): pp. 86–9.

[90] This is the official figure but Arafat had claimed that between 10 and 25,000 were killed.

[91] Morris, *Righteous Victims*, pp. 373–5; also Michael C. Hudson, 'Developments and Setbacks in the Palestinian Resistance Movement 1967–1971', *Journal of Palestine Studies* 1:3 (1972), p. 82.

[92] Morris, *Righteous Victims*, pp. 380–81, 383–5.

[93] Morris, *Righteous Victims*, pp. 348–9.

[94] Morris, *Righteous Victims*, pp. 411, 431–3.

[95] Morris, *Righteous Victims*, p. 434.

[96] Morris, *Righteous Victims*, pp. 452–5. Sadat made efforts for peace with Israel before this as well but was rejected. During his visit Sadat prayed at the al-Aksa Mosque and paid his respects at Yad Vashem, the Israeli Holocaust memorial and museum. In his address to the Knesset, he said, 'For the sake of the lives of all our sons and brothers . . . for the generations to come, for a smile on the face of every child born in our land, for all that I have taken my decision to come to you, despite all the hazards.'

[97] In the aftermath of the Arab Spring there is uncertainty in Israeli circles regarding the future of the peace between the two nations.

[98] Morris, *Righteous Victims*, pp. 477, 489, 492–3; also Oren Barak, 'The Failure of the Israeli–Palestinian Peace Process, 1993–2000', *Journal of Peace Research* 42:6 (Nov. 2005), p. 721. In the midst of the writing of this book, the world has witnessed the events of the 'Arab Spring', sparked by the self-immolation of a despondent young Tunisian fruit seller. As this book was going to press, the events across the Arab Middle East continue to unfold, and naturally, affect relations between Israel and surrounding countries.

[99] Morris, *Righteous Victims*, pp. 499–502.

[100] Morris, *Righteous Victims*, pp. 514–15.

[101] Morris, *Righteous Victims*, pp. 537–8.

[102] Morris, *Righteous Victims*, p. 543. Both international and Israeli commissions were convened to investigate the events and locate responsibility

for those involved 'directly' and 'indirectly' in the massacre. The Israeli Kahan Commission found that the IDF were 'indirectly responsible' and that Ariel Sharon bore 'personal responsibility' for his role in the event. See Ze'ev Schiff and Ehud Ya'ari, *Israel's Lebanon War* (trans. Ina Friedman; New York: Simon & Schuster, 1984), pp. 283–4.

[103] Morris, *Righteous Victims*, pp. 538, 541, 543–8.

[104] Morris, *Righteous Victims*, pp. 551–9.

[105] Morris, *Righteous Victims*, p. 567.

[106] Morris, *Righteous Victims*, pp. 565, 573; Pappé, *History of Modern Palestine*, pp. 234–5.

[107] Morris, *Righteous Victims*, p. 596. Many of the injured and killed were children. See also Lisa Hajjar, 'Human Rights in Israel/Palestine: The History and Politics of a Movement', *Journal of Palestine Studies* 30:4 (Summer 2001), p. 27.

[108] Morris, *Righteous Victims*, p. 577.

[109] Morris, *Righteous Victims*, p. 625; Kimmerling and Migdal, *Palestinian People*, p. 316; Gera, 'Israel and the June 1967 War', p. 238.

[110] Morris, *Righteous Victims*, pp. 635–7.

[111] Morris, *Righteous Victims*, pp. 659–660; Barak, 'Failure of the Israeli-Palestinian Peace Process', p. 723.

2. History and Narrative

[1] David W. Augsburger, *Conflict Mediation across Cultures: Pathways and Patterns* (Louisville, KY: Westminster John Knox, 1992), p. 5.

[2] Barbara Herrnstein Smith, 'Narrative Versions, Narrative Theories', in *On Narrative* (ed. W.J.T. Mitchell; Chicago: University of Chicago Press, 1981), p. 228, as quoted in Shlomith Rimmon-Kenan, 'Concepts of Narrative', in *The Traveling Concept of Narrative* (ed. M. Hyvärinen, A. Korhonen and J. Mykkänen; Helsinki: Helsinki Collegium for Advanced Studies, 2006), p. 10 http://www.helsinki.fi/collegium/e-series/volumes/volume_1/index.htm (accessed 9 Nov. 2011).

[3] Rimmon-Kenan. 'Concepts of Narrative', p. 12

[4] Rimmon-Kenan, 'Concepts of Narrative', p. 12.

[5] Alasdair MacIntyre, *After Virtue: A Study in Moral Theory* (Notre Dame: University of Notre Dame Press, 3rd edn, 2007), p. 216.

[6] MacIntyre, *After Virtue*, p. 216.

[7] Louis O. Mink, 'History and Fiction as Modes of Comprehension', in *Historical Understanding* (ed. Brian Fay, Eugene O. Golob and Richard T. Vann; Ithaca: Cornell University Press, 1987), p. 60, as quoted in Matti Hyvärinen, 'Towards a Conceptual History of Narrative', in *Traveling Concept of Narrative* (ed. Hyvärinen, Korhonen and Mykkänen), p. 23; PDF http://www.helsinki.fi/collegium/e-series/volumes/volume_1/index.htm (accessed 17 Nov. 2011).

[8] Mink, as quoted in Hyvärinen, 'Towards a Conceptual History', p. 25.

[9] David Carr, *Time, Narrative, and History* (Bloomington and Indianapolis: Indiana University Press, 1986), as quoted in Hyvärinen, 'Towards a Conceptual History', p. 27.

[10] Carr, as quoted in Hyvärinen, 'Towards a Conceptual History', p. 27.

[11] Rimmon-Kenan, 'Concepts of Narrative', p. 15.

[12] Catherine MacKinnon, *Women's Lives, Men's Laws* (Cambridge: Harvard University Press, 2005), p. 61.

[13] Shlomith Rimmon-Kenan, 'The Story of "I": Illness and Narrative Identity', *Narrative* 10 (2002): p. 11, as quoted in Hyvärinen, 'Towards a Conceptual History', p. 36; Mark Currie, *Postmodern Narrative Theory* (Houndmills: Palgrave, 1998), p. 2, as quoted in Hyvärinen, 'Towards a Conceptual History', p. 35.

[14] Dan Bar-On and Sami Adwan, 'The Psychology of Better Dialogue between two Separate but Interdependent Narratives', in *Israeli and Palestinian Narratives of Conflict: History's Double Helix* (ed. Robert I. Rotberg; Bloomington: Indiana University Press, 2006), p. 206.

[15] This point on identity is adapted from Daniel Bar-Tal and Gavriel Salomon, 'Israeli-Jewish Narratives of the Israeli–Palestinian Conflict: Evolution, Contents, Functions, and Consequences', in *Israeli and Palestinian Narratives of Conflict* (ed. Rotberg), pp. 28–9.

[16] Robert I. Rotberg, 'Building Legitimacy through Narrative', in *Israeli and Palestinian Narratives of Conflict* (ed. Rotberg), p. 1.

[17] Bar-Tal and Salomon, 'Israeli–Jewish Narratives', p. 23.

[18] Bar-Tal and Salomon, 'Israeli–Jewish Narratives', pp. 20–21.

[19] Bar-Tal and Salomon, 'Israeli–Jewish Narratives', pp. 20–23.

[20] Rotberg, 'Building Legitimacy', p. 2.

[21] Martin Buber, 'Politics and Morality', in *A Land of Two Peoples: Martin Buber on Jews and Arabs* (ed. Paul R. Mendes-Flohr; New York: OUP, 1983), p. 170.

[22] Bar-Tal and Salomon, 'Israeli–Jewish Narratives', p. 24.

[23] Bar-Tal and Salomon, 'Israeli–Jewish Narratives', p. 34.

24 Bar-Tal and Salomon, 'Israeli–Jewish Narratives', p. 40.

25 Ilan Pappé, 'The Bridging Narrative Concept', in *Israeli and Palestinian Narratives of Conflict* (ed. Rotberg), p. 203.

26 Mordechai Bar-On, 'Conflicting Narratives or Narratives of a Conflict: Can the Zionist and Palestinian Narratives of the 1948 War Be Bridged?' in *Israeli and Palestinian Narratives of Conflict* (ed. Rotberg), p. 143.

27 Mordechai Bar On, 'Conflicting Narratives', p.143

28 Mordechai Bar-On, 'Conflicting Narratives', p. 153.

29 Robert I. Rotberg, 'Preface', in *Israeli and Palestinian Narratives of Conflict* (ed. Rotberg), p. vii.

30 Paul Mendes-Flohr, 'Preface', in *A Land of Two Peoples* (ed. Mendes-Flohr), p. xvi. Here, Mendes-Flohr discusses the principle of inclusion in Buber's teaching on dialogue.

3. Israeli–Palestinian Historiography

1 Daniel Bar-Tal and Gavriel Salomon, 'Israeli–Jewish Narratives of the Israeli–Palestinian Conflict: Evolution, Contents, Functions, and Consequences', in *Israeli and Palestinian Narratives of Conflict: History's Double Helix* (ed. Robert I. Rotberg; Bloomington and Indianapolis: Indiana University Press, 2006), pp. 19–46, here pp. 19–20.

2 See Avi Shlaim, 'The War of the Israeli Historians', *Annales* 59:1 (January-February 2004): pp. 161–167, available online at http://users. ox.ac.uk/~ssfc0005/The%20War%20of%20the%20Israeli%20Historians.html (accessed 27 Aug. 2012). See also Bar-Tal and Salomon, 'Israeli–Jewish Narratives' for more information.

3 In 1984 news producer, political writer and advisor Joan Peters received wide acclaim for her book *From Time Immemorial: The Origins of the Arab-Jewish Conflict over Palestine*. She argues that, contrary to popular opinion, Jews did not displace the Arabs in Palestine, but rather Arabs displaced the Jews. She proves her thesis through demographical documentation, and she sees the Palestinian refugee problem as a population exchange. The same year American-Jewish academic Norman Finkelstein wrote a review which later turned into the book *Image and Reality of the Israel-Palestine Conflict* in which he presents the historical evidence and context from which Peters derived her source material, proving that she falsified much of her evidence.

Her book never received the same acclaim in Israel as it did in the United States, and many more authors came to criticize the book and its poor scholarship in the following years. While Peters' ideas did not play a significant role in Israeli historiography, it is still popular in some circles, despite its censure and rejection by the academic world.

⁴ A summarized simplification of the traditional account, as seen in Shlaim, 'War of the Israeli Historians' and Benny Morris, 'The New Historiography: Israel Confronts Its Past', *Tikkun* (Nov.–Dec. 1988): pp. 19–23, 99–102, here p. 20.

⁵ Benny Morris, 'Politics by Other Means', *New Republic* (22 March 2004) http://www.ee.bgu.ac.il/~censor/katz-directory/04-03-22ben-ny-morris-The%20New%20Republic-1.pdf (accessed 27 Aug. 2012).

⁶ His documentary evidence comes largely from the US, British, UN and Israeli archives.

⁷ Benny Morris, 'Derisionist History', *New Republic* (28 November 2009) http://www.tnr.com/article/books-and-arts/derisionist-history?page=0,2 (accessed 27 Aug. 2012).

⁸ Ilan Pappé, 'Histories and Historians in Israel & Palestine', *Transforming Cultures* eJournal 1:1 (March 2006): pp. 33–42, here p. 40.

⁹ Ilan Pappé, 'Histories and Historians', p. 42.

¹⁰ Nur Masalha, *The Palestine Nakba: Decolonising Histroy, Narrating the Subaltern, Reclaiming Memory* (London: Zed Books, 2012), p. 184.

¹¹ Morris, 'New Historiography', p. 20.

¹² This documentation came from State papers, Foreign Ministry papers, and other documentation to researchers in the Central Zionist Archives, the Israel State Archives, the Haganah Archive, the IDF Archive, the Labour Party Archive, and the Ben Gurion Archive.

¹³ Morris, 'New Historiography', pp. 20–21; Shlaim, 'War of the Israeli Historians'.

¹⁴ Shlaim, 'War of the Israeli Historians'.

¹⁵ Anita Shapira, 'The Past Is Not a Foreign Country: The Failure of Israel's "New Historians" to Explain War and Peace', *New Republic* (29 November 1999): pp. 26–36. Also available online: http://ontology.buffalo.edu/smith/courses01/rrtw/Shapira.htm (accessed 27 Aug. 2012).

¹⁶ Shlaim, 'War of the Israeli Historians'.

¹⁷ Shlaim, 'War of the Israeli Historians'.

¹⁸ Morris, 'New Historiography', p. 102.

¹⁹ Shlaim, 'War of the Israeli Historians'.

[20] Hillel Halkin, 'Was Zionism Unjust?' *Commentary* (November 1999) http://www.commentarymagazine.com/article/was-zionism-unjust/ (accessed 27 Aug. 2012).

[21] Morris is commonly accused of not knowing or using Arabic source material; he often responds that this source material would not change his conclusions.

[22] Shapira, 'Past Is Not a Foreign Country'.

[23] Efraim Karsh, 'Rewriting Israel's History', *Middle East Quarterly* (June 1996), pp. 19–29. Also available online http://www.meforum.org/302/rewriting-israels-history (accessed 10 Sept. 2012).

[24] Ian Lustick comments on *Fabricating Israeli History* in Ian S. Lustick, 'Israeli History: Who Is Fabricating What?' *Survival: Global Politics and Strategy* 39:3 (1997), pp. 156–66. Richard Bulliett and Anthony Toth critique his other work: Richard W. Bulliett, 'Empires of the Sand: The Struggle for Mastery in the Middle East, 1789–1923 (Review)' *The Middle East Journal* 54.4 (2000), p. 667; Anthony B. Toth, 'History as Ideology', *Journal of Palestine Studies* 31:2 (Winter 2002): pp. 85–6. See also Morris's review of Karsh's book: Benny Morris, 'Refabricating 1948', *Journal of Palestine Studies* 27:2 (Winter 1998), pp. 81–95.

[25] Ehud Adiv, 'Politics and Identity: A Critical Analysis of Israeli Historiography and Political Thought', in *Across the Wall: Narratives of Israeli–Palestinian History* (ed. Ilan Pappé and Jamil Hilal; London, New York: I.B. Tauris, 2010), pp. 19–44, here p. 34.

[26] Edward Said, 'New History, Old Ideas', *Al-Ahram Weekly On-line*, no. 378 (21–7 May 1998) http://weekly.ahram.org.eg/1998/378/pal2.htm (accessed 27 Aug. 2012).

[27] Masalha, *Palestine Nakba*, pp. 182, 184.

[28] Masalha, *Palestine Nakba*, p. 167. Masalha contrasts Israeli civil rights activists and other intellectuals with the new historians who are 'decidedly not anti-Zionist' but 'liberal Zionists', p. 157.

[29] Masalha, *Palestine Nakba*, p. 168.

[30] Masalha, *Palestine Nakba*, pp. 174–5.

[31] Masalha, *Palestine Nakba*, p. 158.

[32] Tarif Khalidi, 'Palestinian Historiography: 1900–1948', *Journal of Palestine Studies* 9:3 (Aug. 1980): pp. 59–76, here p. 68.

[33] T. Khalidi, 'Palestinian Historiography'.

[34] Saleh Abdel Jawad, 'The Arab and Palestinian Narratives of the 1948 War', in *Israeli and Palestinian Narratives of Conflict* (ed. Rotberg): pp. 72–114, here p. 74.

[35] Jamil Hilal, 'Reflections on Contemporary Palestinian History', in *Across the Wall* (ed. Pappé and Hilal), pp. 177–215, here p. 177.

[36] Hilal, 'Reflections on Contemporary Palestinian History', pp. 177–8.

[37] Abdel Jawad, 'Arab and Palestinian Narratives', p. 74.

[38] Abdel Jawad, 'Arab and Palestinian Narratives', p. 74.

[39] Abdel Jawad, 'Arab and Palestinian Narratives', p. 90.

[40] Abdel Jawad, 'Arab and Palestinian Narratives', p. 90. The five completely depopulated cities were Safad, Majdal, Tiberiade, Beisan and Beer-Saba. The five other almost completely depopulated cities were Jaffa, Haifa, Lod, Ramle and Acre.

[41] Abdel Jawad, 'Arab and Palestinian Narratives', p. 90.

[42] Abdel Jawad, 'Arab and Palestinian Narratives', pp. 90–91, emphasis his.

[43] Abdel Jawad, 'Arab and Palestinian Narratives', pp. 92–3.

[44] Abdel Jawad, 'Arab and Palestinian Narratives'. Yet again, a 'large collection of Palestinian documents was lost when the Israelis occupied the Palestinian Research Center (PRC) and transported its entire contents to Israel. The PRC was the central archive of the Palestinian people, its heritage and memory.' p. 93.

[45] Masalha, *Palestine Nakba*, p. 137.

[46] Abdel Jawad, 'Arab and Palestinian Narratives', pp. 101–2. Quote from p. 101.

[47] Abdel Jawad, 'Arab and Palestinian Narratives', pp. 76–9.

[48] Abdel Jawad, 'Arab and Palestinian Narratives', pp. 76, 79–80. Quote from p. 80.

[49] Abdel Jawad, 'Arab and Palestinian Narratives', p. 76. For more information from Palestinian historiographers, see Moustafa M. al-Dabbagh, *Biladuna Filastin* (Our Country Palestine) (Kofr Qar: Israel, 2nd edn, 1991); Rashid Khalidi, *Palestinian Identity: The Construction of Modern National Consciousness* (New York: Columbia University Press, 1997); Muhammad Y. Muslih, *The Origins of Palestinian Nationalism* (New York: Columbia University Press, 1988); Kamal Abdul Fattah and Wolf-Dieter Hutteroth, *Historical Geography of Palestine, Transjordan and Southern Syria in the Late Sixteenth Century* (Erlangen: Frankische Geographische Ges., 1977); Issa Khalaf, *Politicism in Palestine: Arab Factionalism and Social Disintegration 1939–1948* (New York: State University of New York Press, 1991); Beshara Doumani, *Rediscovering Palestine: Merchants and Peasants in Jabal Nablus, 1700–1900* (Berkeley: University of California Press, 1995); Nafez Nazzal, *The Palestinian*

Exodus from Galilee, 1948 (Beirut: Institute for Palestine Studies, 1978); Nur Masalha, *Expulsion of the Palestinians: The Concept of Transfer in Zionist Political Thought, 1882–1948* (Beirut: Institute for Palestine Studies, 1992); Walid Khalidi, *All that Remains: The Palestinian Villages Occupied and Depopulated by Israel in 1948* (Washington, DC: Institute for Palestine Studies, 2006); Saleh Abdel Jawad, 'The Arab and Palestinian Narratives of the 1948 War', in *Israeli and Palestinian Narratives of Conflict: History's Double Helix* (ed. Robert I. Rotberg; Bloomington: Indiana University Press, 2006), pp. 72–114; Nadim M. Rouhana, 'Zionism's Encounter with the Palestinians: The Dynamics of Force, Fear and Extremism', in *Israeli and Palestinian Narratives of Conflict* (ed. Rotberg), pp. 115–41.

50 Ilan Pappé and Jamil Hilal, *Across the Wall: Narratives of Israeli–Palestinian History* (London, New York: I.B. Tauris, 2010), p. 9.

51 Benny Morris, *The Birth of the Palestinian Refugee Problem Revisited* (Cambridge: CUP, 2004), p. 3.

52 Morris, *Birth of the Palestinian Refugee Problem*, p. 4.

53 Morris, *Birth of the Palestinian Refugee Problem*, p. 4.

54 Avi Shlaim, *The Iron Wall: Israel and the Arab World* (New York: W.W. Norton, 2000), pp. xii–xiii.

55 Zachary J. Foster, 'Arab Historiography in Mandatory Palestine, 1920–1948', Master's thesis (Georgetown University, 2011), p. 44.

56 Foster, 'Arab Historiography', pp. 46–48.

57 Benny Morris, *Birth of the Palestinian Refugee Problem*, p. 42.

58 Edward Said, 'New History, Old Ideas', *Al-Ahram Weekly On-line*, no. 378 (21–7 May 1998).

59 Robert I. Rotberg, 'Preface,' in *Israeli and Palestinian Narratives of Conflict* (ed. Rotberg), p. vii. See also Musalaha's *Curriculum of Reconciliation*, ch. 7 on 'History and Narrative'.

4. An Introduction to Palestinian Christianity

1 Bernard Sabella, 'Socio-Economic Characteristics and Challenges to Palestinian Christians in the Holy Land', in *Palestinian Christians: Religion, Politics and Society in the Holy Land* (ed. Anthony O'Mahony; London: Melisende, 1999), pp. 83–4. See also Bernard Sabella, 'Palestinian Christians: Challenges and Hopes' http://www.al-bushra.org/holyland/sabella.htm (accessed 22 Nov. 2011).

[2] Anthony O'Mahony, 'Palestinian Christians: Religion, Politics and Society, c.1800–1948', in *Palestinian Christians* (ed. O'Mahony), p. 27.

[3] William E. Schwartz, 'Towards Understanding Churches in the Middle East: A Western Evangelical Perspective', *MECC Perspectives* (1986): pp. 43–5.

[4] Gabriel Baramki, 'The Spiritual Significance and Experience of the Churches: The Orthodox Perspective', in *Christians in the Holy Land* (ed. Michael Prior and William Taylor; London: World of Islam Festival Trust, 1994), p. 142.

[5] Mitri Raheb, 'Shaping Communities in times of Crises' http://www.mitriraheb.org/index.php?option=com_content&view=article&id=363:shaping-communities-in-times-of-crises&catid=33:english&Itemid=20 (accessed 27 Feb. 2013).

[6] Salim J. Munayer, 'Beyond Bells and Smells: The Gap between Eastern and Western Christianity' http://www.musalaha.org/articleview.asp?ID=46 (accessed 27 Feb. 2013).

[7] Jos M. Strengholt, *Gospel in the Air: 50 Years of Christian Witness through Radio in the Arab World* (Zoetermeer: Boekencentrum, 2008), p. 183, emphasis original, citing Theresia Hainthaler, *Christliche Araber vor dem Islam* (Leuven: Peeters, 2007), pp. 37–40; Lucas van Rompay, 'Opkomst en groei van onafhankelijke volkskerken in het Oosten tot aan de Arabisch-islamitische veroveringen (451–641)', in *Oosterse Christenen binnen de wereld van de Islam* (ed. H. Teule and A Wessels; Kampen: Kok, 1997), p. 28; Philip Hitti, *History of the Arabs* (New York: Palgrave Macmillan, 2002 [1937]), pp. 28–84.

[8] Strengholt, *Gospel in the Air*, p. 26.

[9] The term 'Arab' has had a number of meanings throughout history. With the onset of the Greek and Roman period, the term Arab referred to anyone from the Arabian Peninsula. In the Islamic period, it variously referred to Bedouins and those who spoke Arabic. In the twentieth century, the term Arab came to refer to those who are connected by language, history and political ambitions. To see more on the history of this term, see the introduction to Bernard Lewis, *The Arabs in History* (Oxford: OUP, 1993).

[10] Tony Maalouf, *Arabs in the Shadow of Israel: The Unfolding of God's Prophetic Plan for Ishmael's Line* (Grand Rapids, MI: Kregel, 2003), p. 20.

[11] Maalouf, *Arabs in the Shadow*, p. 45.

[12] Maalouf, *Arabs in the Shadow*, pp. 199, 122.

[13] Maalouf, *Arabs in the Shadow*, pp. 198–200.

[14] Maalouf, *Arabs in the Shadow*, pp. 208–10.

[15] Baramki, 'Spiritual Significance', pp. 141–2.

[16] Riah Abu El-Assal, 'The Birth and Experience of the Christian Church: The Protestant/Anglican Perspective, Anglican Identity in the Middle East', in *Christians in the Holy Land* (ed. Michael Prior and William Taylor; London: World of Islam Festival Trust, 1994), p. 135.

[17] Irfan Shahîd, *Byzantium and the Arabs in the Fourth Century* (Washington DC: Dumbarton Oaks, 1984).

[18] Milka Rubin, 'Arabization versus Islamization in the Palestinian Melkite Community during the Early Muslim Period', in *Sharing the Sacred: Religious Contacts and Conflicts in the Holy Land, First–Fifteenth Centuries* CE (ed. Arieh Kofsky and Guy G. Stroumsa; Jerusalem: Yad Izhak Ben Zvi, 1998), pp. 149–62.

[19] For more on the development of Eastern churches, see Philip Jenkins, *The Lost History of Christianity: The Thousand-Year Golden Age of the Church in the Middle East, Africa, and Asia – and How It Died* (New York: HarperOne, 2008).

[20] Nestorius became the patriarch of Constantinople in 428 CE, and because of his strong views eventually caused enough controversy for the Council of Ephesus to be convened in 431 ce. He was removed as the patriarch and the Nestorian Church followed his teachings. Strengholt, *Gospel in the Air*, p. 124.

[21] Ronald G. Roberson, *The Eastern Christian Churches: A Brief Survey* (Rome: Pont. Institutum Studiorum Orientalium, rev. edn, 1990), pp. 1, 9, 14, 20.

[22] Albert Aghazarian, 'The Significance of Jerusalem to Christians', in *Christians in the Holy Land* (ed. Prior and Taylor), pp. 100–101.

[23] Roberson, 'Eastern Christian Churches', p. 27.

[24] Strengholt, *Gospel in the Air*, pp. 34–5.

[25] Strengholt, *Gospel in the Air*, pp. 34–5.

[26] Strengholt, *Gospel in the Air*, pp. 26, 29.

[27] Joshua Blau, *A Grammar of Christian Arabic, Based Mainly on South-Palestinian Texts from the First Millennium*, Corpus Scriptorum Christianorum Orientalium, vols 267, 276, 279. Subsidia Tom. 27–9 (Louvain: Secretariat du Corpus SCO, 1966–7), 3 vols: [v] pp. ii, 5–255; [iii] pp. 257–469; [iii] pp. 469–668.

[28] O'Mahony, 'Palestinian Christians', pp. 12–13.

[29] Michael Nizar Ali, 'Christians in the Holy Land', in *Christians in the Holy Land* (ed. Prior and Taylor), p. 163.

[30] Aghazarian, 'Significance of Jerusalem', pp. 102–3.

[31] Jenkins, *Lost History*, p. 120.

[32] Jenkins, *Lost History*, p. 124

[33] Beginning in the nineteenth century, the Arabic word millet became a common term for all non-Muslim communities, whereas prior to the nineteenth century it referred primarily to the accepted minority religious groups in the Ottoman Empire. The millet system allowed these groups a measure of legal autonomy regarding intercommunal issues.

[34] O'Mahony, 'Palestinian Christians', pp. 17–18.

[35] Michael Prior, '"You Will Be My Witnesses in Jerusalem, in All Judaea and Samaria, and to the Ends of the Earth": A Christian Perspective on Jerusalem', in *Palestinian Christians* (ed. O'Mahony), pp. 97. See also O'Mahony, 'Palestinian Christians', p. 23.

[36] O'Mahony, 'Palestinian Christians', p. 41.

[37] O'Mahony, 'Palestinian Christians', pp. 50–51.

[38] O'Mahony, 'Palestinian Christians', p. 51.

[39] O'Mahony, 'Palestinian Christians', p. 51.

[40] O'Mahony, 'Palestinian Christians', p. 41.

[41] O'Mahony, 'Palestinian Christians', p. 41. Arguably, O'Mahony conflates Arab and Palestinian nationalisms, which were opposed to each other in the 1950s and 1960s. One could claim the PLO gave disillusioned Arab nationalists an alternative secular vision that was far more potent, a perspective that O'Mahony's analysis lacks. See, e.g., Rashid Khalidi, 'Arab Nationalism: Historical Problems in the Literature', *American Historical Review* 96:5 (1991).

[42] Sami F. Geraisy, 'Socio-Demographic Characteristics: Reality, Problems and Aspirations within Israel', in *Christians in the Holy Land* (ed. Prior and Taylor), p. 49.

[43] Prior, '"You Will Be My Witnesses"', p. 118.

[44] Michael Dumper, 'Faith and Statecraft: Church–State Relations in Jerusalem after 1948', in *Palestinian Christians* (ed. O'Mahony), pp. 59, 61. The case of Jerusalem was unique because almost no Christians remained after the 1948 war, whereas other Israeli towns, including Haifa, Lyyda and Tel Aviv-Jaffa retained a meaningful Palestinian Christian population. Therefore, when a Christian division of the Israeli Ministry of Religious Affairs was established to deal with the Christian properties acquired during the war, there was no impetus to restore them to the Christian community. Eventually, the officially recognized denominations of the Mandate period were returned their property. Others had more difficulty.

[45] See Amnon Ramon, *Christians and Christianity in the Jewish State* (Jerusalem: Jerusalem Institute for Israel Studies, 2011), forthcoming.

[46] Dumper, 'Faith and Statecraft', p. 66.

[47] Dumper, 'Faith and Statecraft', p. 77.

[48] Although the Palestinian Christian community has generally chosen non-violent forms of resistance, it is important to acknowledge significant exceptions. Some Palestinian Christian individuals – most notable among them George Habash – were involved in the leadership of groups comprising the PLO and were engaged in violence. For more information on the Palestinian Christian response to violence, see Joshua Hammer, *A Season in Bethlehem: Unholy War in a Sacred Place* (New York: Free Press, 2003).

[49] Sabella, 'Socio-Economic Characteristics', p. 93.

[50] Sabella, 'Socio-Economic Characteristics', pp. 92–3.

[51] Baramki, 'Spiritual Significance', p. 142.

[52] Calvin E. Shenk, 'The Middle Eastern Jesus: Messianic Jewish and Palestinian Christian Understandings', *Missiology* 29:4 (2001): p. 408.

[53] Baramki, 'Spiritual Significance', p. 142.

[54] Shenk, 'Middle Eastern Jesus', p. 408.

[55] Shenk, 'Middle Eastern Jesus', p. 408.

[56] See Meron Benvenisti's book, *Sacred Landscape: Buried History of the Holy Land since 1948* (Berkeley: California University Press, 2002).

[57] B. Kimmerling, and J.S. Migdal, *The Palestinian People: A History* (Cambridge: Harvard University Press, 2003), p. 213.

[58] 'Letters of Support – From Jerusalem, a Message of Greeting from Their Betides, Diodorus I, Greek Orthodox Patriarch, Michael Sabbah, Latin Patriarch, and Torkom Manoogian, Armenian Patriarch', in *Christians in the Holy Land* (ed. Prior and Taylor), p. xvi.

[59] O'Mahony, 'Palestinian Christians', p. 9.

[60] Many Protestant Christians visit and worship at the Garden Tomb, which also commemorates Christ's crucifixion and resurrection.

[61] For more on General Gordon and the Garden Tomb, see Peter Walker, *The Weekend that Changed the World: The Mystery of Jerusalem's Empty Tomb* (Louisville, KY: Westminster John Knox, 2000).

5. An Introduction to Israeli Messianic Jewish Identity

[1] For a discussion of identity issues see James D. Fearon, 'What Is Identity (as We Now Use the Word)?'(Stanford University Department of Political Science, 1999) http://www.stanford.edu/~jfearon/papers/iden1v2.pdf (accessed 17 Sept. 2012).

[2] The material in this paragraph is based on social identity theory developed by H. Tajfel and J.C. Turner, 'The Social Identity Theory of Intergroup Behavior', in *Psychology of Intergroup Relations* (ed. S. Worchel and W.G. Austin; Chicago: Nelson-Hall, 2nd edn, 1985), pp. 7–24.

[3] The predominant sects were the Pharisees, Sadducees, Essenes and Zealots. In addition to these major movements, there were a number of smaller sects functioning. See Oskar Skarsaune, *In the Shadow of the Temple* (Downers Grove, IL: InterVarsity Press, 2002), pp. 103–28.

[4] Gal. 4.4.

[5] Acts 2.46: 'Day by day, as they spent much time together in the temple, they broke bread at home and ate their food with glad and generous hearts.'

[6] See Acts 15.

[7] Eusebius, *Ecclesiastical History* 4.5.1–4, in J.A. Stevenson, *A New Eusebius: Documents Illustrating the History of the Church to* AD *337* (London: SPCK, rev. edn. 1985).

[8] The 'parting of the ways' occurred over a period of centuries making it impossible to definitively date the separation of Judaism and Christianity. See Adam H. Becker and Annette Yoshiko Reed, eds, *The Ways that Never Parted: Jews and Christians in Late Antiquity and the Early Middle Ages* (Minneapolis: Fortress, 2007).

[9] See Oskar Skarsaune and Reidar Hvalvik, eds, *Jewish Believers in Jesus: The Early Centuries* (Peabody, MA: Hendrickson, 2007).

[10] See R. Pritz, *Nazarene Jewish Christianity: From the End of the New Testament Period until Its Disappearance in the Fourth Century* (Jerusalem: Magnes, 1992).

[11] Skarsaune and Hvakvik, *Jewish Believers*, p. 552, n. 148.

[12] Edward Flannery, *The Anguish of the Jews: Twenty-Three Centuries of Anti-Semitism* (Mahwah, NJ: Paulist Press, 1965).

[13] Alan T. Davis, *Anti-Semitism and the Christian Mind* (New York: Herder and Herder, 1969), p. 75. The councils of the church were instrumental in institutionalizing anti-Jewishness; particularly the Council of Nicea in 325 CE and the Fourth Lateran Council in 1215 CE.

[14] See K. Kjær-Hansen, *Joseph Rabinowitz and the Messianic Movement: The Herzl of Jewish Christianity* (Grand Rapids, MI: Eerdmans, 1995).

[15] Kjær-Hansen, *Joseph Rabinowitz*.

[16] Shaye J.D. Cohen, *The Beginnings of Jewishness: Boundaries, Varieties, Uncertainties* (London: University of California Press, 1999), p. 3.

[17] Cohen, *Beginnings of Jewishness*, pp. 7–8.

[18] Debra Kaufman, 'Is There Such a Thing as "Jewish Identity"?' http://www.secularjewishculture.org/jewish_identity_.html (accessed 14 Oct. 2012).

[19] Dr. Yedidya Itzhaki, 'What Is Jewish Secularism?' http://www.posen-foundation.com/literaryprojects/haaretzsupplement.html (accessed 14 Oct. 2012).

[20] Felix Posen, 'At the end of the day it is Jewish culture that remains the main possible common denominator and glue that could hold all the disparate groups of different religious views as well as the majority secular Jews together, and around which they could unite if they wanted to and still maintain their individual distinctiveness.' In 'Culture is the Glue to Unite the Numerous Strands of Jewishness' http://www.secular-jewishculture.org/strands_of_jewishness.html (accessed 14 Oct. 2012).

[21] 'Zion' is first of all a biblical term that eventually came to mean the land of Israel, with special reference to Jerusalem.

[22] See Judith Butler, *Parting Ways: Jewishness and the Critique of Zionism* (New York: Columbia University Press, 2012) for a discussion of this topic. She suggests a framework for a new secular Jewish identity, in essence diasporic, centred on living together with the 'other' as the focus and not the margin of 'Jewishness'.

[23] Raffaella A. Del Sarto, 'Israel's Contested Identity and the Mediterranean' (2002) 7 http://ies.berkeley.edu/research/DelSartoIsraelMed.pdf (accessed 14 Oct. 2012).

[24] Del Sarto, 'Israel's Contested Identity', p. 8.

[25] http://www.mfa.gov.il/MFA/Peace+Process/Guide+to+the+Peace+Process/Declaration+of+Establishment+of+State+of+Israel.htm (accessed 19 Oct. 2012).

[26] Del Sarto, 'Israel's Contested Identity', p. 11.

[27] 'David Ben-Gurion, Broadcast to the Nation, May 15, 1948' http://www.jewishvirtuallibrary.org/jsource/History/bgbroad.html (accessed 24 Oct. 2012).

[28] Arab (Israeli Palestinian) citizens of Israel are permitted to serve in the military as is the Druze community. However, very few Israeli

Palestinians choose this option. The Druze community has a tradition of military service. This is in line with their philosophy of being good citizens wherever they reside.

[29] Gili Cohen, 'Study: IDF Officers Identify More as Israeli than Jewish' http://www. /news/diplomacy-defense/study-idf-officers-identify-more-as-israeli-than-j haaretz.comewish.premium-1.469791 (accessed 14 Oct. 2012). (The article noted that the respondents could answer the questions with more than one response, hence the percentages that add up to more than 100 per cent).

[30] Keri Zelson Warshawsky, 'Returning to Their Own Borders: A Social Anthropological Study of Contemporary Messianic Jewish Identity in Israel', unpublished PhD dissertation (The Hebrew University of Jerusalem, 2008), p. 10.

[31] Warshawsky, 'Returning to Their Own Borders', p. 11.

[32] The material for this section is based on material from Gershon Nerel, 'From Death to Life: The Restoration of Jewish Yeshua-Believers in the Land of Israel' (2007), published in *Israel: His People, His Land, His Story* (ed. Fred Wright; Eastbourne: Thankful Books, 2005), pp. 168–88.

[33] G. Nerel, 'Attempts to Establish a "Messianic Jewish Church" in Eretz-Israel', *Mishkan* 28 (1998): pp. 35–44.

[34] G. Nerel, 'Messianic Jews', *Mishkan* 27 (1997): p. 19.

[35] Kelvin Crombie, 'Michael Solomon Alexander and the Controversial Jerusalem Bishopric', *Mishkan* 15 (1991): pp. 1–12.

[36] Joseph Shulam, 'Rabbi Daniel Zion: Chief Rabbi of Bulgarian Jews during World War II', *Mishkan* 15 (1991): pp. 53–7.

[37] The facts surrounding this operation remain unclear, including the actual numbers of persons evacuated. For a discussion of the subject, see 'Operation Mercy and Jewish Believers in 1948', *Mishkan* 61 (2009). The whole of issue number 61 is devoted to this subject and provides a fascinating account of historical detective work.

[38] The Israeli Messianic Jewish community consists of Jews (born of Jewish mothers or converted to Judaism), non-Jewish spouses and children, those with some Jewish heritage (a Jewish father or a Jewish grandparent), and a number of non-Jews who have chosen to live in Israel and identify with Israel and with the Messianic community. It is important to point this out, particularly since the numbers cited often include those from each of the sectors within the community. On a practical level in the life of the community, there is little or no distinction made between those who are 'full Jews', partial Jews or non-Jews.

³⁹ Luke 21.24.

⁴⁰ The following sections, describing the history of the Israeli Messianic Jewish community according to decades, are based on personal involvement and observation and on numerous conversations with large numbers of Israeli Messianic Jewish leaders.

⁴¹ Kai Kjær-Hansen and Bodil F. Skjøtt, eds, *Facts and Myths about the Messianic Congregations in Israel, 1998–1999: A Survey Conducted by Kai Kjaer-Hansen and Bodil F. Skjøtt* (Jerusalem: Caspari Center, 1999).

⁴² By Michael Zinn, the director of Chosen People Ministries in Israel.

⁴³ To be halachicly Jewish means that one is born of a Jewish mother or has converted to Judaism. Israeli citizenship, however, is based on the 'law of return', which grants the right of return and full citizenship to any individual with at least one Jewish grandparent.

⁴⁴ Warshawsky, 'Returning to Their Own Borders', p. 106.

⁴⁵ *Tenach* is the Hebrew word for 'Old Testament'. It is an acronym of the first three letters of the Hebrew words for: *torah* meaning the first five books of the Bible, *nevi'im* meaning the prophets, and *k'tuvim* meaning writings or additional books that are neither torah nor prophets.

⁴⁶ Warshawsky, 'Returning to Their Own Borders', p. 81.

⁴⁷ Until today, there is a common saying in the Hebrew language that each Jew is responsible for every other Jew.

⁴⁸ The content of this section is based on numerous personal conversations with Israeli Messianic Jewish leaders from 2009 to 2012.

6. Reading Scripture as a Palestinian Christian

¹ Murray Rae, *History and Hermeneutics* (London: T&T Clark, 2005), pp. 135–40.

² Kenneth Bailey, *Jesus through Middle Eastern Eyes* (Downers Grove, IL: InterVarsity Press, 2008).

³ Agnes D. Hanania, 'Churches of the Holy Land Obligations and Expectations: A View from the Holy Land', in *Christians in the Holy Land* (ed. Michael Prior and William Taylor; London: World of Islam Festival Trust, 1994), p. 203.

⁴ Michael Prior, 'Pilgrimage to the Holy Land, Yesterday and Today', in *Christians in the Holy Land* (ed. Prior and Taylor), p. 175.

⁵ Salim Munayer, 'The Ethnic Identity of Palestinian Arab Christian Adolescents in Israel', unpublished PhD dissertation (University of

Wales, Cardiff; Oxford Centre for Mission Studies, 2000). See also Daniel Rossing, 'Microcosm and Multiple Minorities: The Christian Communities in Israel', in *Israel Yearbook and Almanac* (ed. N. Greenwood; Jerusalem: IBRT Translation/Documentation, 1999), pp. 28–42.

6 Jørgen S. Nielsen, 'Preface', *Christian Arabic Apologetics during the Abbasid Period (750–1258)* (ed. Samir Khalil Samir and Jørgen S. Nielsen; Leiden: Brill, 1994), p. viii.

7 Nielsen, 'Preface', p. ix.

8 Nielsen, 'Preface', p. x.

9 Yohanna Katanacho, 'Palestinian Protestant Theological Responses to a World Marked by Violence', *Missiology* 36:3 (2006), p. 291.

10 Yohanna Katanacho, 'Introduction to the Church of the Arabs', unpublished as of August 2012, pp. 5–6.

11 Heleen Murre-van den Berg, 'Syriac Christianity', in *The Blackwell Companion to Eastern Christianity* (ed. Ken Parry; Oxford: Blackwell, 2007), p. 252.

12 Timothy Mitchell, *Colonising Egypt* (London: University of California Press, 1991), p. 148–52.

13 Brian Brock, *Singing the Ethos of God: On the Place of Christian Ethics in Scripture* (Grand Rapids, MI: Eerdmans, 2007), p. 125.

14 Roger Chartier, 'Reading Matter and "Popular" Reading: From the Renaissance to the Seventeenth Century', in *A History of Reading in the West* (ed. Guglielmo Cavallo and Roger Chartier; Amherst, MA: University of Massachusetts Press), pp. 276–8.

15 Katanacho, 'Palestinian Protestant Theological Responses', p. 292.

16 Salim Munayer and Phillip E. Goble, *New Creation Book for Muslims* (Pasadena, CA: Mandate Press, 1989).

17 Geries Khoury, *Arab Christians: Rootedness, Presence, Openness* (Jerusalem: Al-Liqa', 2006). The Greek Catholic or Melkite Church began when Kyrillos V, the Greek Orthodox Patriarch of Antioch, recognized the authority of Rome in 1709. While it recognizes the authority of the Roman Catholic Church, the church retains its Greek liturgical practices. See Strengholt, *Gospel in the Air*, pp. 154–5.

18 Khoury, *Arab Christians*, p. 226.

19 Katanacho, 'Palestinian Protestant Theological Responses', p. 294.

20 Riah Abu El-Assal, *Caught in Between: The Story of an Arab Palestinian Christian Israeli* (London: SPCK, 1999), p. 126.

21 Munib Younan and Frederick M. Strickert, *Witnessing for Peace: In Jerusalem and the World* (Minneapolis: Fortress, 2003), p. 133.

[22] Katanacho, 'Palestinian Protestant Theological Responses', p. 295.

[23] Brian Cox of Pepperdine University's PACIS Project in Faith-Based Diplomacy has worked on developing the Abrahamic model of reconciliation. See Brian Cox, *Faith-Based Reconciliation: A Moral Vision that Transforms People and Societies* (USA: Xlibris, 2007).

[24] Michel Sabbah, 'Reading the Bible Today in the Land of the Bible' (1993) http://www.lpj.org/newsite2006/patriarch/pastoral-letters/1993/readingthebible_en.html (accessed 18 Nov. 2011). Although a fuller treatment of this letter is beyond of the scope of this book, the issues Sabbah deals with continue to be as relevant as when the letter was written, including questions of hermeneutics, the moral and ethical questions raised by the Israeli–Palestinian conflict, and theological questions of election, covenant and the biblical land promises.

[25] Paul Tarazi, 'An Orthodox Christian Response to the Inclusive Language Lectionary', *Word Magazine* (April 1984) http://www.orthodoxresearchinstitute.org/articles/bible/tarazi_inclusive_language_lectionary.htm (accessed 18 Nov. 2011).

[26] Tarazi, 'Orthodox Christian Response'.

[27] Tarazi, 'Orthodox Christian Response' (emphasis original).

[28] Paul Nadim Tarazi, *Land and Covenant* (St Paul, MN: OCABS Press, 2009).

[29] Tarazi, *Land and Covenant*, p. 243.

[30] Tarazi, *Land and Covenant*, p. 256.

[31] Tarazi, *Land and Covenant*, p. 257.

[32] Mark Calder, '"Enclosures of Hymns for the Lambs of Your Flock": Syriac Orthodox Scripture, Tradition and Modernity in the Competition for Souls', a paper delivered at the Competition for Souls conference, Van Leer Institute, Jerusalem (14 June 2011).

[33] Sabbah, 'Reading the Bible'.

[34] Sabbah, 'Reading the Bible'.

[35] Horsley, Richard, 'Jesus Confronting Empire', in *Challenging Empire: God, Faithfulness and Resistance* (ed. Naim Ateek, Cedar Duaybis and Maurine Tobin; Jerusalem: Sabeel, 2012): pp. 56–85.

[36] For example, see *The Biblical Text in the Context of Occupation* (ed. Mitri Raheb; Bethlehem: Diyar, 2012).

[37] Katanacho, 'Palestinian Protestant Theological Responses', p. 289.

[38] Alex Awad, *Palestinian Memories: The Story of a Palestinian Mother and Her People* (Bethlehem: Bethlehem Bible College, 2008).

[39] Katanacho, 'Palestinian Protestant Theological Responses', p. 290.

[40] Naim Ateek, *Justice, and Only Justice* (Maryknoll, NY: Orbis Books, 1989), pp. 79–80. Ateek writes, 'The canon of this hermeneutic for the Palestinian Christian is nothing less than Jesus Christ himself' (79). Ateek's more recent *A Palestinian Cry for Justice* (Maryknoll, NY: Orbis Books, 2008) overviews the Palestinian desire for peace, the outbreak of violence, Palestinian liberation theology's challenge to other theologies of the land, its contribution to non-violence and peace, as well as practical obstacles in the way of peace.

[41] Riad Kassis, *Why Don't We Read the Book that Christ Read? Towards a Better Understanding of the Old Testament* (Beirut: Clarion, 2008).

[42] Riad Kassis, *Why Don't We Read*, pp. 13–23.

[43] Salim J. Munayer, 'The Theological Challenge the State of Israel Poses to Palestinian Christians', *St Francis Magazine* 3:4 (2008) http://www.stfrancismagazine.info/ja/pdf/2008/The%20Theological%20Challenge.pdf (accessed 18 Nov. 2011).

[44] Kassis, *Why Don't We Read*, pp. 178–98.

[45] Kairos Palestine Document 2.2.2 (2009) http://www.oikoumene.org/fileadmin/files/wcc-main/2009pdfs/Kairos%20Palestine_En.pdf (accessed 10 Nov. 2010).

[46] Kairos Palestine document 2.2.2.

[47] J. Albert Harrill, 'The Use of the New Testament in the American Slave Controversy: A Case History in the Hermeneutical Tension between Biblical Criticism and Christian Moral Debate', *Religion and American Culture* 10:2 (2000): pp. 149–86.

[48] 'Ben-Gurion also, and crucially, argued that he was fighting all Zionist battles with the help of the Hebrew Bible. Already in his first published work, in Yiddish, entitled: *Eretz Yisrael: Past and Present* (1918), which he co-authored with Yitzhak Ben-Tzvi – later to become the second president of Israel – he argued that the Jewish "return" to Palestine is actually a "repeat" of Joshua's conquest of ancient Palestine.' Nur Masalha, *The Bible and Zionism: Invented Traditions, Archaeology, and Post-Colonialism in Israel–Palestine* (London: Zed Books, 2007), pp. 27–8.

[49] Katanacho, 'Palestinian Protestant Theological Responses', p. 292.

[50] Katanacho, 'Palestinian Protestant Theological Responses', p. 292. It is important to note that a number of Palestinian Brethren churches, particularly in the Galilee, were founded and influenced by Western dispensationalist ministries, and this is reflected in their theology.

51 Hanna Massad, 'The Theological Foundation for Reconciliation between the Palestinian Christians and the Messianic Jews', unpublished PhD dissertation (Fuller Theological Seminary, 2000), p. 212.

52 Massad, 'Theological Foundation', pp. 273–4.

53 Katanacho, 'Palestinian Protestant Theological Responses', p. 297.

54 See also Kenneth Bailey, *Jesus through Middle Eastern Eyes: Cultural Studies in the Gospels* (Downers Grove, IL: InterVarsity Press, 2008).

55 Yohanna Katanacho, 'A Palestinian Reading of Psalm 87: Jerusalem is the City of God', in *The Land Cries Out: Theology of the Land in the Israeli-Palestinian Context* (ed. Salim J. Munayer and Lisa Loden; Eugene, OR: Wipf & Stock, 2012), pp. 181–99; Salim J. Munayer, *Hosea* (ed. Bruce J. Nicholls; Manila: Asia Theological Association, 2010). Munayer makes use of insight from midrashic and mishnaic sources.

56 Munther Isaac, 'Reading the Old Testament in the Palestinian Church Today: Joshua 6 – A Case Study', in *The Land Cries Out* (ed. Munayer and Loden), pp. 217–33. For another example, see Isaac deal with the complex and divisive text of Daniel: Munther Isaac, 'Arab Christian Fundamentalist Reading of the Book of Daniel: A Critique', in *The Biblical Text in the Context of Occupation: Towards a New Hermeneutics of Liberation* (ed. Mitri Raheb; Bethlehem: Diyar, 2012): pp. 247–65.

57 Isaac, 'Reading the Old Testament', p. 219. Within this displayed quote, Isaac refers in footnotes to R. Goetz, 'Joshua, Calvin, and Genocide', *Theology Today* 32 (1975): pp. 263–74; Lawson G. Stone, 'Ethical and Apologetic Tendencies in the Redaction of the Book of Joshua', *Catholic Biblical Quarterly* 53 (1991): pp. 25–35; Esther Epp-Tiessen, 'Conquering the Land', in *Under Vine and Fig Tree* (ed. Alain E. Weaver; Telford, PA: Cascadia, 2007), p. 64; and Michael Prior, '"Power" and "the Other" in Joshua: The Brutal Birthing of a Group Identity', *Mission Studies* 23 (2006): pp. 27–43.

58 Isaac, 'Reading the Old Testament'.

59 Mitri Raheb, 'Contextual Palestinian Theology As It Deals with Realities on the Ground', lecture delivered at Christ at the Checkpoint Conference, Bethlehem (17 March 2010) http://www.christatthecheckpoint.com/lectures/Mitri_Raheb.pdf (accessed 18 Nov 2011).

60 For a recent overview that aptly addresses this issue, see Mitri Raheb, 'Displacement Theopolitics: A Century of Interplay between Theology and Politics in Palestine', in *The Invention of History: A Century of Interplay between Theology and Politics in Palestine* (ed. Mitri Raheb; Bethlehem: Diyar, 2011), pp. 9–32.

[61] That being said, Palestinian Christians have embraced (albeit with tension) some streams of Jewish-Christian expression, such as the Palestinian Catholic Church recognizing the Hebrew Catholic movement in Jerusalem.

[62] Sabbah, 'Reading the Bible'.

[63] A Messianic Jewish critique of the Kairos Document is that it does not fully address the issue of Messianic Jews. This is something we hope to touch on in this work.

7. Reading Scripture as an Israeli Messianic Jew

[1] Boaz Cohen, 'Introduction', in *Everyman's Talmud* (ed. A. Cohen; New York: Schocken Books, 1975), p. iii.

[2] David Hartman, *Israelis and the Jewish Tradition* (New Haven: Yale University Press, 2000), pp. 104–5.

[3] While Messianic Jews are clearly monotheistic, they hold a variety of views on the issue of Christology. Richard Harvey describes five emerging christological views (Theocentric Christology, Recontextualized Nicene Christology, Jewish Mystical Christology, the Hidden Messiah of Post-Missionary Messianic Judaism, and Adoptionist Christology) of the Messianic Jewish community. Richard Harvey, *Mapping Messianic Jewish Theology* (Milton Keynes: Authentic Media, 2009), pp. 104–39.

[4] The Helsinki Consultation theological group, comprised of Jesus-believing Jews from a variety of traditions, published a statement in 2012 on the issue of Torah: 'We as Jewish believers in Yeshua acknowledge the special bond that unites us with Israel's Torah. This bond with Israel's Torah witnesses in the Church to the irrevocability of God's gifts and call to Israel (Rom 11:29). For Yeshua said, "Think not that I have come to destroy the Torah, or the prophets: I have not come to destroy, but to fulfill" (Matt 5:17). We believe in the continuing validity of the Torah even as it is fulfilled in Christ. Moreover, we see Christ as the incarnate Torah, the eternal wisdom of the Father in human flesh. He alone lived out the Torah in perfect form, and he calls his disciples to walk in his ways.' http://www.helsinkiconsultation2012.org/index.php/en/statement-en (accessed 20 Jan. 2013).

[5] Kevin Vanhoozer, *Is There a Meaning in This Text?* (Grand Rapids, MI: Zondervan, 1988), p. 149.

6 R.G. Gruenler, *Meaning and Understanding* (Grand Rapids, MI: Zondervan, 1991), p. xiv.

7 Mark Kinzer, 'Scripture and Tradition', in *Voices of Messianic Judaism* (ed. Dan Cohn-Sherbok; Baltimore: Lederer, 2001), p. 29.

8 Mark Kinzer, *The Nature of Messianic Judaism* (Hartford, CT: Hashivenu Archives, undated), p. 18, and Mark Kinzer, *Post Missionary Messianic Judaism* (Grand Rapids, MI: Braxos, 2005), p. 90.

9 'The promise of the land of Israel is forever, and the plain sense of this is that the Jewish people will possess the land (at least in trusteeship) and live there. To say that the New Covenant transforms this plain sense into an assertion that those who believe in Yeshua come into some vague spiritual "possession" or a spiritual "territory" is intellectual sleight of hand aiming at denying, canceling and reducing to naught a real promise given to a real people in the real world.' David Stern, 'The Land from a Messianic Jewish Perspective', in *The Bible and the Land: An Encounter* (ed. Lisa Loden, Peter Walker and Michael Wood; Jerusalem: Musalaha, 2000), p. 42.

10 David Stern, *Messianic Jewish Manifesto* (Jerusalem: Jewish New Testament Publications, 1988), p. 90.

11 Arnold Fruchtenbaum, 'Eschatology and Messianic Jews: A Theological Perspective', in *Voices of Messianic Judaism: Confronting Critical Issues Facing a Maturing Movement* (ed. Dan Cohn-Sherbok; Baltimore: Lederer, 2001), p. 211.

12 Joseph Shulam, *Hidden Treasures: The First Century Jewish Way of Understanding the Scriptures* (Jerusalem: Netivyah, 2008).

13 For an overview of rabbinic interpretation see http://www.betemunah.org/rules.html.

14 'Pardes' (orchard) is an acronym in Hebrew. Each letter stands for a particular approach to interpretation. P signifies the word *p'shat* which means the plain, simple, grammatical meaning of the text; r signifies *remez* which means hint or allegory, indicating a hidden reference to the numerical value of words or an acronym; d signifies *d'rash*, which means a parabolic, homiletical interpretation; and s signifies *sod* which means secret and implies a mystical or kabbalistic interpretation.

15 Shulam, *Hidden Treasures*.

16 Robert L. Thomas, *Evangelical Hermeneutics: The New Versus the Old* (Grand Rapids, MI: Kregel, 2002), pp. 13–18.

[17] Gershon Nerel, 'Life from the Dead: Modern Jewish Yeshua-Believers and the Historic Churches' (Yad Hashmonah: unpublished paper, 2004), p. 2.

[18] Nerel, 'Life from the Dead', p. 7.

[19] Harvey, *Mapping Messianic Jewish Theology*.

[20] *Halacha* comes from the Hebrew word for 'walk.' Halacha in Judaism is the way in which the Scriptures are lived out and applied in life – how a person 'walks' their faith. The word is spelled in a variety of ways. For this chapter I use 'halacha' unless a different spelling is used by an author who is being quoted.

[21] Richard Harvey, 'A Typology of Messianic Jewish Theology', *Mishkan* 57 (2008): pp. 13–23.

[22] Harvey, *Mapping Messianic Jewish Theology*, pp. 282–3.

[23] See personal interviews in Keri Zelson Warshawsky, 'Returning to Their Own Borders: A Social Anthropological Study of Contemporary Messianic Jewish Identity in Israel', unpublished PhD dissertation (The Hebrew University of Jerusalem, 2008).

[24] Yael Zerubavel, 'A Secular Return to the Bible? Reflections on Israeli Society, National Memory, and the Politics of the Past', *AJS Perspectives*, Association for Jewish Studies: Center for Jewish History, New York, NY (Spring 2011), p. 31.

[25] Warshawsky, 'Returning to Their Own Borders', pp. 142–3.

[26] Warshawsky, 'Returning to Their Own Borders', p. 144.

[27] The Haggadah (telling) is the liturgy for the ceremonial meal that commemorates the exodus from Egypt. The story is meant to be told in its entirety from generation to generation, beginning with deliverance of Israel when the angel of the Lord 'passed over' the house of Israel and the sons of Israel were saved from death, continuing through the deliverance from the armies of Pharaoh at the Red Sea, and ending with the entrance into the Promised Land.

[28] Shaye J.D. Cohen, *The Beginnings of Jewishness: Boundaries, Varieties, Uncertainties* (Berkeley: University of California Press, 1999), p. 348.

[29] Carl Kinbar, 'Israel, Torah and the Knowledge of God', *Kesher* 24 (2010), p. 18/37.

[30] Arnold Fruchtenbaum, *Israelogy: The Missing Link in Systematic Theology* (Tustin, CA: Ariel Ministries, undated), p. 643.

[31] Fruchtenbaum, *Israelogy*, p. 759.

[32] This is a minority position in Israel and among Jews who believe in Jesus worldwide. Out of approximately 150 congregations in Israel

there are currently 5 who would be in substantial agreement with Maoz's Reformed theological position.

[33] Maoz's views, together with a strident critique of 'Torah positive' theology is expressed in his book *Judaism Is Not Jewish: A Friendly Critique of the Messianic Movement* (Ross-shire: Christian Focus, 2003).

[34] Gershon Nerel, 'Torah and Halakhah among Modern Assemblies of Jewish-Yeshua Believers: An Israeli Response to Arnold Fruchtenbaum', in *How Jewish Is Christianity? 2 Views of the Messianic Movement* (ed. Louis Goldberg; Grand Rapids, MI: Zondervan, 2003), pp. 152–65.

[35] Gershon Nerel, '"Post Mission" and "Messianic Judaism" – Semantics and Reality: A Response to Mark Kinzer, "Post Missionary Messianic Judaism Three Years Later: Reflections on a Conversation Just Begun"' (Jerusalem: Robert Lindsey Lectures, 2008), pp. 4–5.

[36] See Daniel Juster, *Growing to Maturity: A Messianic Jewish Guide* (Denver: Union of Messianic Jewish Congregations, 1987); also Daniel Juster, *Jewish Roots: A Foundation of Biblical Theology* (Shippensburg, PA: Destiny Image, 1995); Daniel Juster, 'Messianic Judaism and Torah' (ed. Kai Kjaer Hansen; *Jewish Identity and Faith in Jesus* (Jerusalem: Caspari Center, 1996), pp. 113–21.

[37] http://www.tikkunministries.org/newsletters/dj-dec08.asp (emphasis in the original; accessed 3 Feb. 2013).

[38] David H. Stern, *Messianic Jewish Manifesto* (Jerusalem: Jewish New Testament, 1988), pp. 125–54.

[39] A short list would include Mark Kinzer, Stuart Dauerman, John Fischer, Carl Kinbar, Rich Nichols and David Rudolf. This reflects the fact that theological discourse is much more on the agenda of Diaspora Messianic Jews than for their Israeli brothers and sisters.

[40] Zvi Sadan, 'Halakic Authority in the Life of the Messianic Community', *Kesher* 24 (Summer 2010) http://www.kesherjournal.com/pdf/Issue-24/Halakic-Authority-in-the-Life-of-the-Messianic-Community.pdf 7/17 (accessed 2 Feb. 2013).

[41] Sadan, 'Halakic Authority', p. 14/17.

[42] From a lecture given by Joseph Shulam.

[43] Joseph Shulam: 'we must make a very serious effort to know and study and understand what do the Pharisees who sit in Moses' seat say and teach on a variety of issues that we all face as Jews living in a post-modern world.' http://www.netivyah.org/articles/Doing_Messianic_Jewish_Halacha.pdf, p. 5 (accessed 3 Feb. 2013).

[44] Shulam, 'Doing Messianic Jewish Halacha', p. 3.

[45] Ariel and Devorah Berkowitz, *Torah Rediscovered: Challenging Centuries of Misinterpretation and Neglect* (Lakewood, CO: First Fruits of Zion, 1996), p. 3.

[46] Berkowitz, *Torah Rediscovered*, pp. 8–9.

[47] Berkowitz, *Torah Rediscovered*, pp. 130–31.

[48] Genesis 17.7–8.

[49] David Stern, 'The Land from a Messianic Jewish Perspective', in *The Bible and the Land* (ed. Loden, Walker and Wood), p. 42.

[50] Gershon Nerel, 'Messianic Jews and the Modern Zionist Movement', in *Israel and Yeshua* (ed. Torlief Elgvin; Jerusalem: Caspari Center, 1993), p. 75.

[51] Harvey, *Mapping Messianic Jewish Theology*, p. 224.

[52] David Stern, 'The Land from a Messianic Jewish Perspective', p. 42.

[53] Genesis 15.7; 17.8.

[54] Abraham Joshua Heschel, *God in Search of Man: A Philosophy of Judaism* (New York: Farrar, Strauss and Giroux; 1976), p. 425.

[55] Mark Kinzer notes this connection in 'Beginning with the End: the Place of Eschatology in the Messianic Jewish Canonical Narrative', in *Israel's Messiah and the People of God* (ed. Jennifer M. Rosner, Eugene, OR: Cascade Books, 2011), p. 99.

[56] Rabbi Shlomo Itzhaki (1040–1105), famed French medieval scholar and commentator on Torah and Talmud. His writings are widely respected and continue to be studied in Jewish circles today.

[57] Hartman, *Israelis and the Jewish Tradition*, pp. 128–9.

[58] Ian S. Lustick, *For the Land and the Lord: Jewish Fundamentalism in Israel* (USA: Council on Foreign Relations, 1988), pp. 72–90.

[59] Hartman, *Israelis and the Jewish Tradition*, p. 15.

[60] Bodil Skjøtt, 'Messianic Believers and the Land of Israel: A Survey', *Mishkan* 26:1 (1997), pp. 72–81.

[61] Richard Harvey, *Towards a Messianic Jewish Theology of Reconciliation* (UK: Richard Harvey, 2012), pp. 18–20.

[62] Harvey, *Messianic Jewish Theology*, p. 19, n. 61; p. 20, nn. 61, 62; p. 21, n. 67.

[63] Philip D. Ben-Shmuel, 'Hagshama: A Theology for an Alternate Messianic Jewish Zionism', in *The Land Cries Out: Theology of the Land in the Israeli-Palestinian Context* (ed. Salim J. Munayer and Lisa Loden: Eugene, OR; Wipf & Stock, 2012), p. 147.

[64] Ben-Shmuel, 'Hagshama', p. 145.

[65] Ben-Shmuel, 'Hagshama', p. 154.

[66] Ben-Shmuel, 'Hagshama', p. 166.

8. Theological Disagreements

[1] Paul Nadim Tarazi, 'Covenant, Land and City: Finding God's Will in Palestine', *The Reformed Journal* 29 (1979), p. 11.

[2] David Holwerda, *Jesus and Israel: One Covenant or Two?* (Grand Rapids, MI: Eerdmans, 1995), p. 156.

[3] Paul Nadim Tarazi, *Land and Covenant* (St Paul, MN: OCABS Press, 2009), p. 257.

[4] See Gen. 12.1–3; 15; 17; 26.2–5; 28.10–15.

[5] Michael Wyshogrod, *The Body of Faith: Judaism's Corporeal Election* (New York: Seabury, 1983), pp. 64–5.

[6] Matt. 10.5–6; cf. Matt. 19.28; Acts 13.14; 14.1; 17.10; 18.4; 19.8.

[7] Rom. 5.6; Eph. 2.8–9.

[8] For further reading and various perspectives on a theology of the land, see *The Land Cries Out: Theology of the Land in the Israeli-Palestinian Context* (ed. Salim J. Munayer and Lisa Loden; Eugene, OR: Wipf & Stock, 2012).

[9] Canon Naim Ateek, 'Putting Christ at the Centre: The Land from a Palestinian Christian perspective', in *The Bible and the Land: An Encounter* (ed. Lisa Loden, Peter Walker and Michael Wood; Jerusalem: Musalaha, 2000), p. 56.

[10] For his entire article, see *The Bible and the Land* (ed. Loden, Walker and Wood), pp. 55–63.

[11] Yohanna Katanacho, 'Christ Is the Owner of Haaretz', *Christian Scholar's Review* 34 (2005), pp. 425–41.

[12] Merism is a figure of speech by which something is referred to by a conventional phrase that enumerates several of its constituents or traits. It is also a rhetorical term for a pair of contrasting words used to express totality or completeness. When combined with 'spatial', the term relates to space or location.

[13] Salim J. Munayer, 'Theology of the Land: From a Land of Strife to a Land of Reconciliation', in *The Land Cries Out* (ed. Munayer and Loden), p. 249.

[14] Munayer, 'Theology of the Land', pp. 234–64 for the entire article.

[15] Palestine Kairos Document 2.3.

[16] See Ps. 24.1.

[17] Gen. 10.

[18] Lisa Loden, 'Messianic Jewish Views on Israel's Rebirth and Survival in Light of Scripture', in *Christian Perspectives on the Israeli–Palestinian Conflict* (ed. W. Brown and P. Penner; Pasadena, CA: William Carey University Press, 2008), p. 46.

[19] D. Stern, 'The Land from a Messianic Jewish Perspective', in *The Bible and the Land* (ed. Loden, Walker and Wood), p. 37.

[20] Baruch Maoz, 'Jerusalem and Justice: A Messianic Jewish Perspective', in *Jerusalem Past and Present in the Purposes of God* (ed. P.W.L. Walker; Cambridge: Tyndale House, 1992), p. 157.

[21] Maoz, 'Jerusalem and Justice', p. 158, citing Lev. 2.24–25; 23.22.

[22] Maoz, 'Jerusalem and Justice', p. 159

[23] Maoz, 'Jerusalem and Justice', p. 155

[24] Maoz, 'Jerusalem and Justice', p. 159.

[25] Maoz, 'Jerusalem and Justice', p. 159.

[26] Salim J. Munayer, *Hosea*, Asia Bible Commentary Series (eds. Bruce J. Nicholls and Sang-Bok David Kim; Manila, Philippines: Asia Theological Association, 2010), pp. 8–19, 313–19.

[27] Munther Isaac, *A Biblical Theology of the Land: with a Special Emphasis on the Palestinian Church* (Oxford Centre for Mission Studies), forthcoming in 2014.

[28] Isaac referencing Robert P. Gordon, *Holy Land, Holy City: Sacred Geography and the Interpretation of the Bible* (Carlisle: Paternoster, 2004), pp. 104–6, and Christopher Wright, 'A Christian Approach to Old Testament Prophecy Concerning Israel', in *Jerusalem: Past and Present in the Purposes of God* (ed. Peter Walker; Cambridge: Tyndale House, 1992), p. 6. For further references to make clear this understanding of 'forever', see Exod. 29.9; Num. 25.10–13; 1 Chr. 23.13; Jer. 35.19.

[29] Norman Solomon, 'Covenant' (Oxford, 2001) http://www.bc.edu/dam/files/research_sites/cjl/texts/center/conferences/solomon.htm (accessed 30 Apr. 2013).

[30] The five covenants are: Noahic, Gen. 9; Abrahamic, Gen. 12; 13; 15; 17; Mosaic, Exod. 19:3–8; Davidic, 2 Sam. 7; and the new covenant, Jer. 31.30–34.

[31] http://www.yale.edu/faith/jewishchristianconference/documents/Gerald_McDermott.pdf (accessed 1 June 2013).

[32] David Stern, *Messianic Jewish Manifesto* (Jerusalem: Jewish New Testament, 1991), p. 100.

[33] Stern, *Messianic Jewish Manifesto*, p. 100.

[34] Stern, *Messianic Jewish Manifesto*, p. 100.

[35] Stern, *Messianic Jewish Manifesto*, p. 100. Stern spells this out in a later chapter.

[36] Stern focuses on Rev. 20.4, which describes Christ's followers reigning with him (cf. Matt 19.28).

[37] Stern, *Messianic Jewish Manifesto*, p. 101. Messianic Jews point out that the context of the new covenant is that it is cut with the house of Israel and the house of Judah (Jer. 31.31); this is often overlooked by Christian interpreters.

[38] Dan Juster, 'Covenant and Dispensation', *Mishkan* 1:2 (Jerusalem: 1985): pp. 34–5.

[39] Dan Juster, 'Covenant and Dispensation', p. 41.

[40] Keith Allen Regehr, 'Justice and Forgiveness: Restorative Justice Practice and the Recovery of Theological Memory', unpublished MTh thesis, University of Waterloo: Ontario, 2007), p. 47, referencing J. Scullion, 'Righteousness, Old Testament', in *Anchor Bible Dictionary*, vol. 5 (ed. David Freedman; Toronto: Doubleday, 1992), pp. 724–36. Available online: http://uwspace.uwaterloo.ca/bitstream/10012/3489/1/Keith%20Regehr%20Thesis.pdf (accessed 1 Apr. 2013).

[41] See Ps. 101.1; Mic. 6.8.

[42] John E. Toews, *Romans* (Scottdale, PA: Herald, 2004), p. 401.

[43] Richard Hayes, *The Moral Vision of the New Testament* (New York: HarperCollins, 1996), p. 98.

[44] Regehr, 'Justice and Forgiveness', p. 60.

[45] 'Mercy and truth are met together; righteousness and peace have kissed each other' (Ps. 85.10 AV).

[46] Regehr, 'Justice and Forgiveness', p. 50.

[47] Regehr, 'Justice and Forgiveness', p. 57.

[48] Regehr, 'Justice and Forgiveness', p. 59.

[49] Mae Elise Cannon, *Social Justice Handbook: Small Steps for a Better World* (Downers Grove, IL: InterVarsity Press, 2009), p. 21.

[50] Glen H. Stassen, *Just Peacemaking: Transforming Initiatives for Justice and Peace* (Louisville, KY: Westminster John Knox, 1992), p. 72.

[51] Miroslav Volf, *Exclusion and Embrace: A Theological Exploration of Identity, Otherness, and Reconciliation* (Nashville: Abingdon Press, 1996), p. 221.

[52] Edward W. Said, *Orientalism* (New York: Vintage Books, 1978), p. 6.

[53] Mitri Raheb, *The Invention of History: A Century of Interplay between Theology and Politics in Palestine* (Jerusalem: Diyar, 2011), p. 16.

[54] Raheb, *Invention of History*, p. 12.

[55] Shlomo Sand, *The Invention of the Jewish People* (London: Verso), 2009, p. 73.

[56] 'A Moment of Truth (Kairos Palestine): A Word of Faith, Hope, and Love from the Heart of Palestinian Suffering' (Bethlehem, 2009).

[57] Chaim Gans, 'Palestinians Were Made to Pay an Unfair Price', *Ha'aretz* (27 June 2009) http://www.haaretz.com/hasen/spages/1094908.html (accessed 18 Nov. 2011).

[58] Gans, 'Palestinians Were Made to Pay'.

[59] Naim Ateek, *Justice, and Only Justice* (Maryknoll, NY: Orbis, 1989).

[60] Ateek, *Justice*, pp. 110–11.

[61] Dan Juster, 'A Messianic Jew Looks at the Land Promises', in *The Land Cries Out* (ed. Munayer and Loden), p. 67. Juster (ibid., n. 6) commends the clarity of Macintyre's discussion of justice in Alasdair Macintyre, *Whose Justice? Which Rationality?* (Notre Dame: University of Notre Dame Press, 1988).

[62] Juster, 'A Messianic Jew', p. 67.

[63] Juster, 'A Messianic Jew', p. 67 (emphasis original).

[64] Juster, 'A Messianic Jew', p. 67 (emphasis original).

[65] Dan Juster http://www.tikkunamerica.org/halachah/intro-dj.php (accessed 1 June 2013).

[66] Juster, 'A Messianic Jew', p. 67, citing Gen. 12.1–20.

[67] Juster, 'A Messianic Jew', p. 68.

[68] Juster, 'A Messianic Jew', p. 68.

[69] Juster, 'A Messianic Jew', p. 68.

[70] Juster, 'A Messianic Jew', p. 79.

[71] Maoz, 'Jerusalem and Justice', p. 159.

[72] Richard Harvey, 'Toward a Messianic Jewish Theology of Reconciliation in the Light of the Arab-Israeli Conflict: Neither Dispensationalist nor Supersessionist?', in *The Land Cries Out* (ed. Munayer and Loden), pp. 82–103.

[73] Harvey, 'Toward a Messianic Jewish Theology', p. 83.

[74] The Brethren missionary influence in the Galilee region church was influential in cultivating a premillennial dispensational theological approach to the biblical hermeneutics among the predominantly Orthodox Palestinian Christians who embraced Plymouth Brethren teaching. For an Arabic-language biographical document on a significant Brethren leader in region, see Suheil Madanat, *The Life of Roy Whitman* (publisher unknown, 1995).

75 Kendall Soulen, *The God of Israel and Christian Theology* (Minneapolis: Fortress, 1996), pp. 30–31.

76 Martin Luther, 'On the Jews and Their Lies', in *Luther's Works, American Edition* (55 vols; ed. Jaroslav Pelikan and Helmut T. Lehmann; Philadelphia: Muehlenberg and Fortress, and St Louis: Concordia, 1955–86), 47:267.

77 Soulen, *God of Israel*, p. 29.

78 Soulen, *God of Israel*, p. 32 (emphasis in original).

79 Although diasporic Jews refer to the Nazi annihilation of six million Jews in death camps as the Holocaust, derived from a word in the Septuagint meaning 'whole burnt offering', Israelis prefer the Hebrew term *Shoah* (catastrophe).

80 Daniel Rossing, 'The Twelve Points of Berlin Viewed through the Prism of Jewish-Christian Relations in Israel Today', paper presented at the Jerusalem Rainbow Club, Jerusalem (December 2009).

81 Nahum N. Glatzer, *Franz Rosenzweig: His Life and Thought* (New York: Schocken, 1961), p. 341.

82 For an expression of redefined Christian theology that results in such two-covenant theology, see Rosemary Reuther, *Faith and Fratricide: The Theological Roots of Anti-Semitism* (New York: Seabury, 1974); and Reuther, *To Change the World* (New York: Crossroad, 1981), 'Theologically, anti-Judaism developed as the left hand of Christology' (31).

83 C.I. Scofield, *Rightly Dividing the Word of Truth* (New Jersey: Loizeaux Brothers, n.d. [1896]), pp. 12–16.

84 Lawrence Davidson, 'Christian Zionism as a Representation of American Manifest Destiny', *Critique: Critical Middle Eastern Studies* 14 (2005), pp. 157–69.

85 Richard J. Mouw, 'What the Old Dispensationalists Taught Me', *Christianity Today* 39:3 (6 March 1995), p. 34.

86 For Israeli Messianic Jews, doing military service is a normal, natural part of their civic life since all Jewish Israelis are required to serve. To refuse to serve would entail a deliberate refusal to participate in Israeli civil society. For Palestinian Christians the situation is quite different; there is no Palestinian army in which to serve.

9. Towards a Theology of Reconciliation

[1] See especially Matt Jenson, *The Gravity of Sin: Augustine, Luther and Barth on 'homo incurvatus in se'* (London: T&T Clark, 2006). Jenson explores Luther's cogent description of humanity's fallen state as *'homo incurvates in se'* – literally 'man turned in on himself'. Relationally, sin is 'dissociation and relationlessness', and a sinner (metaphorically) is a person without relations, a person who tries to *not* relate to God or to others. Sin can be viewed as 'incurvature'. We attempt to orbit ourselves, to curve in on ourselves. In our redemption and adoption by God, through Christ's cross, God reorients us to himself, facing us out of ourselves and out of self-preoccupation. At the cross one enters relationship with God and with other people in such a way that Christ will *not* permit us to not relate.

[2] 'For God was pleased to have all his fulness dwell in [the Son], and through him to reconcile to himself all things, whether things on earth or things in heaven, by making peace through his blood, shed on the cross' (Col. 1.19–20 NIV).

[3] 'See, just as the LORD my God has charged me, I now teach you statutes and ordinances for you to observe in the land that you are about to enter and occupy. You must observe them diligently, for this will show your wisdom and discernment to the peoples, who, when they hear all these statutes, will say, "Surely this great nation is a wise and discerning people!"' (Deut. 4.5–6).

[4] The intent here is not to claim that Christology was the solution to partisan and doctrinal divisions in the early church when in fact, christological differences were a major cause of splits and abundant heresies. The point is that a true understanding of Jesus, keeping him as the focus, is the answer to false theologies.

[5] 'What Jesus did on the cross is not, therefore, simply an example, even the supreme example, of some general truth either about how people should behave or about what God is like. The cross only becomes an example, as and when it does, because it is first an achievement, an accomplishment. We can only truly speak of following Jesus on the way of the cross if we have first stood back and watched in awe and gratitude as he walks it alone on our behalf.' N.T. Wright, *Way of the Lord* (Grand Rapids, MI: Eerdmans, 1999), pp. 96–7.

[6] See Oliver O'Donovan, *Desire of Nations* (Cambridge: CUP, 1999), p. 27. O'Donovan makes this argument concerning 'mutual witness' as

it concerns political theology and what it means to be a nation. The same is true for theological refection more generally.

7 Chris Wright, *The Mission of God* (Downers Grove, IL: InterVarsity Press, 2006), p. 39.

8 Palestinian Christians and Israeli Messianic Jews are, of course, not enemies but rather spiritual siblings born of the same spiritual father. However, the dominant political atmosphere in Israel-Palestine affects everyone, and the real spiritual enmity between our respective peoples easily spills over into our believing communities, especially during times of heightened conflict.

9 Miroslav Volf, *Exclusion and Embrace: A Theological Exploration of Identity, Otherness, and Reconciliation* (Nashville: Abingdon, 1996), p. 216 (emphasis ours).

10 Jürgen Moltmann, *The Crucified God* (London: SCM, 2001), p. xvii.

11 Oliver O'Donovan, 'The Political Thought of the Book of Revelation', *Tyndale Bulletin* 37 (1986), p. 71.

12 Vern Neufeld Redekop, *From Violence to Blessing: How an Understanding of Deep-Rooted Conflict Can Open Paths to Reconciliation* (Ottawa: Novalis, 2002), pp. 31–54. Redekop lists the five basic needs that are essential to the psychological health of human beings. If any one of them is denied or threatened, conflict usually ensues.

13 Daniel Bar-Tal, *Living with the Conflict: Socio-Psychological Analysis of the Jewish Society in Israel* ([Hebrew] Jerusalem: Carmel, 2007).

14 Michael Hogg, 'Intragroup Processes, Group Structure and Social Identity', in *Social Group and Identities: Developing the Legacy of Henri Tajfel* (Oxford: Butterworth-Heinemann, 1996), pp. 65–94.

15 N.T. Wright, *Paul: In Fresh Perspective* (Minneapolis: Fortress, 1995), p. 120.

16 N.T. Wright, *Paul*, pp. 112–13.

17 N.T. Wright, *Paul*, p. 113, emphasis his.

18 N.T. Wright, *Paul*, pp. 120–21.

19 See IVP New Testament Commentary Series on Philippians for more information regarding the elite status of the various identifiers Paul lists.

20 Salim J. Munayer, 'The Cross and Reconciliation', in *Journey through the Storm: Musalaha and the Reconciliation Process* (Jerusalem: Musalaha Ministry of Reconciliation, 2011), pp. 69–81, here pp. 75–8.

21 Although the Mishnah (the earliest extant 'rabbinic' literature) was codified c.200 CE, at times it surely reflects *halakot* (Judaism's legal

rulings) from Second Temple times. Whole *masektot* (tractates within the Mishnah's six *Sedarim* [Orders]) take up issues that directly impinge on minimal social intercourse with Gentiles, e.g. tractate *Avodah Zarah* ('Strange Worship', laws related to idolatry), Yadim ('Hands', ways in which one's hands may become ritually contaminated), etc.

22 S. McKnight, s.v. 'Gentiles', in *Dictionary of Jesus and the Gospels* (ed. Joel B. Green and Scot McKnight; Downers Grove, IL; InterVarsity Press, 1992).

23 S. Cohen notes, 'Following the lead of Ezra, the Jews of the second temple period grew more and more intolerant of marriages with foreigners. Even Philo admired the zeal of Phineas, who killed an Israelite chieftain for consorting publicly with a Midianite woman (Num. 25). The Jews also buried their dead separately, thus maintaining separation from gentiles in death as in life. They refused to participate in public ceremonies that involved worship either of the pagan gods or of the emperor; in other words, they refused to participate in practically all the communal events of ancient society'. *From the Maccabees to the Mishnah* (Philadelphia: Westminster, 1987), p. 46.

24 Flusser explains the connection between Israel's opposition to paganism and their national hope for the kingdom (rule) of God, noting that 'Second Temple Judaism both in Palestine and the Diaspora always linked the hope of the disappearance of paganism to the hope of the manifestation of the kingdom of God: idolatry will vanish and God will be the sole king of the world'. D. Flusser, 'Paganism in Palestine', in *The Jewish People in the First Century* (ed. S. Safrai and M. Stern; Amsterdam: Van Gorcum, 1976), 2:1097.

25 Flusser, 'Paganism in Palestine', p. 1097.

26 We assume here that Paul is the author of Ephesians.

27 Tet-Lim N. Yee, *Jews, Gentiles and Ethnic Reconciliation: Paul's Jewish Identity and Ephesians*, Society for New Testament Studies Monograph Series 130 (Cambridge: CUP, 2005), p. 102. An example of this is circumcision, not practised by Gentiles, which was the physical symbol of belonging to the Jewish people.

28 Eli Lizorkin: 'The context of 1 Maccabees indicates that the prevailing Jewish understanding of Gentiles referred to their status as unbelievers, rather than their non-Jewish ethnicity. In 1 Maccabees, the covenant-keepers within Israel battle Gentile forces and their Jewish sympathizers, who are enemies of theirs and consequently of their covenant god: "Judas had raised a mixed force of believers

and seasoned fighters" (3:13) against Seron of Syria, who "therefore launched another expedition, with a strong army of unbelievers to support him" (3:15) . . . It is interesting that 1 Maccabees 1–7 refers to the non-Jews as Gentiles (*ethnos*) 34 times, but when the negative political climate has changed to the positive in chapters 8 – 16, the word Gentile is used only twice (12:53; 13:41–42). Chapter 8 starts with a Roman takeover and the beginning of a new era, which initially displays a positive attitude towards the Jews. As we consider this drop in frequency from thirty four to just two, we should present a reasonable explanation/s. Without assuming too much and jumping to far reaching conclusions with relatively little data, it is safe to conclude that the word nations (*ethnos*) as opposed to people (*laos*) was used more often when the circumstantial relationships with non-Jewish nations were generally negative. If I am correct in my suggestion, then the word Gentile in this work would not be applicable to non-Jews in general, but rather be used to describe a hostile non-Jew in particular.' http://jewishstudies.eteacherbiblical.com/2012/08/the-jewish-sabbath-what-took-place-in-between-the-testaments/#_ftn65 (accessed 19 May 2013).

29 Yee, *Jews, Gentiles*, p. 105.

30 Yee, *Jews, Gentiles*, pp. 104–7.

31 In the Diaspora, Jews were favourable to Gentiles. Actually, Jews were more strict and hostile to groups within Judaism than they were towards Gentiles. As long as Gentiles gave up their idol worship and abstained from eating blood and things dedicated/sacrificed to idols and moral impurity, they were welcome in the synagogue. They were still peripheral; but definitive, broader lines were not drawn during the time spoken about here. The separation between Jews and Christians was a gradual process that took place over several centuries.

32 This interpretation of the text is found from the time of the early church fathers but does not reflect the understanding of the text during the Second Temple period.

33 Yee, *Jews, Gentiles*, p. 143.

34 Yee, *Jews, Gentiles*, pp. 127–8, 135–6.

35 The occasion was the celebration of Shavuot/Pentecost, one of the three great pilgrim feasts of Israel, during which time male Jews were commanded to present themselves before God in the Jerusalem temple. Jews and proselytes from the Diaspora were present in large numbers.

[36] M. Barth, 'Conversion and Conversation: Israel and the Church in Paul's Epistle to the Ephesians', *Interpretation* 17 (1963), pp. 3–24, here p. 6.

[37] Gordon T. Smith, *A Holy Meal: The Lord's Supper in the Life of the Church* (Grand Rapids, MI: Baker, 2005), pp. 47–55.

[38] The Samaritan was not an enemy; he was the 'other'. The Judeans (the Jews) did not consider the Samaritans as being part of the children of Israel (*Bnei Israel*).

[39] Francis Zerwick, 'The Good Samaritan', *The Furrow* 6 (1955), pp. 291–5.

[40] This stance of distance from the subject is especially clear in Hebrew: '*the one* who . . .' (*Zeh* sheh, זה ש).

[41] See 1 Kings 17 for the Hebrew Bible's historical perspective of the Samaritans and their origins.

[42] R.J. Coggins, 'The Samaritans in Josephus', in *Josephus, Judaism and Christianity* (ed. L.H. Feldman and G. Hata; Detroit: E.J. Brill, 1987), pp. 257–73.

[43] See David I. Smith, *Learning from the Stranger: Christian Faith and Cultural Diversity* (Grand Rapids, MI: Eerdmans, 2009), pp. 65–6 for many of the insights offered in this paragraph.

[44] Joshua Schwartz, 'On Priests and Jericho in the Second Temple Period', *Jewish Quarterly Review* 79 (July 1988), pp. 23–48.

[45] The Mishnah contains oral traditions from the Second Temple period, but was formally edited and written down c.200 CE.

[46] E.g. 'And they further said before him [R. Aqiba], R. Eliezer used to say, One who eats bread [baked by] Samaritans is like one who eats pork', Mishnah, tractate *Shevi'it* [Seventh Year] 8:10 (trans. Jacob Neusner; New Haven, CT: Yale University Press, 1988).

[47] www.throughmyenemyseyes.info; www.iprecon.info

Appendix: Stages of Reconciliation

[1] Ron Kraybill, 'The Cycle of Reconciliation', in *Seeking and Pursuing Peace: The Process, the Pain, and the Product* (ed. Salim J. Munayer; Jerusalem: Musalaha, 1998), p. 73. See also Shoshana Steinberg and Dan Bar-On, 'Dialogue in the Midst of an Ongoing Conflict: A Group Process of Israeli Jewish and Palestinian Students', in *Beyond Bullets and Bombs* (ed. Judy Kuriansky; Westport, CT: Praeger, 2007), p. 148.

[2] This list is taken from John Dawson, 'Hatred's End: A Christian Proposal to Peacemaking in a New Century', in *Forgiveness and Reconciliation: Religion, Public Policy, and Conflict Transformation* (ed. Raymond G. Helmick, S. J., and Rodney L. Peterson; Radnor: Templeton Foundation Press, 2001), p. 236.

[3] Sari Hanafi, 'Dancing Tango during Peacebuilding: Palestinian-Israeli People-to-People Programs for Conflict Resolution', in *Beyond Bullets and Bombs* (ed. Kuriansky), p. 69. See also Rabah Halabi and Nava Sonnenschein, 'School for Peace: Between Hard Reality and the Jewish–Palestinian Encounters', in *Beyond Bullets and Bombs* (ed. Kuriansky), pp. 278–9.

[4] Haggai Kupermintz and Gavriel Saloman, 'Lessons to Be Learned from Research on Peace Education in the Context of Intractable Conflict', 44:4 (2005), p. 295.

[5] Steinberg and Bar-On, 'Dialogue in the Midst of an Ongoing Conflict', pp. 148–9.

[6] How each side participates in or assists the conflict is a point of contention among Israeli and Palestinian believers. Israeli Jews are required to enlist in the Israeli army but are not required to join a combat unit. However, many Israeli Messianic Jews volunteer for elite combat units out of a desire to excel in their contribution to the country's national defence force. They also do so in order to be accepted and further integrated into Israeli-Jewish society. This fact upsets most Palestinian Christians, who generally choose, as a community, to resist calls by their Muslim neighbours to join in violent resistance against Israel. However, as we have noted earlier, Palestinian Christians were leaders in the early days of the Palestinian nationalist movement and were prominent in the formation of the PLO. Overall, though, the majority of Palestinian Christians have favoured non-violent methods of resistance, which are viewed as threatening by the Israeli Messianic community.

[7] Kraybill, 'Cycle of Reconciliation', p. 75.

[8] John Paul Lederach, *The Journey toward Reconciliation* (Scottdale, PA: Herald, 1999), p. 23.

[9] See, e.g., Jonathan McRay, *You Have Heard It Said: Events of Reconciliation* (Eugene, OR: Wipf & Stock, 2010); and *Journey through the Storm: Musalaha and the Process of Reconciliation* (ed. by Salim J. Munayer; Jerusalem: Musalaha, 2011).

Index